MAGICAL IMAGINATIONS:
INSTRUMENTAL AESTHETICS
IN THE ENGLISH
RENAISSANCE

GENEVIEVE JULIETTE GUENTHER

Magical Imaginations

Instrumental Aesthetics in the English Renaissance

UNIVERSITY OF TORONTO PRESS
Toronto Buffalo London

© University of Toronto Press 2012
Toronto Buffalo London
www.utppublishing.com
Printed in Canada

ISBN 978-1-4426-4241-6

Printed on acid-free, 100% post-consumer recycled paper with
vegetable-based inks.

Library and Archives Canada Cataloguing in Publication

Guenther, Genevieve
Magical imaginations : instrumental aesthetics in the English Renaissance /
Genevieve Guenther.

Includes bibliographical references and index.
ISBN 978-1-4426-4241-6

1. English poetry – Early modern, 1500–1700 – History and criticism.
2. English drama – Early modern and Elizabethan, 1500–1600 – History
and criticism.   3. Magic in literature.   4. Aesthetics in literature.   I. Title.

PR525.M24G83 2012   821'.309377   C2011-906835-4

University of Toronto Press gratefully acknowledges the financial assistance
of the University of Rochester in the publication of this book.

University of Toronto Press acknowledges the financial assistance to its
publishing program of the Canada Council for the Arts and the Ontario
Arts Council.

Canada Council   Conseil des Arts   ONTARIO ARTS COUNCIL
for the Arts   du Canada   CONSEIL DES ARTS DE L'ONTARIO

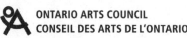

University of Toronto Press acknowledges the financial support of the
Government of Canada through the Canada Book Fund for our publishing
activities.

People speak with justice of 'the magic of art' and compare artists to magicians. But the comparison is perhaps more significant than it claims to be. There can be no doubt that art did not begin as art for art's sake.

Sigmund Freud, Totem and Taboo

Contents

Acknowledgments

My thanks go first to the institutions that supported me with grants and fellowships: the Andrew W. Mellon Foundation, the Townsend Center for the Humanities at the University of California, Berkeley, the Mabelle McLeod Lewis Memorial Fund, and the Frances Bacon Foundation at the Huntington Library. *English Literary Renaissance* 36.2 (April 2006) published an early version of chapter 2 as 'Spenser's Magic, or Instrumental Aesthetics in the 1590 *Faerie Queene*'; material from chapter 3 was published in *Modern Philology* 109.1 (August 2011). I am grateful to the editors of both journals for permission to reproduce my work here. And I thank Suzanne Rancourt for giving *Magical Imaginations* a most welcome home at the University of Toronto Press.

I am especially beholden to friends and colleagues for reading drafts of chapters, as well as for supplementing the limits of my interdisciplinary knowledge and helping me to prepare the manuscript. My most profound gratitude goes to Jeffrey Knapp, Randolph Starn, and Paul Alpers, who inspired and guided me at every stage of this project. I am lucky indeed to have such brilliant and generous mentors. I am also grateful to the late Janet Adelman, Alp Aker, Charles Altieri, Penelope Anderson, Harry Berger, Brooke Conti, Julie Cooper, Kasey Evans, Andrew Escobedo, Mike Farry, Amy Greenstadt, Kenneth Gross, Richard Halpern, Katherine Ibbett, Rosemary Kegel, Peggy Knapp, James Longenbach, Sasha McGee, John Michael, Anne Prescott, David Riggs, Damion Searls, Rob Stillman, Richard Strier, Erich Strong, Holly Watkins, Travis Williams, Herb Wilson, Michael Witmore, Susan Zieger, the members of the 2002–3 fellows group at the Townsend Center for the Humanities at Berkeley, the staff of the Manuscripts Reading Room at the British Library, and the anonymous readers, particularly 'Reader A,' chosen by University of Toronto Press.

I thank all these people for the ways in which they made *Magical Imaginations* a better book. Certainly the errors or infelicities remaining in the work are my own.

I have relied above all on the unconditional support of my husband, Neal Cardwell. He has my deepest thanks and love.

Magical Imaginations is dedicated to the poets it studies and to my son, Theodore, in small recompense for great joy.

A Note on Texts

I have modernized the spelling in quotations of English Renaissance texts, with the exception of the deliberately archaic *The Faerie Queene*. Unless otherwise noted translations from the Latin, French, and German are my own.

MAGICAL IMAGINATIONS: INSTRUMENTAL AESTHETICS IN THE ENGLISH RENAISSANCE

Introduction

There may be some natural operation in the generation and pronunciation of words with an intent and desire of working, so that not without good cause we use to say that a lively voice is of great efficacy: not because it has that virtue which the Magicians dream of, [nor because] it is able to make and alter as others think, but because it is as nature has ordained. We must therefore be very circumspect in these things, for a man may easily tread awry, and many err in both parts: some deny that there is any operation, but others exceed and fly unto Magic.

Roger Bacon, A Most Excellent and Learned Discourse of the
Admirable Force and Efficacie of Art and Nature

In his *Defense of Poesy*, Sir Philip Sidney claims that the 'charming force' of poetry can lead even 'hard-hearted evil men' who enjoy only 'indulgere genio' to 'see the form of goodness (which seen they cannot but love) ere themselves be aware.' *Magical Imaginations* was conceived when I became interested in this claim, particularly in the way it afforded literary pleasure ideological efficacy, as if poetic delight could make resistant readers love 'goodness' without alerting them that their dispositions were being disciplined. This intriguing and perhaps disquieting suggestion made me newly curious about Edmund Spenser's statement that his 1590 *Faerie Queene* is meant 'to fashion a gentleman or noble person in virtuous and gentle discipline' with 'allegorical devises' that are 'delightful and pleasing to the commune sense.' Spenser's desire to use pleasing devices to inspire gentle discipline seemed to me to reappear in *The Tempest*, where Prospero attempts to discipline the ethics and politics of his enemies by deploying artistic devices meant ultimately, as he tells the audience, 'to please.'

Rewriting the Renaissance commonplace that literature should teach and delight, all these texts suggest that literature teaches *by delighting*: that literary pleasure itself produces, or is meant to produce, normative ethical and social effects in readers and spectators.[1] Taking my cue from Sidney – who writes that poetry is an 'instrumental cause' of virtue, 'the ending end of earthly learning' – I adopted the phrase *instrumental aesthetics* to identify this theory of efficacious beauty and the poetic and theatrical practices it motivated. I then set out to recover the historical conditions of possibility for these aesthetics, the intellectual and cultural assumptions that sustained their striking literary vitality.[2]

The lines of my historical inquiry came into focus when I noticed that in his more exuberant statements about the poet, Sidney sounds almost exactly like Cornelius Agrippa, the early modern magician who in *Three Books of Occult Philosophy* vaunts the adept's power to ascend into a transcendent realm of Platonic Ideas, whose representation, Agrippa argues, can transform social and even material life. I might have dismissed this resemblance as a trace of the Renaissance celebration of the centralized, omnipotent subject, except for the fact that in other places in the *Defense*, Sidney seems highly concerned to *distinguish* the poet from the magician. Following his famous statement, for instance, that the poet 'nothing affirmeth ... so never lieth,' Sidney immediately goes on to say that 'the poet never draweth circles about your imagination to conjure you to believe for true what he writes.' The circles to which Sidney refers are those that early modern magicians drew around themselves for protection when they attempted to conjure devils. And I later discovered that even some mainstream Protestants held devils to be the very source of Platonic Ideas. Once I began to map the field on which Sidney mimics yet disavows the Renaissance magician, I began to see historical significance in the fact that Spenser begins and ends his 1590 *Faerie Queene* with representations of evil magicians who double for the poet, as well as the fact that the 'art' Prospero renounces at the end of *The Tempest* is at once magic and theatre. These depictions of conjurers suggest that poets were either feeling or exploiting a considerable anxiety that the magician's methods all too closely resembled those of the poet who attempted to use the beauty of language to produce ideological effects.

It turns out that this anxiety was inevitable. As Keith Thomas has long since demonstrated in his magisterial social history of religion and magic in early modern England, the Reformation focused pastoral attention on the scriptural injunction against magic – 'thou shalt not suffer a witch to live' (Exod. 22:18) – and called into question the Florentine humanist idea that knowledge and magic were linked.[3] Yet the very discourses that enabled poets to imagine that literature could be used as an ideological instrument also provided the assumptions that sustained magical practice. When contemporary faculty psychology, for example, argued that people were roused to action by the sensuous beauty of concepts appearing as pictures in the mind's eye, it cautioned that those alluring mental images could be implanted by conjured demons. Such a theory of mind allowed poets to assume that their representations could affect their readers' behaviour, yet it enabled magicians to imagine that their rites could influence others as well. For early modern thinkers – who relied on the framework of Christian cosmology and metaphysics even in allegedly secular fields – the imaginative and the diabolical, the ideational and the real, the subjective and the numinous were domains with overlapping boundaries, connected by the mediation of language itself. Poets and magicians alike adopted classical theories of rhetorical persuasion in developing their arts. Demonologists argued about conjuration using terms that we now find in ordinary language philosophy, debating whether signifiers had inherent performative efficacy or whether devils appeared to human beings in a satanic theatrical deception intended to win souls for hell. In debating the sources of linguistic efficacy, these arguments over the power of the signifier in conjuration spoke directly to the issues that informed early modern instrumental aesthetics; thus Marlowe's *Doctor Faustus*, in which Faustus and Mephistopheles explicitly discuss the issue of the magical signifier's performative power, also emerges in the network of relations between magic and instrumental aesthetics that I trace here. Indeed, Marlowe's play raises important questions about the power of aesthetic representation to produce ideological effects, not least because sixteenth-century performances of the play were occasionally stopped when both actors and audiences believed that the dramatic staging of Faustus's conjuration had managed to invoke actual devils. *Magical Imaginations* examines these texts by Sidney, Spenser, Marlowe, and Shakespeare, then, because they all explore how language might turn imagined metaphysical forces to social ends. The power to use language as a metaphysical instrument was the goal of both early modern magical practice and the early modern literature that attempted to fashion the ideological orientation of its readers and audiences.

In arguing that English Renaissance magic centred on the way language might turn metaphysical forces to social ends, I hope to revise our current paradigm for the study of the relationship between magic and literature in early modern England, which has been dominated by the historical narrative first advanced by Frances Yates in the early 1960s. In the Yatesian narrative, magic is the ardent expression of a heroic individualism that uses occult ideas and practices to resist institutional orthodoxy, and that finds its teleological justification in the discoveries of modern scientific inquiry.[4] By showing that magical aspirations motivated Italian Renaissance philosophers to contest Thomist and Aristotelian dogma, Yates's story has inspired important work in intellectual history and the history of science.[5] But her account has a more limited application to the study of magic's relationship to poetry and drama, for in this context it merely facilitates either identifications of hermetic doctrine in early modern texts or readings of literary works as reflections of historical 'progress.'[6] Recently cultural historians have applied Foucauldian and Derridean models to the study of Renaissance magic, producing epistemic genealogies and histories of the present.[7] But to examine the relationship between magic and literature in early modern England, I will take an eclectic but essentially anthropological approach to magic, reading magic not as a form of empirical experimentation, but as a rhetorical practice, whose particular content is grounded in enabling cosmological or ideological constructs, and whose performance allows individual subjects to appear to mediate sacred forces in a way that enables them to ratify or transform social relations.

In so reading magic, I will develop the insights of Kenneth Burke, who recommends that we pay attention to the 'rhetorical *function* in magic,' to what gives magic its 'pragmatic sanction.'[8] Burke proposes that we view magical discourse not as a form of proto-science, but as a 'transference of linguistic function to an area for which it [is] not fit.' In this view, 'the realistic use of addressed language to *induce action in people*' is analogous to 'the magical use of addressed language to *induce motion in things* (things by nature alien to purely linguistic orders of motivation).'[9] My concern will be, then, to understand the stakes of the notion that the magician attempts to use the power of both the formal organization of his words and the charismatic pathos of his enunciation to turn purported devils into instruments of his worldly desires.[10] To contextualize rhetorical performances of magic theoretically, I will also draw on the work of Stanley Tambiah, who likewise argues that 'in ritual operations by word and object manipulation' the action 'conforms to the "persuasive" rather than the "scientific" model.' Tambiah usefully expands the category of the rhetorically persuasive to include performative utterances, under which he classifies magical rites: 'like "illocutionary" and "performative" acts,' Tambiah explains, ritual acts aim to 'have consequences and effect changes; they structure situations not in the idiom of ... "rationality" but in terms of convention and normative judgment.'[11] Following Tambiah, I will pay close attention to the early modern English conventions and normative judgments that provided the contexts for attempts at magical performativity. Honouring the historical specificity of such contexts, I will, finally, situate what follows in light of recent studies by historians of the Reformation, who have built on Keith Thomas's work to examine the complex ways representations of magical practices served as forums for Reformation debates.[12] I will, however, be interested less in these debates themselves, and more in the way they reveal how Protestant polemics produced and mandated magical beliefs while implicitly and explicitly connecting magic and literature.

Protestant theologies were not simply polemical or doctrinal positions, I will show; rather, they were a shifting but ever-present set of interpretive protocols through which putatively secular discourses and practices were given magical valence. As I have suggested and will detail further in chapter 1, to adhere to *sola scriptura*, for instance, was potentially to understand Platonic metaphysics as diabolically motivated. Or, as I will discuss in chapter 4, to accept the monarch as head of the national church in Jacobean England was to participate in the ideology of monarchical sanctity that designated the witch and magician as traitors. It will also be important to remember that while theologies provided the assumptions that allowed magical beliefs to circulate, magical beliefs in turn reinforced the assumptions of these theologies. And they did so even when magic was put to the test and failed. An exemplary tale in John Foxe's life of William Tyndale illustrates how even unsuccessful conjurations could confirm theological premises. Foxe narrates an incident that supposedly took place 'at Antwerp, on a time amongst a company of Merchants as they were at supper.' With the merchants was

a certain juggler, which through his diabolical enchantments or Art Magical, would fetch all kinds of viands and wine from any place they would, and set it upon the table incontinent before them ... The fame of this juggler being much talked of, it chanced that as Master Tyndall heard of it, he desired certain of the Merchants, that he might also be present at supper, to see him play his parts. To be brief, the supper was appointed, and the Merchants with Tyndall were there present. Then the juggler being required to ply his feats, and to show his cunning, after his wonted boldness began, to utter all that he could do, but all was in vain. At the last, with his labor sweating and toiling, when he saw that nothing would go forward, but that all his enchantments were void, he was compelled openly to confess, that there was some man present at supper, which disturbed and letted all his doings. So that a man even in the Martyrs of these our days, cannot lack the miracles of true faith, if miracles were now to be desired.[13]

What is crucial about this anecdote is that Foxe proclaims the *failure* of the juggler's conjuration to be the miracle, as if only the naked strength of Tyndale's extraordinary faith had prevented the meat and wine from appearing. Apparently taking it for granted that a magician could in fact 'utter ... enchantments' that would conjure devils to procure delicacies for his patrons (as Faustus will have Mephistopheles procure grapes for the pregnant duchess), Foxe represents an unsuccessful or infelicitous conjuration – what from a scientific perspective would appear as an empirical demonstration that magic lacked efficacy – as an obvious proof that God has providentially sanctified the English elect. Even secular writers who explicitly argued that conjuration was impossible did so in ways that affirmed the theological premises enabling magical beliefs in the first place. Sir Walter Ralegh, for example, maintains in his *History of the World* that magical ambitions are utterly in vain, yet he justifies his argument not by pointing out that devils do not actually exist, but by insisting that human beings are too dependent on God's grace to have the spiritual power to control them with words. 'Doubtless they forget,' Ralegh argues pointedly, 'that the devil is not terrified of doing ill ... no, not by the fearful word of the Almighty; [but] forgetting these proud parts of his, an unworthy wretch will yet resolve himself, that he can draw the devil out of hell, and terrify him with a phrase.'[14] What passes for Ralegh's scepticism, then, is his denial that human beings may 'terrify' the devil with a phrase. But this denial simply reaffirms the doctrine that Satan lives and acts in the world with the permission of God. (And as a piece of historical evidence, it also suggests that the belief that the magician could in fact conjure had sufficient credibility in the early seventeenth century that it needed to be explicitly rejected.) Thus even accounts of the futility of magic linked the worldly and the sacred in ways that enabled magicians to argue that they could use their utterances to conjure spirits.

Like magic in Renaissance England, the poetry and drama I study in *Magical Imaginations* either claims or stages the claim that the mediation of metaphysical entities – whether Platonic Ideas or putatively transcendent truths embodied by allegorical devices or impersonations of spirits in theatrical spectacles – can produce ethical, social, and soteriological effects. Hence my objective in the chapters that follow will be to demonstrate that Renaissance literature was by no means an 'aesthetically disinterested' production. Yet in recovering the unique ways certain literary texts mobilized and sought to influence their cultural contexts, I intend also to show that Renaissance literature was not simply one site among others for discursive circulation. And by doing so I hope to contest the terms of our current debates about Renaissance literary aesthetics. These terms have been indelibly determined by a nominally Kantian paradigm in which aesthetic judgments claim universal validity precisely insofar as they are disinterested, or detached from the particular contingencies of political interest and sensual desire. Modern American literary critics – that is, the New Critics – selectively appropriated Kant's work on aesthetics to argue that literature presents readers with a permanent and always disinterested enactment of universal human experience, one re-enacted and made available to contemplation by the process of close reading. Postmodern critics who were particularly concerned with what they took to be the conservative politics of the New Criticism – that is, the New Historicists – argued, by contrast, that all representation is interested, and no particular experience can be universally valid, and that literary aesthetic is, therefore, merely constructed as having aesthetic autonomy, in essence by twentieth-century New Critics. For this reason, they maintained, the ethical critic should avoid aesthetic analysis and should instead trace ideologically charged discourses as they circulate through the text of culture as a whole. And yet both these critical schools assume that the autonomy of the literary aesthetic relies on the purposelessness of beauty and the disinterestedness of aesthetic analysis: New Critics by maintaining that literature has no other end than the expression of its own essential core of meaning, and New Historicists by asserting that literature has no essence at all, since meaning is so clearly made and remade by readers and communities to non-literary ends. But this conflation of the aesthetically distinctive and the socially disinterested is merely post-Kantian. As such, it is itself historically contingent and, more important for my purposes, historically anachronistic in the context of Renaissance literary criticism. The literature that espoused or performed an instrumental aesthetic in early modern England composed neither an autonomous sphere constructed to be disinterested nor merely one site among others for cultural contestation. It was, rather, the producer of effects not to be found in other cultural sites and a discourse explicitly interested in the instrumental ends such effects might have in social and political life.

Nevertheless, the New Critics downplayed the instrumentality of Renaissance literature. For instance, in their survey of Western literary criticism, William Wimsatt and Cleanth Brooks's discussion of Sidney's

Defense overlooks Sidney's statements about the ideological efficacy of poetry and instead focuses on his pronouncements about the freedom and range of the poet's imagination.[15] This focus enables them to posit that creation, like consumption, escapes the necessities of historical determination, manifesting instead an ideal autonomy. This theory of autonomy would be severely compromised if the critic acknowledged the author's interest in producing social effects. As John Crowe Ransom puts it in 'Criticism, Inc.': both Aristotle and the Broadway producer 'are concerned with the effects [of literature]. Such concern seems to reflect the view that art comes into being because the artist, or the employer behind him, has designs upon the public, whether high moral designs or box-office ones. It is an odious view in either case, because it denies the autonomy of the artist as one who interests himself in the artistic object in his own right, and likewise the autonomy of the works as existing for its own sake.'[16] Thus in *The Verbal Icon*, Wimsatt argues that New Critics should 'inquire ... not about origins, nor about effects, but about the work insofar as it can be considered by itself as a body of meaning.'[17] And what that means for critical practice, according to Ransom, is that criticism *itself* 'shall be objective, shall cite the nature of the object rather than its effects upon the subject.'[18] As an object described by an objective practice, literature, in this story, claims for its 'meaning' the same transhistorical or even transcendent permanence afforded to mathematical equations, things expressible and valid in every context. For New Criticism, then, literature's autonomy relies not only on its disinterest, its objectivity rather than its ability to effect an end, but also on its permanent validity and universality. Yet it is clear that literature does not so much express this disinterested universality as it produces its fantasy in the reading of the critic: in 'The Affective Fallacy,' Wimsatt and Monroe Beardsley show the ends of their own method when they represent poetry as 'a way of *fixing* emotions, or *making them* more permanently perceptible when objects have undergone a functional change from culture to culture.'[19] And they reveal their institutional goals when they argue that an account of these fixed emotions – what they call 'the poem itself' – will be 'an account of what the poem is likely to produce in other – sufficiently informed – readers.'[20] Literature's ability to fix experience, to anchor it in the stream of historical flux, relies on the critic's production of a community of readers modelled after the critic himself, who thus stands in for the universal subject who has unmediated access to the aesthetic objects of a supposedly timeless Western culture. This subject is, then, as much an exclusionary construction of the New Criticism as the putatively disinterested poem.

New Historicism explicitly situated itself as the negation of these philosophical assumptions and critical practices. In *Practicing New Historicism*, Catharine Gallagher and Stephen Greenblatt state outright that to them, at least, '"new historicism" at first signified an impatience with American New Criticism.'[21] To be sure, in their impatience Gallagher and Greenblatt were not alone: postmodern literary theory generally established the universal subject implied by the idea of disinterested aesthetic autonomy as the main focus of critique, and made the destabilization of the transcendent aesthetic object the correlative goal of most critical endeavour. Indeed, New Critical ideas were held so utterly bankrupt at the turn of the 1980s that in the introduction to *The Power of Forms in the English Renaissance*, the New Historical edition of *Genre*, Greenblatt mounted a devastating attack on what we now call the old historicism by accusing it of being a species of formalism. Greenblatt's particular target was John Dover Wilson, who had argued that Shakespeare's *Richard II* upholds and stabilizes monarchical authority with its sympathetic portrayal of the hapless king and its prophesy that Richard's deposition by Bolingbroke would lead to the Wars of the Roses. To counter Dover Wilson's argument, Greenblatt discusses two historical facts: first, that someone paid Shakespeare's company forty shillings to revive *Richard II* on the eve of Essex's rebellion against the queen, and second, that Elizabeth herself seemed to have tremendous anxiety about this particular play. Greenblatt quotes her as exclaiming: 'I *am* Richard II; know ye not that?' Together these facts imply, of course, that Shakespeare's play might have been taken, and indeed was taken, to subvert rather than to stabilize the queen's authority. But Greenblatt never explicitly accuses Dover Wilson of having gotten his history wrong, or of having attempted to advance a conservative political reading of the play; rather, Greenblatt accuses him of having practised a kind of bad literary criticism, that is, *New Criticism*. For Dover Wilson, Greenblatt asserts, 'historical research has the effect of conferring autonomy and fixity upon the text.'[22] Now, what is curious about this claim is how strongly it suggests that New Historicism in fact shared New Critical assumptions about the literary aesthetic. Literary 'autonomy' for Greenblatt is here synonymous with (or at least in apposition to) 'fixity.' And since 'fixity' implies, as Greenblatt puts it, 'a stable core of meaning ... that unites disparate and even contradictory parts into an organic whole' (2253) and that reflects 'a stable point of reference, beyond contingency' (2254), literary autonomy itself, in this reading, implies such a unity beyond contingency. Moreover, Greenblatt connects literary autonomy not only with essential fixity, but with the idea of disinterestedness.

Every time he cites the interest that power takes in representations, or that representations take in power, he begins to speak about the play as if he were not speaking about a piece of literature at all. Indeed, he argues that what made the play threatening to Elizabeth is that it *ceased* to be literary as such, that it broke 'out of the boundaries of the playhouse, where such stories are clearly marked as powerful illusions' (2252). No longer an aesthetic illusion, in Greenblatt's argument, the play now becomes like any other form of representation. Elizabeth, Greenblatt writes, 'is clearly responding ... to the presence of *any* representation of deposition' (2253, emphasis in the original). Elizabeth, like a new historicist *avant la lettre*, has 'a conception of art that has no respect whatsoever for the integrity of the text' (2253). What Greenblatt is arguing here is that there was no distinct literary discourse in the English Renaissance – that *Richard II* has the same status as '*any* representation of deposition' – precisely because the play has such clear political interest, or, rather, because it has such a clear potential for political effects. 'How can tragedy,' Greenblatt asks, 'be strictly a literary term when the queen's own life is endangered by the play?' (2252). This question works rhetorically only if we assume that literary language must be disinterested, that it must have no further end than the production of the illusion of its own fixed unity.

But perhaps we should ask whether *Richard II* seemed to endanger the life of the queen precisely because it was literary, and as such was believed to present a *more* compelling model for action than another kind of representation, say a chronicle, would have.[23] Indeed, defenders and detractors of literature both assumed that literature was distinctive precisely because it, like no other discourse, enticed readers and audiences to imitate in life what they read in texts or saw on the stage. Italian Renaissance literary critics in particular defended imaginative writing from anti-poetical attacks by arguing that poetry's beauty could serve as an instrument to the production of a well-ordered republic, and English poets adopted these arguments when they justified themselves and their practice to those who, in Thomas Nashe's words, demanded 'what fruits the poets of our time bring forth, or wherein they are able to prove themselves serviceable to the state.'[24] And poets mounted their justifications not as rearguard actions, but as advances seeking to establish the value of literature on the field of cultural production at a time when, as David Kastan points out, 'English literature' as such 'had not yet even formed as a category of collection and organization.'[25] If instrumental aesthetics were, then, meant to transform the dispositions of readers and audiences by giving them pleasure, their ultimate purpose was to use the promise of transformation to produce and augment the cultural value of poetry and theatre.

Thus Sir Philip Sidney wrote his *The Defense of Poesy* to persuade his fellow aristocrats to patronize poetry for its usefulness to the Elizabethan regime, and he attempted to demonstrate poetry's usefulness by importing and adapting the instrumental aesthetics of Italian literary theory into his essay. Sidney's literary project was appreciably complicated, I will argue in chapter 1, by the fact that his instrumental aesthetics were intertwined with magic in a double bind. Sidney appropriated theories of rhetorical coercion that emerged equally in magical tracts by Agrippa, Bruno, and lesser-known English magicians. And he attempted to justify his claims for poetry's coercive effect with the argument that it arose automatically from poetry's conveyance of metaphysical ideas of perfection, but this argument also related his instrumental aesthetics to magic, namely to the magical Neoplatonism that zealous Protestantism characterized as a diabolical form of heresy. Although the Elizabethan court was interested in magic, I will show, for the ways it might help them secure continental alliances and raise extra tax revenues, Elizabeth's ministers and the spokesmen for her conformist church repeatedly warned their parishioners that both magic and poetry were sorceries outlawed by God. In the face of such accusations, Sidney attempted to distinguish poetry from magic by suggesting that poetry embodied what nineteenth- and twentieth-century literary critics would retrospectively identify as a disinterested aesthetic, but he could never sustain this distinction because he never abandoned his claim to be able to influence social and political life with his art. Instead, ending the *Defense* with a parody of conjuration, Sidney diffused the theological problems entailed in the imbrications of poetry and magic by recasting them as material for a joke. This joke, this mock conjuration, thus locates the cultural problem that shadowed Sidney's instrumental aesthetics: the Elizabethan magician was the twin, or rather the evil twin, of Sidney's efficacious poet.

Like Sidney, Spenser claimed in the beginning of his career that poetry might be useful to the Elizabethan state: he famously cast his 1590 *Faerie Queene* as an instrument whose 'general end' was 'to fashion a gentleman or noble person in virtuous and gentle discipline.' But unlike Sidney, I will argue in chapter 2, Spenser seemed to doubt that conveying images of metaphysical beauty in verse would automatically produce a disciplinary effect. *The Faerie Queene* implies that Spenser was richly aware of both the Protestant critique of Neoplatonic metaphysics and the discourse of faculty psychology, which held that subjects become aroused to action by the aesthetic beauty of concepts appearing in the mind's eye, but which also warned that mental images might be implanted by conjured demons. Spenser framed his attempt to fashion disciplined subjects in terms of this psychological demonology, instructing his reader at once to be motivated by his desire for beautiful images and to remain fiercely sceptical of their ontological provenance. Hence in the very beginning of the 1590 *Faerie Queene*, the wicked magician Archimago manipulates Spenser's romance hero by seducing him with a conjured demon who impersonates the allegorical personification of truth.

Yet Spenser was less interested in providing object lessons for his reader than in attempting to enact an instrumental aesthetics that would train him in the bi-fold intellectual habit, at once desiring and sceptical, of his disciplined subject. Spenser sought to train his reader by representing the magical practices of Merlin and Busirane with verse so artfully ambiguous that it remained impossible for the reader to decide whether the pictures in his mind's eye were poetic or demonic or both. This blurring of ontological boundaries was understood in sixteenth-century terms as inspiring wonder, the reaction to extraordinary things both marvellously beautiful and frighteningly inexplicable. For Spenser wonder was an instrumental aesthetic effect, not only because as a psychological experience it was analogous to the bi-fold model of the disciplined mind theorized by faculty psychology, but also because it was inward looking, having been inspired by mental images that were always at once allegorical vehicles and demons. For the reader who believed in the possibility that demons could wind their way into the imagination, this inward-looking wonder, this desire for images coupled with suspicion about their origins, enacted the anxious self-regulation that characterizes the disciplined subject the 1590 *Faerie Queene* attempted to fashion.

If Sidney and Spenser attempted to found the cultural value of their poetry on its claim to generate normative ideological effects, Marlowe attempted more pragmatically to increase the charisma and therefore the market value of his theatre by transgressing normativity, and staging a Protestant doctrinal conflation of theatre and magic that seemed to call actual devils to the stage. Taking up the rumors that performances of *Doctor Faustus* were stopped because actors and audiences feared that actual devils had appeared in the playhouse, chapter 3 will recover the interplay of cultural conditions and aesthetic strategies that enabled Marlowe's theatrical representation of conjuration to have metadramatic performative effects in its own historical context. In a wide polemic campaign at the end of the sixteenth century, zealous Protestant ministers began to argue that devils tricked hapless people into their damnation by staging conjuration as a theatrical spectacle. This spectacle, the reformers argued, inspired participants and spectators to think thoughts and feel emotions that would anger God and cause him to withdraw his salvific grace. Knowing a dramatic occasion when he saw one, Marlowe represented Faustus's magic in just these terms. The reformers argued that magical language had no essential performative efficacy, that it served merely as a scripted cue for a devil to appear and act as if he had been commanded. And in the beginning of *Faustus*, Mephistopheles tells Faustus that his conjuration worked only *per accidens*, as a sign that cued him to appear in the hope he could win Faustus's soul for hell. By characterizing Faustus's magic in the reformer's terms, Marlowe made it possible for spectators who knew and feared what their ministers were saying about magic to imagine that God was watching and judging their responses to the spectacles they were witnessing, so that their absorption in onstage events would appear as inward evidence of their own reprobation. At times this evidence appeared overwhelming enough to cause collective hysterias, as if whole groups of people suddenly panicked that God had judged them irredeemable for their investment in the play, and became convinced that devils had therefore appeared on the scene. In *Doctor Faustus*, then, Marlowe created a drama whose aesthetic pleasures seemed instrumentally to produce the spiritual consequences of magic itself, and whose theatrical performativity therefore managed to produce the spectacular results that off-stage performativity quite obviously could not.

Although recently *The Tempest* has been read as a document of early British colonialism, the play may be equally well understood as the consummate example of instrumental aesthetics in the English Renaissance. In *The Tempest*, I will show in chapter 4, Shakespeare used James I's own beliefs about magic to establish the theatre as an utterly autonomous cultural zone. In both his political writings and in his legislation, James characterized magicians as traitors who should be tortured and executed without pardon for their desire to accrue power through the instrumentality of magic. In this political context, the fact that Prospero asked the audience to pardon him for his magic served as an oblique challenge to James's authority. Yet James apparently liked *The Tempest*; at the very least he allowed it to be staged as his daughter's wedding. This contrast between the content of the play and its success at court indicates the power of Shakespeare's instrumental aesthetics, which produced the drama's autonomy and freedom from political law. If Prospero first appears in *The Tempest* as the magician of James's anxious fantasies, the form of the play itself – its interplay of dramatic modes, its development of information through the juxtaposition of scenes, its structuring of Prospero's dramatic arc – serves to transform the magician from a feared figure into an object of mercy, and to transmute magic, which at first seemed like a technology of power, into a mode of aesthetic experience whose only effect is to provide consolation for death. By the epilogue, in which Prospero asks the audience to pardon him by applauding, magic has been so subsumed into disinterested theatrical play that pardon appears as nothing more than an expression of delight. But for those fleeting, glimmering moments in which James himself applauded, *The Tempest* fulfilled the promise of instrumental aesthetics. By applauding, not only did the king behave as if he had undergone an ethical transformation – his merciful renunciation of his right to torture and execute the magician – but that performance produced the theatre as a culturally sovereign space in which the laws of play triumphed even over the laws of the realm.

Finally, in a coda to *Magical Imaginations*, I will revisit the theoretical questions about the literary aesthetic that I have discussed in this Introduction. I will propose that our common understanding of aesthetics, which underlies both New Critical and New Historicist approaches to Renaissance literature, is based on a misreading of Kant in which beauty is characterized as a purposeless quality appreciated only by disinterested judgment. I will suggest, by contrast, that the actual aesthetics Kant laid out in the *Critique of Judgment* are not in fact disinterested, but themselves instrumental. In the third *Critique*, Kant argues that taste remains 'barbaric' if it is influenced by 'charm' (*der Reiz*). In both sixteenth-century German and English, the word 'charm' denoted a magical incantation or spell. And in the instrumental aesthetics of the English Renaissance, the charm and the poem had yet to be entirely distinguished. Thus, as we shall see, the Elizabethan parliament outlawed the magical practice of 'charming' as a felony in 1563, and English theologians worried over the etymological connections between 'charm' and '*carmen*' (the Latin for 'poem'), but Sidney still attributed poetry's efficacy to its 'charming force.' Spenser called the spells of his demonic magicians both 'verses' and 'charms.' The Protestant ministers whose account of conjuration Marlowe appropriated into *Doctor Faustus* insisted that any signs used to spiritual ends without God's scriptural authorization should be called 'charms.' And Shakespeare staged Prospero's power over his enemies as an effect of his 'high charms.' This connection between magic and poetry became purely metaphorical in the eighteenth century, when 'charm' emerged as a term in British empiricist aesthetics designating the merely natural, if alluring force of beauty. In the third *Critique*, distancing himself from the history connecting magic and beauty, Kant initially rejects the idea that beauty might be an alluring force, and instead theorizes an aesthetics based not on the subject's submission to beauty's power, but on his mastery of a style of consumption that seemingly confirms his autonomy and freedom from compulsion. Yet in the end Kant too, I will show, attempts to justify aesthetic experience not only by instrumentalizing it to moral ends but also by continuing to base this salutary instrumentality on the pleasure of charm.

1 Conjuration and *The Defense of Poesy*

> To be led unknowing down paths unchosen ... what can we call that but
> magic?
>
> Plotinus, *Enneads*

In a moment that exemplifies his charming critical persona, Sir Philip Sidney ends his 1581 essay of literary theory, *The Defense of Poesy*, by engaging in a witty extended parody. Having argued eloquently for poetry's cultural value, in his *peroratio* Sidney switches modes, and adopts the self-mocking role of a magician who hyperbolically conjures his readers to believe for true all that he has written:

> I conjure you all that have had the evil luck to read this ink-wasting toy of mine, even in the name of the Nine Muses, no more to scorn the sacred mysteries of Poesy ... but to believe, with Aristotle, that they were the ancient treasurers of the Grecian's divinity; to believe, with Bembus, that they were first bringers-in of all civility; to believe, with Scaliger, that no philosopher's precepts can sooner make you an honest man than the reading of Virgil ... to believe, with me, that there are many mysteries contained in poetry, which of purpose were written darkly, lest by profane wits it should be abused ... lastly to believe themselves, when they tell you they will make you immortal by their verses.[1]

So why does Sidney end his essay in this way? Recent accounts of the *Defense* generally argue that the facetious tone in this passage is unmistakable, and that Sidney is so tongue-in-cheek here, because he wants to emphasize his own self-fashioning as someone who maintains a distanced, ironic stance to his own poetic endeavours.[2] But we might say that such readings misidentify the actual target of Sidney's irony. That target is not in fact poetry per se, but poetry's relation to magic. Indeed, if Sidney is engaging in self-parody here it is of himself precisely as a magician. The form of the mock conjuration – that is, 'in the name of X, I conjure you no more to do Y, but to do Z' – matches exactly those of conjurations found in contemporaneous manuscripts, such as British Library Add. MS 36674, Article One.[3] This suggests not only that Sidney was familiar with magical discourse but also that he wanted his ventriloquism of that discourse to seem eerily accurate. Furthermore, by conjuring us to believe that the 'mysteries' contained in poetry were 'of purpose ... written darkly, lest by profane wits [they] should be abused,' Sidney is rehearsing the standard magical caveat that the occult text at hand is an allegory, written 'darkly' so that magical power cannot be abused by the 'profane.' Similarly, Cornelius Agrippa claims in his *Three Books of Occult Philosophy* that he has 'writ many things, rather narratively than affirmatively' so that he might deliver 'this art in such a manner, that it may not be hid from the prudent and intelligent, and yet may not admit the wicked and incredulous to the mysteries of these secrets.'[4] Having thus confused the boundaries between poetry and magic, Sidney pulls out of his hat the most hyperbolic promise for the efficacy of poetry, the most ridiculous and brilliant conflation of printer's dedication and supernatural performance: the claim that poets 'will make you immortal by their verses.' With this conflation, Sidney performs a double operation. He transforms the poet's promise to his patron into a mock magical power, and he distances poetry from magic by turning the gift of immortality into nothing more than the standard form of literary fame.

But why should Sidney want to distance poetry from magic by mocking each discourse for being like the other? Why should Sidney end his *Defense* by parodying himself for being a sort of magician? He does so, I shall argue, because the poetry he constructed in the *Defense* and the practice of early modern magic were intertwined in a double knot. To make his aesthetics instrumental, Sidney employed theories of coercive rhetorical persuasion that emerged also in magical tracts by Agrippa and Giordano Bruno as well as a variety of English magicians. Further, Sidney's argument that poetry's coercive effects are justified because they arise not from poetry's contingent rhetorical force, but from its conveyance of metaphysical Ideas of perfection, also connected his instrumental aesthetics with magic, namely with the magical Neoplatonism that strict Protestantism characterized as a form of heresy. Knowing that his contemporaries were aware of the discursive symbiosis of poetry and magic, Sidney attempted in the *Defense* to distinguish the two practices in order to evade the theological and social problems entailed in their relationship. He could not do so, though, without abandoning his desire to influence social and political life with his art, so instead he took recourse in humour. He concluded his *Defense* with a parody of conjuration, which diffused the implications of the interconnection of poetry and magic by recasting it as material for a joke. This joke, this mock conjuration, thus expresses the hidden anxiety haunting Sidney's instrumental aesthetics: that the Elizabethan magician was the doppelgänger of the efficacious poet.

Sixteenth-century Italian literary theory was born from the necessity of defending poetry against the charge that imaginative literature and theatre had deleterious social effects. Though in England this anti-poetic attitude took on new urgency among Protestants concerned about the rise of the public playhouses, the charge may, of course, be traced back to Plato. It goes something as follows: imaginative writing represents images of unethical action, but its style has such a powerful emotional and cognitive effect that it entices readers and audiences into emulation, which in turn makes them behave unethically.[5] Responding to this challenge, Italian literary critics conceded that poetry inspires emulation, but they also insisted that poetry representing virtue could be used as an instrument to generate moral and civic virtue in its readers. Thus Antonio Sebastiano Minturno began his 1559 *De Poeta*, parts of which Sidney wove into his own text, by praising the 'power of poetry ... with which you can educate children in all disciplines, exhort men to all virtues ... enlighten the people with wonderful pleasure and lead them where you will, or from whatever place it may please you.'[6] And Julius Caesar Scaliger in his 1561 *Poetices libri septem*, which Sidney also used to compose the *Defense*, proposed in a more cynical mode that there is 'no imitation for its own sake, for it goes without saying that every art looks beyond itself toward somebody's advantage.'[7] Sidney imported this Italian literary theory into his essay in order to argue that verse written by 'right poets' (102) is useful to the well-ordered Protestant state, because the aesthetic delight that poetry generates moulds the moral and political dispositions of even its resistant readers, making them inclined to act according to the cultural ideals represented in poetry's fictions. At his most extreme, Sidney even suggests that poetry has an imperial, state-building function: 'Even among the most barbarous and simple Indians where no writing is,' there are 'poets who make and sing songs, which they call *areytos* ... a sufficient probability that, if ever learning come among them, it must be by having their hard dull wits softened and sharpened with the sweet delights of Poetry' (98). Sidney thus addressed himself to the nascent imperial ambitions of his fellow activist Protestants at court, and not just to the objections of disgruntled polemicists like Stephen Gosson. In his *Defense*, that is, he attempted to persuade his fellow aristocrats, those who would be made 'immortal' by the poet's verses, to patronize poets with their social and monetary capital. Sidney sought, then, to establish poetry as a culturally and materially valued production on the basis of its instrumentality to the ends of the powerful.[8]

Poetry, Sidney argues, is 'not wholly imaginative, as we are wont to say by them that build castles in the air; but so far substantially it worketh, not only to make a Cyrus ... but to bestow a Cyrus upon the world to make many Cyruses, if they will learn aright why and how that maker made him' (101). This remarkable claim for poetry's efficacy goes far beyond the Horatian commonplace that poetry should 'teach and delight.' The idea that poetry bestows a Cyrus upon the world to make many Cyruses grants generative agency to imaginative language, affording it the ability to reproduce human copies of the heroic models it represents. Poetry reproduces these models, Sidney argues, by inspiring readers to emulate what they read: indeed, Sidney nominates poetry 'the monarch' of 'all the sciences' (113) for its power to move readers to 'virtuous action,' which he calls 'the ending end of all earthly learning' (104).[9] What inspires the reader to virtuous action is poetry's beauty, which engenders the delight that 'move[s] men to take that goodness in hand, which without delight they would fly as from a stranger' (103).[10] This delight is an 'instrumental cause' (115), the 'end of well-doing and not well-knowing only' (104); it produces 'not *gnosis* but *praxis*' (112). Indeed, if poetry teaches 'moral doctrine' (112), according to Sidney, it does so only in retrospect, 'to make [readers] know that goodness whereunto they are moved' (103). In the instrumental aesthetics that Sidney articulates in the *Defense*, then, poetry does not simply teach and delight, it teaches *by* delight, transforming the reader into an ethical subject by the pleasure of reading, even before the reader understands what he has become.

This promise that poetry may transform its reader without the reader's conscious knowledge or consent lies at the heart of Sidney's claim for poetry's usefulness to England, for it allows him to argue that poetry will transform the social behaviour even of 'hard-hearted evil men' who 'know no other good but *indulgere genio* ... [yet who] will content to be delighted – which is all the good-fellow poet seemeth to promise – and [who will] so steal to see the form of goodness (which seen they cannot but love) ere themselves be aware' (114). Sidney here relies on the premise that poetic delight has a manipulative, or even automatic efficacy in stealing evil men 'to see the form of goodness (which seen they cannot but love).' Indeed, his argument affords a kind of disciplinary coercion to literary pleasure, a coercion insidiously if paradoxically experienced as libidinal arousal. Later in the *Defense*, Sidney compares aesthetic delight to the sensation of being 'ravished with delight to see a fair woman' (136), as if poetry's beauty had an erotic force that overwhelmed the reader with admiration and desire for ideological ideals. In contrast, philosophy 'teacheth them that are already taught' (109), producing only 'a wordish description' that 'doth neither strike, pierce, nor possess the sight of the soul' (110). And history, like philosophy, also lacks ravishing force: its mundane examples of virtue, obscured by too many contextualizing facts, utterly fail to overwhelm and move the reader. When you read history, Sidney asks, 'how will you discern what to follow but by your own discretion, which you had without reading Quintus Curtius?' (110). In dismissing history's ethical efficacy, Sidney implicitly characterizes poetry as a discourse that overmasters 'your own discretion,' leading or even compelling you towards virtue, whether or not you consciously discern what to follow. This is why Sidney imagines poetry can transform readers who have no idea they are subject to persuasion, like those 'hard-hearted evil men' who 'know no other good but *indulgere genio*,' and who are simply 'content to be delighted.' The most effective coercion for Sidney is the experience of pleasure or play: the poet 'with a tale forsooth ... cometh unto you ... and pretending no more, doth intend the winning of the mind from wickedness to virtue' (113). Under the pretense of providing only entertainment, a compelling yet entirely disinterested pleasure that has no further end, the poet attempts with a kind of persuasion by legerdemain to induce his reader to fall in love with the ideological ideal.

Now, to understand the relationship between Sidney's instrumental aesthetics and Elizabethan magic, we must begin by seeing how magicians themselves characterized persuasion as a fundamental occult power. Thus Francis Coxe, a physician convicted by the Privy Council in 1561 for 'employment of certain sinistral [*sic*] and devilish arts,' explains in his public confession that when magic has 'credit with men,' they judge not only 'the source of natural things thereby to be governed, but also that part which God hath and doth reserve to himself, and his determination, as the mind of man, and such like.'[11] Agrippa claims that 'the magicians do not only search out natural things, but them also, which accompany nature' such as 'the movings, numbers, figures, sounds, voices' that command 'the affections of the mind,' and that 'oftentimes do bring forth some marvellous effect.'[12] And in his *Essays on Magic*, Giordano Bruno argues that it is necessary for the magician to govern the affections of men's minds if his magical operations are to work. Asserting that the 'magical bond ... consists of faith or credibility [and] of love and of strong emotions,' Bruno states without a trace of irony that 'a magician is most fortunate if many believe in him, and if he commands great persuasion.'[13] Indeed, for Bruno persuasion is ultimately what is operative in magic, and it has an equal, and equally magical force on spirits and people: 'Great results are produced by those bonds which come from the words of a man of eloquence, by which a certain disposition arises and flourishes in the imagination, which is the only entrance for all internal feelings and is the bond of bonds ... [This applies] to any type of magic or to any power identified by a different title, for, in the act of binding, the imagination must be stimulated or else one can hardly motivate anyone by other means' (141).

Accordingly, Bruno accounts for the obvious difficulty in compelling spirits to obey his will as a *rhetorical* difficulty: 'Our Latin, Greek, and Italian sounds,' he writes, 'sometimes fail to be heard and understood by higher and eternal sprits, which differ from us in species; thus, it is no easier for us to be able to communicate with the spirits than it is for an eagle to converse with a human' (115). Yet within his own species Bruno takes the magician's talent for persuasion to be nearly limitless. Because the subject of magic lacks 'deliberate choice' (138) over the images his imagination apprehends, according to Bruno, the persuasion of magical eloquence may occur without the subject's consent, or even without his conscious knowledge. Bruno argues that magical representations may work in the thoughts over time – with what he calls 'an occult murmur' (135) – so that those subjected to magic may find themselves eventually bound to perform actions by the inclinations that have slowly arisen in their dispositions.

This claim brings us back to Sidney's promise that poetry works on 'hard-hearted evil men' by making them love goodness 'ere themselves be aware.' To be sure, in the *Defense* Sidney wants to prove that poetry is unique in this power: 'The poet,' he says, 'with the same hand of delight, doth draw the mind more effectually than any other art doth' (115). Yet this drawing of the mind itself invokes the Hercules Gallicus, Alciati's emblem for rhetoric, who leads his followers along with chains of gold and amber that bind their ears to his tongue.[14] In turn, those chains are emblematic of Bruno's 'magical bond,' which consists 'of love and ... strong emotions.' Of course, unlike Sidney, Bruno was happy to afford such binding force to 'any type of magic or to any power identified by a different title,' but then in his essays on magic, Bruno is not exactly trying to establish the cultural legitimacy of his magical practice. Unlike Bruno, however, Sidney in the *Defense* is attempting to establish poetry as a legitimate practice. He must, therefore, not only produce its value as a powerful tool to normative ends, but also legitimize poetry's power by naturalizing it, making it seem inherent to the very beauty that poetry conveys to the reader.

Sidney attempts to naturalize poetic efficacy by locating poetry's coercive force not in the dangerously contingent power of the operator's eloquence, but rather in the essential beauty of the metaphysical referent that poetry represents – in the '*Idea* or fore-conceit of the work, and not in the work itself' (101). In adducing the 'Idea' into his instrumental aesthetics, Sidney appropriates the Neoplatonic justification for poetry, a critical response to Plato's claim that 'the imitative poet puts a bad constitution in the soul of each individual by making images that are far removed from the truth.'[15] Plato and Neoplatonists alike imagine the universe as a hierarchy that can be divided most simply into three parts. At the top level are the forms, or Ideas, the eternal models of all things in the universe, which reside in the mind of God as pure Being. Richard Hooker calls Ideas 'those principal and mother elements of the world, whereof all things in this lower world are made.'[16] One ontological step down is what Sidney calls 'Nature' with a capital *N*, or what Plato in the *Timaeus* characterizes as 'an imitation of the model, something that possesses becoming.'[17] This Nature, *natura naturans*, mediates between the celestial Ideas and the phenomenal world; it imitates Ideas by infusing them into matter in a temporal process of coming-to-be (a process never fully realized because matter is fallen). By infusing Ideas into matter, generative Nature produces the lowest ontological level: what Sidney characterizes as 'nature' with a small *n*, the phenomenal and social world, *natura naturata*, or the corrupted mimetic approximation of the Idea's true being.[18] Plato objects to poetry in part because he sees its representations of the phenomenal world as imitations of an already-defective imitation, as third-order representations of true Being.

Neoplatonists counter Plato by pointing out that because the world exists only insofar as it represents eternal Ideas, one could characterize 'nature herself as an enigmatic poesy,' as does Montaigne after reading 'a divine saying' in Plato himself.[19] And, the Neoplatonic argument continues, as nature and poetry are analogous imitations of the Ideas, poetry may well be the better copy of the supersensuous original, especially since it is 'not tied to the laws of matter,' as Bacon points out in *The Advance-*

ment of Learning.[20] Indeed, as Plotinus insists, art does not represent already-created objects in 'a bare reproduction of the thing seen'; rather, working by 'the Idea' of 'the beautiful object it is to produce,' art goes 'back to the Reason-Principles from which Nature itself derives' and conveys a clearer, more powerful beauty that 'adds where nature is lacking.'[21] In Neoplatonic aesthetics, then, the idea (or Idea) in the poet's mind can claim metaphysical validity and objectivity, and his inner notions can enjoy supernatural and superindividual existence.[22] This conflation of the ideational and the metaphysical in the concept of the poetic Idea was well captured by the English translator Thomas Cooper in his *Thesaurus* of 1565: 'Idea: a figure conceived in Imagination, as it were a substance perpetual, being a pattern of all other sort or kind, as of one seal proceeds many prints so of one Idea of man proceed many thousands of men.'[23] Here the Idea is at once a figure conceived in the imagination and a pattern of sorts or kinds (like a 'substance perpetual'). And Cooper's assumption that 'of one Idea of man proceed many thousands of men' bears a striking resemblance to Sidney's claim that poetry 'worketh ... to bestow a Cyrus upon the world to make many Cyruses, if they will learn aright why and how that maker made him.'

The resemblance neatly locates the identity of the metaphysical and the aesthetic in the *Defense*, for Sidney indeed argues that the men represented in right poetry, those who embody the virtue to which poetry forcefully moves the reader, are themselves imitations of metaphysical Ideas. More excellent than any men who actually exist in the world, these literary characters have a greater fidelity to the transcendent 'reason principles' that give subjects their virtues. As Sidney puts it, 'Nature' has never 'brought forth so true a lover as Theagenes, so constant a friend as Pylades, so valiant a man as Orlando, so right a prince as Xenophon's Cyrus, so excellent a man in every way as Virgil's Aeneas' (100). In Neoplatonic terms, these literary characters manifest the Ideas that inform them, and their actions emanate directly from those Ideas: the fidelity of Theagenes, for example, emanates from his manifesting the form of Lover, and the political rightness of Cyrus arises from his manifesting the form of Prince. Sidney argues that the poet brings forth these ideal types because the force of his imagination allows him conceptually to ascend to the celestial sphere where the Ideas dwell. 'Only the poet,' Sidney famously proclaims, 'lifted up with the vigour of his own invention doth grow in effect into another nature, in making things either better than Nature bringeth forth, or, quite anew, forms such as never were in Nature ... so as he goeth hand in hand with Nature, not enclosed within the narrow warrant of her gifts, but freely ranging only within the zodiac of his own wit' (100).[24] Here are the two natures of the Neoplatonic cosmos: the generative Nature that embodies forth forms, and the phenomenal nature that manifests what Nature produces. The poet works 'hand in hand' with generative Nature, ranging in the 'zodiac of his own wit' to discover and imitate metaphysical Ideas that have never yet come to be in the world.

Lest we think that he speaks only metaphorically or 'jestingly' about the poet's ability to represent metaphysically objective forms, Sidney insists that it matters not that 'the works of one [Nature] be essential, the other [poetry] in imitation or fiction,' for the value of any production is found 'in that Idea or fore-conceit of the work, and not in the work itself.' And, Sidney continues, 'that the poet hath that Idea is manifest, by delivering them forth in such excellency as he hath imagined them' (101). In other words, with some circular logic, Sidney argues that the beauty of poetic representation displays the essence of the metaphysical objects of that representation. Of course, from a materialist perspective, as Adorno points out, 'the artifactual more does not in itself guarantee the metaphysical substance of art.'[25] But in Sidney's idealist instrumental aesthetics, the beautiful essentially entails both the true *and* the good, which is why for him poetry 'doth teach and move to a truth' (119) and why truth is not 'wholly imaginative,' but rather bestows 'a Cyrus upon the world to make many Cyruses, if [readers] will learn aright why and how that maker made him' (101). To learn why and how the maker made Cyrus is to see the Idea of Cyrus that the poet apprehended in his mind and conveyed to the reader. And, Sidney asserts, to see that Idea is to see the form of beauty and also 'to see the form of goodness (which seen [readers] cannot but love) ere themselves be aware' (114). Readers, even 'hard-hearted evil men' (114), cannot help but love the 'form of goodness' because the beauty of the form itself compels their libidinal response, overmastering their discretion and possessing their imagination without their conscious consent. Founding his instrumental aesthetics on the Neoplatonic Idea, then, Sidney is able to position poetry as representing essences that transcend historical contingency, poetry's instrumentality as deriving from those essences, and the poet as the conduit of a metaphysical realm that exists beyond either rhetorical manipulation or political calculation, beyond time or history, indeed beyond the mundane world itself.

Thus does the Neoplatonic justification for poetry differentiate instrumental aesthetics from sophisticated rhetoric. Yet in its own historical context this Neoplatonic justification does little to make poetry seem less magical. Sixteenth-century magicians themselves constantly invoke the

Idea to naturalize their claims to occult efficacy. Bruno, as I have pointed out, argues that magicians may use their eloquence to perform whatever they wish, but he also recommends that the practitioners who desire to act 'in accordance with nature' should study the 'idea, which is generally present everywhere' and 'especially understand this ideal principle.'[26] On his part, Agrippa cannot even imagine separating the instrumental and the ideal. He views the magician's ability to ascend to the sphere of Ideas as the very basis of his supernatural power. 'Seeing there is a three-fold world, Elementary, Celestial, and Intellectual,' Agrippa begins his *Three Books of Occult Philosophy*, 'wise men conceive it no way irrational that it should be possible for us to ascend by the same degrees through each World ... and to draw new virtues from above.'[27] Having ascended to the zodiac of God's own wit, the magician, according to Agrippa, draws down virtues from above by representing Ideas in spells: such representations have 'a certain and sure foundation, not fortuitous, nor casual, but efficacious, powerful, and sufficient, doing nothing in vain' (27). For Agrippa, Ideas are quite literally angels, which he calls 'celestial souls,' and which he imagines influence 'various effects, inclinations, and dispositions' (28). John Dee also conflates Ideas and angels when he praises 'celestial influences' for graciously pouring themselves down 'into our imaginative spirit so that they coalesce more intensely, as in a mirror, and show us wonders and work wonders within us.'[28] By blurring the boundaries between metaphysical Ideas, celestial spirits, and imaginative influences, Neoplatonic magicians and poets alike collapse the distinction between, as Sidney puts it, the 'essential' works of the Idea in Nature and those in 'imitation or fiction,' enabling them both to claim that they mediate a transcendent realm whose representation automatically has transformative effects.

It is perhaps unsurprising, then, that Neoplatonism itself, with its conflation of ideas and spirits, is often characterized by Protestants as a diabolical heresy. Samuel Harsnett, arguably one of the most talented propagandists of the conformist church, relentlessly mocks what he calls 'Plato's *Ideae*' of essences 'made pendulous in the air': he calls these Ideas 'Italian Monsters, hatched of the eggs of school Crocodiles, the winding serpentine wits of profane uncircumcised spirits that take liberty to descant upon Almighty God.'[29] According to Harsnett, and to Protestants across sectarian lines, the only spirit who enjoys the liberty to descant upon God is the Holy Spirit mediated by scripture. 'I would fain know of these men [the Neoplatonists], by whose inspiration they are carried up so high,' Calvin asks wryly in the *Institution of the Christian Religion*, implying that the Neoplatonists are carried 'high' by devils. It is not 'the office' of the Holy Spirit, Calvin goes on to point out, 'to feign new and unheard-of revelations, or to coin a new kind of doctrine.' And Neoplatonism could not have been disseminated by the Spirit, Calvin argues, for its Ideas and angels appear nowhere in the Bible: Paul himself was 'ravished up into the third heaven,' but said nothing in his writings about metaphysical essences suspended in a celestial sphere.[30] Having thus implied that Neoplatonic philosophy is the work of devils, Calvin finally proposes, in a typically sententious conclusion, that we should 'forsake that Platonic philosophy, [of seeking] the way to God by Angels' (69). Having noted Calvin's implication that only evil spirits feign 'unheard-of revelations,' in *A Discourse Upon Devils and Spirits* (the appendix to *The Discoverie of Witchcraft*), Reginald Scot makes the argument explicit. Scot insists that human beings can have no commerce with the metaphysical world. To mediate transcendence, he says, is 'neither within the compass of mans capacity, nor yet of his knowledge,' because 'no carnal man can discern the things of the spirit.'[31] (Unlike Sidney, Scot makes no distinction between the 'erected wit' that enables us to 'know what perfection is' and the 'infected will' that keeps us 'from reaching unto it.')[32] Hence, Scot goes on to argue, the 'Ideae' that Plato claimed existed among 'the nine several orders of Spirits' must have been 'evil spirits,' for 'Paul was rapt into the third heaven and reported no such matters' as eternal Ideas. Such Protestant critiques of Platonic metaphysics indicate that the very Neoplatonic justification for poetry is itself profoundly unstable.[33] The metaphysical objects that poetry putatively represents are ominously connected to the devil, and the poet's claim to mediate these objects emerges as a dangerous attempt to deploy entities condemned by God.

This belief that poets traffic with the devil, or at least do his work on earth, and are thus 'accursed ... by the mouth of God' – as Stephen Gosson puts it in *The School of Abuse*, his anti-poetical polemic dedicated to Sidney – goes hand in hand with Elizabethan Puritans' conflation of poetry and magic.[34] Hence Gosson himself accuses the poet of being like a 'juggler' who 'casts a mist to work the close' (A2r). To call a man a 'juggler' is to call him a stage magician, a prestidigitator. This title in itself does not always carry a negative theological charge: the excellent handbook *The Anatomie of Legerdemaine, or the Arte of Juggling*, by Hocus Pocus Junior, gives instructions for such spiritually innocuous tricks as 'how to seem to pull a rope through your nose' and 'how to make two or three eggs dance upon a staff.'[35] Yet many Protestants – like John Foxe, as we saw in the Introduction – characterize jugglers as diabolical agents.

William Perkins, for instance, insists that 'magic operative' should be divided into 'two parts: juggling and enchantments,' and he defines juggling as an art 'whereby, through the devil's conveyance, many great and very hard matters, are in show effected.'[36] The devil works with the juggler, in some accounts, to produce feigned 'wonders' rather than the true miracles attributable solely to God. In his commentary on the book of Daniel, Andrew Willet, for instance, argues that 'divine miracles are not counterfeit tricks, such as are the *juggling feats* of Magicians' for 'God only makes true wonders.'[37] And, to take a poetic example, in his *Mask*, Milton's Lady calls the sorcerer Comus a 'Juggler' who can 'charm' her 'eyes' with 'dazzling Spells' that make him appear to her as a lowly shepherd rather than a devilish enemy.[38] To call a poet a 'juggler,' then, is to accuse him of being a magician who mediates diabolical deceptions in order to confuse true belief.[39] The poet's diabolical deceptions are quite simply poems, narratives, and stage plays themselves. Thus Edward Dering, a zealous conformist minister who preached before Elizabeth in 1569, and whose collected sermons became popular enough to merit three printings between 1590 and 1614, warns his flock that 'Songs and Sonnets ... Palaces of Pleasure ... unchaste fables and Tragedies' are all 'sorceries,' or 'spiritual enchantments' because they are not only 'boldly printed' but 'plausible taken.'[40] Dering locates the deceptive sorcery or enchantment of poetry in its beauty and persuasiveness – 'plausible' here means *pleasurable*, or worthy of applause, as well as *believable* – and we should not assume that Dering sees poetry's enchantment as only metaphorically magical. Enchantment and sorcery, along with witchcraft and 'the Conjuration of Evil Spirits,' were actual magical practices outlawed by Elizabeth's statute against magic, legislated by a 1563 Act of Parliament.[41] In calling poems 'sorceries' and 'enchantments,' Dering gives a *literalist* bite to his accusation that 'there is no one thing more enemy to the word of GOD, then these vain and sinful imaginations of our own unbridled wits.'[42]

Sidney's instrumental aesthetics were, then, intertwined with magic in a double bind: his claims for the overwhelming force of language were echoed by magicians such as Agrippa and Bruno, and zealous Protestants regarded the Neoplatonism with which he justified his claims as a kind of diabolical magic, which only reinforced such Protestants' accusations that poetry was a form of sorcery or enchantment. But how aware was Sidney of this perceived relationship between poetry and magic? How familiar was he with magicians and with magical practice? There are more gaps than texts in the historical record, but we may start to answer these questions first by pointing out that Bruno dedicated two of the four books he published while he was in England to Sidney, whom he called that 'most illustrious and excellent cavalier.'[43] Bruno's most personal dedication came with the last of these books, *The Heroic Frenzies* (*De gl'heroici fuori*), which Bruno presented to Sidney 'without fear, because here the Italian reasons with someone who understands him.'[44] A sequence of sonnets with extended commentary, *The Heroic Frenzies* was intended allegorically to 'signify divine contemplation and to present the eye and ear with other frenzies, not those caused by vulgar love, but those caused by heroic love' (145) – heroic love in this case meaning 'the instruments and effects by which this divine light enters, shows itself, and takes possession of the soul, in order to raise it and convert it unto God' (146). Of course, this Neoplatonic allegory for spiritual ascent would have been understood by any Englishman with an Italianate education, yet Bruno suggested that the text was a contribution to a dialogue he had been carrying out with Sidney himself. Indeed, to hear Bruno tell it in *The Ash Wednesday Supper*, once he settled in England he became part of Sidney's circle of friends: 'the most excellent Sir Francis' (Walsingham, that is), along with 'the most illustrious Milord Count Robert Dudley' and 'the must illustrious and excellent cavalier, Sir Philip Sidney,' by their own instigation, dined on more than one occasion with Bruno at the house of Fulke Greville, and thereby 'with the light of their great nobility [became] sufficient to dissipate and extinguish darkness; and with warm and loving courtesy to polish and clean any rudeness and rusticity that may occur not only among the Britons but also among the Scythians, Arabs, Tartars, Cannibals and Anthropofags' (83–4). As his listing them with the 'Cannibals and Anthropofags' suggests, Bruno did not end up liking the 'Britons' that much (nor, for that matter, did they think much of him), so Bruno may have seized on whatever courtesy Sidney showed towards him and interpreted it as a sign of friendship.

Yet it is also the case that Sidney's close friends and family were the members of Elizabeth's court most inclined to patronize men associated with magic. Sidney's great aunt Jane Dudley, the duchess of Northumberland, commissioned two works from John Dee in 1553, early in his career, one of which was entitled *The Philosophical and Poetical Original Occasions of the Configurations, and Names of the Heavenly Asterisms*, and she corresponded with him on multiple topics throughout her life. Sidney's great friend Edward Dyer was remarkably close to Dee: he mediated requests from the Privy Council to Dee, and, although of no blood relation, stood as godfather to Dee's first son, Arthur.[45] The only one to whom Dyer had closer personal ties was Sidney.[46] And Sidney's uncle, Robert Dudley, the earl of Leicester, engaged Dee in all his political manoeuvrings, from employing him to calculate the most favourable day for Elizabeth's coronation to trotting out both Dee and Bruno as part of his political campaign to create a Protestant alliance on the Continent.[47] When the Polish prince Albert Laski visited England, Leicester set up Bruno's debate at Oxford as part of the entertainments to be held in Laski's honour.[48] And on the way to Oxford from London, Leicester's train – including Laski, Leicester, Bruno, and Dyer – stopped at Dee's residence in order that Laski might formally meet Dee. Laski himself had written a treatise on magic, and Leicester was attempting to impress his guest by introducing him not only to the Nolan, as Bruno called himself, but to the English magus with the widest Continental reputation.[49] On her part, although less excited than Leicester by the idea of a Protestant military alliance, the queen had no reluctance to support Dee's social advancement. So that he could host a formal dinner for the Laski party on the night they stopped with him, Elizabeth reportedly sent money out of her own coffers to finance the necessarily lavish affair. But Elizabeth not only patronized magicians with gifts and favour, in the 1563 Act of Parliament to which I have already referred, she even enabled the laws against magic to be changed to accord with her lenient attitude towards magical practice. Under previous Henrican law it had been a felony, and therefore a capital offence, not only to practise witchcraft, enchantment, or sorcery, but also to conjure spirits of any variety.[50] In Elizabeth's law, invoking spirits per se was no longer a crime; only the deliberate invocation of *evil* spirits merited punishment. Such a statutory construction allowed the possibility that spirits could indeed be benevolent, and thus enabled the idea that there could be 'white magicians' or 'spiritual magicians' who could practise lawfully. Keith Thomas comments aptly that 'this leniency contrasted sharply with the attitude of those theologians who would have liked to see all magicians, black or white, consigned to speedy execution.'[51]

It seems that Elizabeth and her Privy Council were more inclined to permit activities that they thought could be useful to the realm than to worry about the theological niceties of Promethean endeavours. The notorious epistolary exchange between the statesman Lord Burghley and Edward Kelly, the con man and erstwhile scryer for John Dee, makes this abundantly clear.[52] In the late 1580s, Dee and Kelly were completing a long residency in Bohemia, where a breach had opened between the two men, because Kelly was purportedly doing intensive alchemical experiments without Dee's collaboration, which offended Dee deeply.[53] In 1589

Dee began his slow return to England, and Kelly moved on to take a place at the court of Rudolph II. Within a year, reports began to trickle back to England through Dyer – at that point the queen's agent in Germany – that Kelly had indeed managed to discover an alchemical substance that would transmute metals into gold. Burghley wrote immediately to solicit Dyer to convince Kelly to come back to his native country and bestow his treasure on his queen, glossing over theological questions to focus on the benefit that such occult powers could provide the treasury.[54] Burghley claimed the worldly situation was really pressing. He told Dyer that even if Kelly could not return immediately, he should 'in some secret box, send to her majesty a token, some such portion, as might be to her a sum reasonable to defer her charges for this summer for her navy, which we are now preparing to the sea, to withstand the strong navy of Spain, discovered on our coasts between Breton and Cornwall within these two days.'[55] Burghley also corresponded with Kelly directly, in order to reassure him that he need not 'fear severe punishment' on his return to England, for either unlawful magic on one hand or 'imposturing' on the other:

> Such is my persuasion of your ability to perform what Mr. Dyer has reported (by reason of the estimation, honor, and credit I see that you have gotten by your behaviour), that I rest only unsatisfied in your delay of coming; and I am expressly commanded by Her Majesty to require you to have regard to her honour, and according to the tenor of her former letters, to assure yourself singularly favoured in respect of the benefit you may bring to Her Majesty.[56]

The substance of this letter exemplifies Bruno's dictum that 'a magician is most fortunate if many believe in him, and if he commands great persuasion.' Everything turns on the 'credit,' or the belief, that Burghley has in Dyer, and on the 'estimation, honor, and credit' he bestows on Kelly (which recalls Coxe's lament that magic has grown 'into such credit with men' that they judge 'the source of natural things thereby to be governed'). Of course, Burghley's 'persuasion' of Kelly's 'ability to perform what Mr. Dyer has reported' must in part have been facilitated by his dreams of 'the benefit' alchemical success might bring to his queen, a supernatural financial utility that could solve the eternal problems of debt and taxation. Needless to say, Burghley's persuasion in itself could not enable Kelly to transmute lead into gold, but it could move money from one sphere to another by motivating Burghley to promise Kelly great 'worldly reward.' Moreover, it could afford self-proclaimed practitioners of magic a place in courtly culture: when Burghley spoke of his 'allowance' of Kelly's 'loyal profession,' with great politic ambiguity he was assuring Kelly that he believed in his profession of desire to return to England, and also obliquely offering honour to a theologically complicated occupation.[57] It seems that the court related to its servants who practised magic as it did to its servants who wrote poetry: when persuaded it was in its interests to do so, the court allowed that they could be useful, and provided them with rewards for their service under such conditions.

But what of Sidney? Unlike Dyer, Sidney seemed distinctly ambivalent about the efficacy of magic. In an epistolary exchange with Hubert Languet, for example, he expressed something like sly disdain for occult speculations. Writing to Sidney in a vaguely strained attempt at extended wit, Languet described reading an extremely nationalistic history of Cambria by one Humfrey Lhuid (in which, among other scholarly outrages, various figures of Roman history had been made Welsh).[58] Illustrating the boredom the book inspired in him, Languet told Sidney about dozing off over the text and letting some pages catch the fire from his candle, and he finished his letter by threatening to send Sidney 'the scorched remains of my poor Cambrian, that you might desire your Griffin his countryman [Sidney's manservant] to perform his obsequies, while you offered a laugh to appease his ghost.'[59] In his reply Sidney responded to this threat by lightly chiding Languet for the 'handsome treatment' the 'poor Cambro-Briton' received at his hands, and then by parrying a mock threat of his own. He bade that Languet 'reflect, and it is a serious matter':'that our unknown god [deus ignotus], whoever he may be, who is of the same country and quality, may be ill pleased that you should raise such a laugh at his cousin after the flesh: and so perchance in his anger may wield against you his hieroglyphical monad, like Jove's lightening. Such is the wrath of heavenly spirits.'[60] The 'deus ignotus' was, of course, John Dee, who had presented Languet's lord, the Holy Roman emperor Maximilian, with his *Monas Hieroglyphica* in 1564.[61] And the joke here was surely at Dee's expense: even though Sidney was warning Languet, lest he make some sort of more public blunder, that the question of British nationalism was more serious than he seemed to realize, he was also slyly agreeing that Welshmen were indeed ridiculous, by implying that Dee, like his countryman Lhuid, was absurd.

Sidney reveals himself here as someone who is happy to laugh at claims for magical efficacy (and, indeed, there is something quite silly about the image of Dee wielding his little drawing in wrath). Yet we know that Sidney officially consulted Dee on at least one occasion, with Leicester at his side.[62] Like his opinion of the idea of poetic *furor*, Sidney's attitude towards magic is ultimately elusive. It seems clear, though, that distancing himself with wit from things in which he is actually invested is one of Sidney's trademarks. If his authorial persona in the *Defense*, for instance, may be characterized by his impassioned celebration of poetry's ability to make us love 'that unspeakable and everlasting beauty to be seen by the eyes of the mind' (99), it may equally well be defined by the strategies Sidney uses in order not to seem foolish – his amused, knowing self-mockery (the Pugliano anecdote of the *exordium*, for example) and his reflexive self-distancing (the ever-present acknowledgment that he must speak contingently so that 'the truth may be more palpable' [101]). On one hand, the ambivalence of his voice points to the power of Sidney's rhetorical performance in the *Defense*, which so fundamentally depends on his ability to improvise the fitting argument and the proper tone for whatever issue may be under discussion at any moment; on the other hand, it also suggests how vigilantly Sidney qualifies his claims in order to avoid appearing naive or self-deceived.

But whatever his worries about appearing naive, and whatever his scepticism about the efficacy's of Dee's *Monas*, in the *Defense* Sidney himself affords poetry a kind of occult force. To be sure, he does so uncomfortably, when he warns that poetry's efficacy may be 'abused,' or used to undesireable ends. Nonetheless, he seems to imagine that poetry has a magical power that works automatically, like a spell: thus, he argues, 'poesy may not only be abused, but that being abused, by the reason of his sweet charming force, it can do more hurt than any other army of words' (125). That he imagines poetry's sweet force as magical is telegraphed by his witty pun on 'charming.' This pun leads etymologically back to antiquity, when magic and poetry were on one continuum. In pre-Socratic Greece magical spells were written in metered verse to be sung in incantations; this formal equivalence of spells and verses gave poetry the name, 'charm' (*thelkterion*).[63] The Romans also conflated magical spells and metered verse; hence *carmen*, the Latin for poem, also signifies an incantation or charm. The connection between the charm and the poem enters English from the Latin via the French: as James Mason reminds us in his *Anatomie of Sorcerie*, 'It is certain that the word *charm* is derived of the Latin word *carmen*.'[64] Sidney rehearses this aspect of poetry's genealogy when he discusses 'the reasonableness of this word *vates*' (99), or diviner, that the Romans used to describe their poets: 'although it were a very vain and godless superstition, as also it was to think that spirits were commanded by such verses – whereupon this word charms, derived of *carmina*, cometh – so yet serves it to show the great reverence those wits were held in' (98). Thus we find a neat encapsulation of Sidney's ambivalence about the relationship between magic and poetry: Sidney concedes that it is 'vain and godless superstition' to think that spirits might be commanded by verses, yet he imagines that the very name, *vates*, which identifies poets as magicians, serves 'to show the great reverence those wits were held in.' But of course, whether or not the Romans revered their poet-magicians, the conflation of magic and poetry is a tremendous problem for Sidney, and not only because it associates poetic efficacy with godless superstition (allowing anti-poetic ministers like Dering to claim that 'there is no one thing more enemy to the word of GOD, then these vain and sinful imaginations of our own unbridled wits'). *Charming* was an actual magical practice in early modern England: a practice outlawed by the same 1563 statute that outlawed the conjuration of evil spirits, sorcery, and enchantment.[65] Indeed, in early modern English 'charm' did not yet refer to the attractiveness of someone's demeanour: according to the *OED*, that definition only took hold in the mid-eighteenth century.[66]

Sidney attempts to deal with the problem that poetry seems to have magical instrumentality by explicitly distinguishing poetry and magic, and he does so when addressing the charge that the poet lies. Explaining that in his view 'to lie is to affirm that to be true which is false,' Sidney argues that the poet 'nothing affirms, and therefore never lieth' (123), and he goes on immediately to insist that 'the poet never maketh circles about your imagination to conjure you to believe for true what he writes' (124). The circles to which he refers here are the charmed circles that magicians draw around themselves when they invoke spirits. As much as it tells that Sidney needs to distinguish between the poet as the producer of illusions and the magician as the conjurer of delusions, it is perhaps equally significant for literary history that twentieth-century critics took Sidney's statement that the poet 'nothing affirms' to epitomize his literary aesthetics. They did so because Sidney in this particular moment characterizes poetic language as something autonomous and disinterested, which post-Kantian criticism has defined as 'the Aesthetic,' abstracted as a philosophical and critical category. That is, modern critics read Sidney's statement that the poet 'nothing affirms' as a declaration that poetic language has no interest in anything outside itself – that it makes no assertions about the world, and consequently neither claims metaphysical objectivity for its representations nor seeks to produce the belief in the ideological value of its content necessary for instrumental persuasion. Rather, they continue, Sidney is suggesting here that poetry merely produces the attitude that Coleridge later defined as the 'suspension of disbelief ... that *negative* faith,' which simply entertains the images presented to the imagination 'without either denial or affirmation of their real existence by the judgment.'[67]

Accordingly, Harry Berger argues that in this moment Sidney abandons 'the truth of correspondence' in order to 'disjoin the imaginary from the actual field of experience, to win for it greater freedom and autonomy.' He further argues that this sort of autonomy requires an awareness that 'we are only playing, only making believe.'[68] Taking Sidney's statement that the poet 'nothing affirms' as exemplary, Graham Hammill assumes that Sidney views literary language as requiring us at once to suspend and 'to sustain' our disbelief, in effect to maintain an attitude that prevents us from feeling that, as Sidney says elsewhere in the *Defense*, poetry instrumentally 'doth teach and move to a truth' (119).[69] Finally, Ronald Levao argues that Sidney's 'double justification' for poetry on the basis of its instrumentality and its metaphysical objectivity is entirely undone by Sidney's claim that the poet 'nothing affirms.'[70] According to Levao it demonstrates that Sidney thinks poetry 'is the greatest of the arts' not because, as Sidney argues throughout the *Defense*, it 'move[s] men to take that goodness in hand, which without delight they would fly as from a stranger' (103), but because poetry 'is the only one to realize that it is not anchored to a fixed and objective truth' (150).

What all these readings elide is history: the very fact that Sidney produced his statement that the poet 'nothing affirms' in the context of his attempt to distinguish the poet from the magician, whom he set up as a straw man who 'maketh circles about your imagination to conjure you to believe.' Of course, Sidney set up the magician as the straw man so *he* could evade or elide the negative cultural consequences of his claim for poetic efficacy. Indeed, Sidney produced a disinterested rather than instrumental literary aesthetic here only contingently, improvisationally, under the pressure of the cultural forces that required him to distinguish poetic from magical efficacy. In reality, Sidney could not sustain this distinction in any robust way, for its very terms collapse into themselves: far from being a touchstone of a theory of disinterested fiction, the claim that the poet 'nothing affirms' is as much a *magical* as a literary strategy, one that enables an author to evade the political consequences of his text's reception. As we have seen at the beginning of this chapter, in his *Three Books of Occult Philosophy*, Agrippa too claims that he nothing affirms – or, in his own words, that he writes 'many things, rather narratively than affirmatively' so that he might deliver 'this art in such a manner, that it may not be hid from the prudent and intelligent, and yet may not admit the wicked and incredulous to the mysteries of these secrets.' Moreover, as we have seen, Sidney *does* make circles about our imaginations to conjure us to believe for true what he writes ('I conjure you all ... to believe, with me, that there are many mysteries contained in poetry, which of purpose were written darkly, lest by profane wits it should be abused'). Indeed, Sidney ends his *Defense* with his parody of conjuration precisely because he wants his readers to believe that poetry has cultural value for its very instrumentality, and because the discursive materials of efficacious poetry and magic cannot be separated, as a persuasive strategy Sidney diffuses the implications of their symbiotic relationship by recasting it as material for a joke. The very pretense of the joke's disinterest, of the poet's uncommitted irony, provides the cover under which Sidney intends to convince his readers that they need not feel anxious about magic when they attempt to serve their own ideological interests by patronizing poetry.

In the context of English literary history, the parodic conjuration that ends Sidney's *Defense* locates a moment when poetry sought to derive its cultural value from its ideological instrumentality and was thus inextricably linked to magical practice. Sidney wanted poetry to fashion disciplined subjects, to produce readers with docile affective dispositions and ideologically normative attitudes, by calling upon poetry's ability to 'strike, pierce [and] possess the sight of the soul,' and by that possession to make 'hard-hearted evil men' love goodness 'ere themselves be aware.' Yet, as I have argued, if poetry's efficacy seems to arise from the overwhelming sweetness of its rhetorical force, then Sidney's poet stands, like the magician, as a manipulative operator who might persuade people into ideological and spiritual transgression. And further, if poetry's efficacy appears grounded on its claim to mediate a transformative metaphysical truth, Sidney's poet becomes, like the magician, a heretical overreacher who has commerce with the diabolical. Sidney's *Defense* cannot entirely diffuse Puritan accusations that the poet attempts to gain illegitimate authority over the minds of his readers by deploying enchantments and sorceries condemned by the Christian God. Indeed, Sidney himself warns against the abuse of poetry's 'sweet, charming force.' Sidney's instrumental literary aesthetics are, therefore, bound up with the history of Elizabethan magic, and aesthetics and magic will continue to be so intertwined as long as literary representations of beauty are imagined to effect powerful ends in cultural and political life.

2 The Demonology of Spenserian Discipline

He makes their minds like the thing he writes.

Ben Jonson on Spenser, in Discoveries

In his 1590 *Faerie Queene*, Spenser represents demonic conjuration in terms that could well describe poetic creation. His diabolical magician Archimago, for instance, conjures malevolent spirits using 'verses' (1.1.27) from his magic books, and he fashions his spirits to make 'false showes' that 'abuse [the] fantasy' (1.1.46) of the Redcrosse knight.[1] Indeed, ever since A. Bartlett Giamatti first noticed that the demonic 'false shewes' conjured by Archimago's verses are akin to the imaginative images invoked by Spenser's poetry, it has become commonplace to read the magician as Spenser's allegorical figure for the poet. Hence critics generally characterize Archimago and the equally sinister Busirane as contrivers of illusory fictions, while they interpret Merlin, Spenser's benevolent magician, in Giamatti's terms as 'the creator [not] of false images, but of true reflections – from another perspective the poet *par excellence*.'[2] In characterizing poetry as a discourse that either distorts or reflects truth, such readings assume that Spenser's magic is a metaphor for an art that finds its greatest virtue in mimetic fidelity to transcendent reality.[3] But in *The Faerie Queene*, Spenser identifies his poetry with magic not because magic is mimetic, but because it is instrumental.[4] Hence Archimago's verses, for example, are performative: they call spirits out of the 'deepe darknes dredd' (1.1.38). And Archimago uses the poetic images he fashions out of spirits to influence the allegorical society around him: 'he applyes' them, as Spenser puts it, 'to aide his friendes, or fray his enimies' (1.1.38). Archimago uses his demonic Una to manipulate Redcrosse into abandoning the true Una, and when he sees that he has achieved

> Th'end of his drift, he praise[s] ... diuelish arts,
> That had such might over true meaning harts:
> Yet rests not so, but other meanes doth make,
> How he may worke vnto her further smarts
> For her he hated as the hissing snake ...   (1.2.9)

Archimago is, then, a poetic maker, but he 'means doth make.' With a wit as much 'practick' as creative, and with a rhetorician's 'fayre fyled tonge' (2.1.3), he produces allegorical images that seem to have 'might over true meaning harts,' and that move his victims to perform the social or theological error that is always his 'aymed end.' Nor is Archimago's concern with means and ends a symptom of his particular nature; all magic in *The Faerie Queene* is instrumental, whether to good ends or bad. When Glauce and Britomart come upon the beneficent Merlin in his secret cave, 'writing straunge characters in the ground, / With which the stubborne feendes he to his service bound,' they find him thus 'deepe busied bout worke of wondrous end' (3.3.14).

If magic, for Spenser, served as an instrumental endeavour that used spirits to produce wondrous ends, in *The Faerie Queene* Spenser represented the poet as a demonic conjurer because he situated his own poetic endeavour specifically in relation to magical practice. He did so not only because his own aesthetics are explicitly instrumental, but also because their claim to instrumentality occupied the same discursive field as magical claims to occult efficacy. When in his 'Letter to Ralegh,' appended to the 1590 edition of *The Faerie Queene*, Spenser proclaims that 'the generall end of all [his] booke' is 'to fashion a gentleman or noble person in vertuous and gentle discipline,' he was, as Gordon Teskey has pointed out, advertising his allegory as 'an instrument for improving secular life, which is identified [by the poem] unambiguously with political life.'[5] Spenser was also, as Richard Helgerson has described, staking the production of his own literary career on the claim that poetry contributed to the good of the realm through its ability to have an ethical effect even on England's more unruly subjects.[6] As I argued in chapter 1, Sidney made this same claim in his *Defense of Poesy*, in which he promised that poetry could transform the social behaviour of 'hard-hearted evil men who know no other good than *indulgere genio*,' because its 'charming force,' its very aesthetic delight, would irresistibly move those men to virtuous action.[7] Although the idea that aesthetic delight has a 'charming force' was absolutely essential to early modern conceptions of aesthetic instrumentality, it also neatly located the worrisome identity of poetic and magical power in those conceptions. 'Charming' was an actual magical practice outlawed by a 1563 Act of Parliament, along with the practices of witchcraft, sorcery, demonic conjuration, and enchantment.[8] Spenser invoked this very sense that the rhetorical power of poetic beauty is a magical force. When he proposed in *The Faerie Queene* that 'pleasing words are like to magic art, / That doth the charmed snake in slomber lay' (3.2.15), he was observing the way that 'pleasing words' can overwhelmingly soothe the inner senses, and suggesting that such words and magical charms work in the same way.

But neither Sidney nor Spenser grounded his claim for the ideological efficacy of poetry on a theory of magical rhetoric. In *The Faerie Queene* it is first and foremost guileful Archimago who possesses a 'fayre fyled tonge' (2.1.3), and whose arts move hapless knights like Redcrosse into the erroneous action that is always his 'aymed end.' On his part, Sidney attempted to justify poetry's charming force by claiming that it derives not from the power of the poet's voice, but from the inherent beauty of the metaphysical truth – the Neoplatonic '*Idea* or fore-conceit of the work' – that poetry conveys to the reader in images.[9] Yet as we saw in chapter 1, this recourse to Neoplatonism did not enable the poet to escape the shadow of the magician. Zealous Protestants, both Puritan and conformist, tended to view Neoplatonism as an idolatrous pagan heresy, arguing that the concept of the Ideas themselves, as metaphysical entities not represented in the Bible, could be implanted in the imagination by devils. That the origin of mental phenomena might potentially be diabolical made the ontology of early modern thought extremely problematic. For instance, in his discussion of angels and devils in *The Institution of the Christian Religion*, Calvin conflates 'affections of minds' with discrete 'minds or spirits.' To 'confute them that fondly say, that devils are nothing else but evil affections or perturbations of the mind, that are thrust into us by our flesh,' Calvin cites 'testimonies of Scripture' showing that devils who appear inwardly cannot be mere 'motions or affections of minds,' but rather 'as they be called minds or spirits endued with sense and understanding.' Thus, it was extremely important for active Protestants to question the nature of their own mental 'perturbations,' lest, as Calvin warns, 'any entangled with the error, while they think they have none to stand against them, should wax more slow and unprovided to resist.'[10]

Apparently, Spenser was richly aware of this discourse about the demonic potential of thought, for *The Faerie Queene* maintains an epistemological problematic in the foreground of its instrumental aesthetics. It does so by developing the aesthetic effect of wonder, which here relies on the possibility that demons may wind their way into the imagination. In broad sixteenth-century terms, wonder is the characteristic human reaction to things at once marvellous and frightening; in Spenser's aesthetics, wonder entails simultaneous marvel over the extraordinary beauty of poetic images and doubt over their ontological provenance. This bi-fold aesthetic orientation was instrumental to the fashioning of disciplined sixteenth-century readers, for it enacted the interiority of the self-regulating subject theorized by early modern faculty psychology, which posited that the subject must feel desire for images in the imagination and frame those images with a sceptical 'discourse of the understanding' for the subject to act according to cultural norms. Moral psychologists developed this model of intellectual habits in conjunction with the belief that demons could implant images into the imagination; more specifically, they developed it as a model that enabled the subject to resist demonic deception. Hence, in *The Faerie Queene* Spenser not only represented wonder as the disciplined subject's proper response to demonic apparitions, he also attempted to enact wonder in the reader by representing magic with verse so artfully ambiguous that it became impossible for the reader to decide whether the pictures in his mind's eye were poetic or demonic, or both.

Thus we could call the moment Archimago tells a demon to go to Redcrosse and 'with false shewes abuse his fantasy' (1.1.46) one in which the poem offers its contemporaneous reader instructions for its own interpretation, for we may use the phrase 'false shewes' equally to describe the images implanted in Redcrosse's imagination by Archimago's demons and the images generated in the mind's eye by the vehicles of allegory. To be sure, we need some historical empathy to inhabit the sense that images in the mind's eye could potentially be demonic and thereby real; yet as John Guillory tartly points out in his work on Spenser and the early modern imagination, 'the opposition between imagination and reality is very post-Cartesian.' Guillory goes on to say that he would 'not consider Spenser, or most Renaissance thinkers, incapable of intuiting this distinction (obviously, Hobbes is already thinking at times on the other side of the Cartesian divide), but their notion of the real should not be confused with the concept of the "really existent." Phantasms, such as those which appear to Redcrosse in his demonically inspired dream, are *real* but not *true*.'[11] And indeed, *The Faerie Queene* represents the pictures that appear to the mind's eye as coming from an external, spiritual source. In Phantastes' chamber, there are 'idle thoughts and fantasies' as well as all things 'feigned,' but there are also phenomena that were understood as coming from demons – such as 'shews, visions, sooth-sayes, and prophesies' (2.9.51) – and 'infinite shapes of things dispersed thin ... as in the world were neuer yet, / Ne can deuized be of mortal wit' (2.9.50, emphasis added). The immortal wit that creates these shapes remains unidentified, but that the poem represents immortal forces as in play at all can help us recognize the stakes of Spenser's attempt to produce wonder in the reader with pleasing words that are like to magic art. With such stakes, magic in The Faerie Queene cannot be merely a trope for writing, for Spenser sought to fashion disciplined subjects by rhetorically manipulating potentially demonic phantasms in the imagination. To show how Spenser attempted to fashion his reader, I will now turn to early modern beliefs in the presence of demons in everyday life and psychological theories of demonic influence over the imagination. Then, moving to The Faerie Queene, I will look at the role of wonder in enacting the intellectual habit of Spenser's disciplined subject, and illustrate how and why Spenser sought to produce wonder in the reader by discussing Arthur's encounter with Glorianna and Britomart's journey through Busirane's castle.

Despite the murderous factionalism of the Reformation, early modern Catholics and Protestants of all varieties generally agreed that the cosmos is populated by invisible spirits, and that angels and devils not only exist but act in the world by the permission of God. Belief in spirits was necessarily bundled together with Christian belief in the immortality of the soul: to deny the reality of spirits was to deny, as Hobbes puts it, that 'the souls of men' live on as 'substances distinct from their bodies,'[12] and thereby to espouse atheism or 'Sadduceism,' as it was more commonly characterized. So Randall Hutchins, in his 1593 treatise On Specters, exhorts his reader at the last to 'flee from all atheists, who do not recognize demons appearing in assumed forms, nor God as taking care of human affairs with certain infinite providence.'[13] And so Calvin, in his Institution, cries out against 'the old time opinion of the Sadduces, that by Angels is meant nothing else, but either the motions that God doth inspire in men, or the tokens that he shows of his power,' and by devils nothing else 'but evil affections or perturbations of the mind, that are thrust into us by our flesh.' Calvin insists that 'against this errour cry out so many testimonies of Scripture, that it is a marvel that so gross ignorance could be suffered in that people.' As he asks, rhetorically, 'how fond should these speeches be [Matt. 8:29, 25:41 and Jude 1.9], that the Devils are ordained to eternal judgment, that fire is prepared for them, that they are now already tormented and vexed by the glory of Christ: if there were no devils at all?'[14]

'Tormented and vexed' as they may be, demons, in the sixteenth-century English imagination, enjoy a good deal of liberty to move and act in the world, where, under the eye of God, they use their freedom to attempt to lead humanity ever further into perdition. According to the eschatological narrative adopted by Elizabethan conformity, demons live in the human sphere because they were cast out of heaven after they rebelled against heaven's throne. As Richard Hooker explains it, after their fall these angels were 'dispersed some in the air, some on the earth, some in the water, some amongst the minerals, dens, and caves, that are under the earth: they have by all means laboured to effect an universal rebellion against the laws, and as far as in them lies, utter destruction of the works of God.'[15] Thus in *The Faerie Queene* Spenser describes the demon shaped into the false Florimell as:

> A wicked Spright fraught with fawning guyle
> And fayre resemblance aboue the rest,
> Which with the Prince of Darkenes fell somewhyle,
> From heauens blis and euerlasting rest.   (3.8.8)

Interwoven into the elements, such demons are part of the fabric of the fallen world, where, independently and in collaboration with evil magicians, they attempt to ruin what goodness remains after the fall.

A favourite, arguably the favourite, way demons attempt to wreak postlapsarian havoc is by attacking the human mind, which was understood commonly and in scientific discourse to be subject to diabolical influence.[16] Renaissance psychologists argued that angels and demons can affect the human mind, both its cognitive processes and its governance of the will, by manipulating the pictures that appear in the imagination. (Early modern faculty psychology identified imagination, which it sometimes called 'phantasy' or 'fancie,' as the visual part of thought that we might call 'the mind's eye.') Thus, in *The Anatomy of Melancholy* Robert Burton counsels his readers that 'tis true they [demons] have, by God's permission, power over us, and we find by experience that they can hurt not only our fields, cattle, goods, but our bodies and minds.'[17] Burton goes on to explain that, to gain his power, a demon 'begins first with the phantasy, & moves that so strongly, that no reason is able to resist' (174). Elsewhere he warns that this devilish movement of the phantasy occurs in waking life as well as in the production of 'demoniacal' (140) dreams (such as, for instance, the one imposed on Redcrosse by Archimago's spright). Edward Reynolds, in *A Treatise on the Passions and Faculties of the Soule of Man*, places demonic action within a basic classification of unwholesome influences over the imagination. Along with 'imposture' of the senses and imbalanced humours, he lists 'the ministry of evil Angels, who can easily cast into the fancy strange and false species, with such subtlety, as shall easily gain them plausible credit and admittance.'[18] Finally, in *The Passions of the Minde in Generall*, Thomas Wright argues not only that demons can infiltrate the phantasy and disturb proper imaginative function, but by so doing they can influence the subject's moral orientation: 'A spirit, by secret means can enter into the former part of our brain and there chop and change our imaginations: he can represent pleasures with a goodly show; he can propound Virtue as a most bitter object ... which cause [*sic*] a tedious loathsomeness in us.'[19]

As Wright suggests, in faculty psychology's moral scheme, the visual representation of concepts in the mind's eye directly affects the subject's will. Attractive images incite desire in the subject towards acquisitive action. Thus Reynolds proposes that images in the imagination act directly upon the will 'to quicken, allure, and sharpen its desire towards some convenient object.'[20] In the same terms, as we have seen, Wright asserts that images representing concepts of virtue as 'most bitter' objects can inspire the aversion to virtuous behaviour that Wright calls 'loathsomeness.' In a more hierarchical formulation, Nicholas Coffeteau's *A Table of Human Passions* explains that the imagination first sends 'phantasms' to the appetite 'under the appearance of things that are *pleasing* or *troublesom*, that is to say under the form of Good and Evil,' while the understanding 'under the appearance of things that are *profitable* or *hurtful* ... represents them to the will.'[21] This link between the pleasing and the profitable is exactly what allowed poets to claim that a beautiful representation of virtue leads to virtuous behaviour. As Francis Bacon notes in *The Advancement of Learning*, 'Reason' itself must send its dictates 'over to Imagination before the Decree can be acted,' for the imagination must represent the end of action as desirable before the subject will feel motivated to act. For this reason, Bacon sententiously declares, 'Imagination ever precedes Voluntary Motion.'[22]

The reliance of the will on pleasing, desirable images in the imagination leaves virtue on very unstable ground, for the desire produced by images could in theological terms be idolatrous. To the Renaissance faculty psychologists, it is precisely for this reason that demons could so readily deprave human beings by implanting beautiful images in their imaginations. Demons can represent things in the imagination deceptively ('pleasures with a goodly show' and 'virtue as a most bitter object,' as Wright puts it). But with the help of the appetite (the locus of animal impulses related to but different from the will), they can also provoke the imagination to tyrannize the mind so that their deceptions cannot be recognized as such. Coffeteau best characterizes this problem: 'So as suddenly when as phantasy offers to the Appetite, the forms which she receives ... under the show of Good or Evil; he [the appetite] without stay to have them judged by the discourse of the Understanding, and chosen by the will, commands of himself the moving power & makes it act according to his pleasure.'[23] When the phantasy acts, or is acted upon, so 'suddenly' that reason cannot provide a 'stay' to its productions, the appetite 'commands' the 'moving power' and impels the subject towards its desired object, whatever its ideological or theological value may be. Wright suggests that when imagination and appetite team up like this, 'the imagination puts green spectacles before the eyes of our wit, to make it see nothing but green.'[24] In other words, when an overwhelming desire that cannot be seen from any perspective but inside itself colours everything in the mind's eye, the mind fixates on the object of desire, and the 'phantasy commands of himself the moving power & makes it act according to his pleasure.'

The solution, according to these accounts, is not, as we might assume, to master imagination with the force of reason. As we have seen, the subject needs strong desire inspired by the imaginative image to motivate his actions towards even normative goals. As Coffeteau explains: 'Provident *Nature* hath prescribed certain ends to all the Creatures of this Universe, whom She hath clothed with certain qualities and allurements fit to inflame them with their *Love*; so there is not any one in this world but doth endeavour by all means to attain unto those ends which are propounded.'[25] Essentially, these faculty psychologies propose that desire and reason should work in tandem. More specifically, they propose that both the imagination and what Coffeteau calls 'the discourse of the Understanding' should be engaged simultaneously, so that the imagination holds up images that inflame the subject with love, and 'the discourse of the Understanding' frames those images in terms of their proper use. Hence Coffeteau goes on to argue that Nature, as she has given her creatures their ends, has also given them 'as it were two wings to raise them up' (A5v): 'Desire alone were not sufficient, for that is fastened in the Appetite, which is a blind power, and requires some light to guide and conduct it in its motion. [But] neither were knowledge alone sufficient, for that proceeds from a faculty which being borne to give light, doth necessarily presuppose another power, which doth receive the beams of her light ... In this manner then if things knew their ends and did not desire them, or if they desired them without the knowledge, they could not be drawn to endeavor to get them' (A6v–A7r, A7v). In this psychological model of agency, the desire produced by the imagination and the knowledge produced by the understanding engage simultaneously to incite the subject to embrace 'Nature's' ethical design. And this is the model of agency, with its account of the bifold nature of the mind, which informs the instrumental aesthetics of *The Faerie Queene*.

As we might expect, though, Spenser's model of the mind is more nuanced than that of the psychologists. As Spenser allegorizes and enacts it in *The Faerie Queene*, the discourse of the understanding provides a stay to imaginative desire not by judging the ideological or theological worth of images in the imagination, but simply by contextualizing those images from multiple points of view, or by taking on what Paul Alpers has called 'the provisional adopting of attitudes and evaluations' about the activity of the imagination.[26] It is exactly the constant psychological reorientation in provisional attitudes, in hypothetical judgments that never resolve all doubts, that, in the psychologists' terms, frames or provides a stay for imaginative images of desire, thus preventing them from either overwhelmingly arousing the appetite or generating an obsession that would obscure the vagaries of social action. Yet the poem suggests, paradoxically, that the faculty of the understanding must be engaged absolutely – it must never cease to produce these provisional evaluations – for without a constant engagement of both the imagination and the understanding, human beings will begin to lose their perspective, as it were; they will begin to fixate on images of desire, becoming so obsessed with their cathected objects that they become unable to function in a world that makes multiple and shifting demands on their allegiances.

To emphasize the epistemological and theological stakes of this psychology, in *The Faerie Queene* Spenser represents the overcoming of the mind by obsession as a form of demonic possession that transforms the subject into the demon from which his or her imagination cannot free itself. This demonic possession emerges as at once cause and effect of the emotional fixation that forecloses the possibility of disciplined behaviour. The ethical import of this allegory of possession complicates Angus Fletcher's long-influential argument that the activity of the allegorical hero 'conforms to the type of behavior manifested by people who are thought (however unscientifically) to be possessed by a demon' – or, as he puts it elsewhere, that the allegorical hero manifests a kind of 'daemonic agency' insofar as he is 'obsessed with only one idea, or [has] an absolutely one-track mind ... frozen into an eternally fixed form, an "idea" in the Platonic sense of the term.'[27] In *The Faerie Queene* it is not Arthur whose mind seems one-track, frozen into a fixed form; it is Malbecco, whom Spenser names as the personified form of 'Gelosy' (3.10.60) exactly as the man turns into the demon of his own jealous obsession. The formal and the demonic transformations occur simultaneously: having lost both the conjugal and pecuniary property he was so jealously guarding, Malbecco becomes 'all desperate of his fore-damned spright' (3.10.56). This 'spright' has a double valence. On the one hand, it signifies Malbecco's internal life, his character or esprit, 'fore-damned' by the choices that the fabliaux cuckold must make (such as marrying a much younger woman who proves to have a buxom sexual appetite); on the other hand, the word 'spright' recalls the demonic 'Sprights' that Archimago conjured up in his hermitage, 'fore-damned' to hell, or, in this case, to a craggy cave where they would sit alone 'in dreary darkness' and 'continual fear' (3.10.58), eating the bitter frogs and toads that creep about on the filthy floor. This demonic valence is only reinforced when Malbecco throws himself off his cliff in a suicidal leap, but does not die, because

> through long anguish, and selfe-murduring thought
> He was so wasted and forpined quight,
> That all his substance was consumed to nought
> And nothing left, but like an aery Spright,
> That on the rockes he fell so flit and light
> That he thereby receiu'd no hurt at all.   (3.10.57)

Malbecco's transformation into an 'aery Spright' makes explicit the identity of the effects of psychic obsession and demonic possession.[28] Malbecco's obsessive, one-track mind does nothing to enable his agency; on the contrary, it produces only 'selfe-murduring thought' that corrodes and consumes the 'substance' of a human life and transforms it into a form of hell.

Yet I should not use Malbecco to overstate the costs of obsession, for there is indeed something compulsive, even demonic, about the desire propelling Spenser's heroes.[29] Arthur's quest is motivated by incessant longing for the potentially demonic Fairy Queen who appears and makes 'lovely blandishment' (1.9.14) to him during the night, and who vanishes leaving 'nought but pressed gras where she had lyen' (1.9.15), marking the very absence or lack that constitutes desire. Britomart, too, rides off into the wilderness of Faerie Lond to seek the 'shade and semblant of a knight' (3.2.38) who appears to her in Merlin's magic mirror. This shade of Arthegall clearly has demonic valence, since in magical as well as literary discourse demons were thought to communicate with human beings by being conjured to display allegorical scenes and images in the magician's crystal ball.[30] Nevertheless, these knights do not turn their desire into action by becoming compulsively obsessed by the objects of their desire; rather, they apply their desire instrumentally by setting the image of the object cathected in the imagination within the 'stay' fashioned by the discourse of the understanding. In this sense, the mind of the Spenserian subject is not the 'one-track mind' of Fletcher's allegorical theory, but, as it were, the 'two-track' mind of Elizabethan faculty psychology. Britomart, for example, having fallen in love with the magical image of Arthegall, initially develops the symptoms of demonic possession, becoming tormented by obsessive thoughts and dreams until, like Malbecco, she becomes 'like a pyned ghost' through 'long languour, and hart-burning brame' (3.3.18). Her fixated desire is transformed into agency only by her witnessing Merlin's prophesy of the Tudor dynasty that she and Arthegall will found, for the prophesy functions in relation to her imaginative desire as does the discourse of the understanding.[31] Though the prophesy does not give Britomart understanding as knowledge per se – it ends in utter enigma, with Merlin breaking off 'ouercomen of the spirites powre, / Or other ghastly spectacle dismayd' (3.3.50) – it does afford her at least a provisional context in which to place the imaginative image of Arthegall. This context neither resolves all of Britomart's doubts nor tells her exactly what to do; rather, it organizes the psychic energies of her love for Arthegall's image in a way that allows her to take up her quest, and to improvise solutions to its challenges as they arise. Under the influence of Merlin's ambiguously demonic productions, then, Britomart develops the bi-fold intellectual habit of the disciplined subject, enabling her to act to fulfil her allegorical (and political) function.

Like Britomart, Arthur is also trained in his habit of mind by Merlin (although we do not witness this instruction; we only hear that the magician would often visit Arthur when he was a child, since Merlin 'had charge' of Arthur's 'discipline to frame' [1.9.5]). As the fully realized subject of the poem, Arthur also thinks with a two-track mind, providing the basis for his heroic agency. When Arthur recounts the effects of his encounter with Glorianna, for example, he does so in a way that suggests that he simultaneously apprehended his desire and placed that desire in the framework of his understanding. Arthur speaks to Una:

> When I awoke, and found her place deuoyd,
> And nought but pressed gras where she had lyen,
> I sorrowed all so much, as earst I ioyd,
> And washed all her place with watry eyen.
> From that day forth I lou'ed that face diuyne;
> From that day forth I cast in carefull mind,
> To seek her out with labor, and long tyne.   (1.9.15.1–7)

The apposition of 'from that day forth I lou'ed that face diuyne' and 'from that day forth I cast in carefull mind' suggests that Arthur simultaneously loved and cast that love in careful mind. Moreover, the enjambment of line six gives the verb 'cast' a double meaning: once line six becomes line seven, and the reader sees that Arthur has 'cast ... To seek her out,' *cast* clearly becomes *decided*, but in line 6, where Arthur has simply 'cast in carefull mind,' it also appears that Arthur's love for the 'face diuyne' was instantaneously cast or contextualized in the frame of his 'careful mind,' suggesting again that Arthur's loving and his casting that love in careful mind happened both at once, and with equal force.

That Spenser's disciplined subject displays a 'two-track' mind suggests that his instrumental aesthetics will attempt to produce this bi-fold psychological disposition in the reader, whose desire for beautiful poetic images will be framed by the contextualizations of the discourse of the understanding. And indeed, in contrast to Neoplatonic aesthetics of imitation, Spenser's instrumental aesthetics are those of *wonder*. They seek to train the reader in an intellectual disposition that both uses the desire inspired by beauty to motivate action and resists the effects of beauty's force, which Spenser, like the faculty psychologists, represents as appropriable by demons, or for that matter, the magicians that deploy them. As Caroline Bynum has demonstrated, the theological strand of the medieval discourse of wonder that Spenser inherits specifically distinguishes wonder, or *admiratio*, from *imitatio*: 'The phrase *non imitandum sed admirandum* (not to be imitated but to be marvelled at) had been used to express the distance between heroes and martyrs, on one hand, and the ordinary faithful, on the other.'[32] Wonder involves, then, not the obsessive identification with the beautiful image that fosters imitation, but the recognition of the otherness of beauty, of its singular and inappropriable character. This recognition distantiates the reader from the beautiful images produced by the text. Rather than a form of disinterest, this distantiation is, as Descartes formulates it, 'a sudden surprise of the soul which makes [the mind] tend to consider attentively those objects which seem to it rare and extraordinary.'[33] Wonder thus includes a sensation of surprise, as well as admiration or marvelling. These affects in turn engender curiosity, or even bewilderment and suspicion. As Mary Campbell points out in *Wonder and Science*, wonder in the sixteenth century has 'a valence with horror and terror.'[34] In *Hamlet*, for example, Horatio cries out that the vision of old Hamlet's ghost 'harrows' him 'with fear and wonder' (1.1.44). Wondrous objects are potentially threatening because they are, as Bynum puts it, 'events or phenomena in which ontological and moral boundaries are crossed, confused, or erased.'[35] This erasure of ontological boundaries makes wondrous phenomena essentially unpredictable, or impossible to explain with either common knowledge or logic. Bynum formulates this dynamic most elegantly: 'Human beings' she writes, 'cannot wonder at what is not there; but neither can we wonder at that which we fully understand' (39). Wondering is thus characterized by the experience of a particular kind of doubt, one that fundamentally relies on belief (doubt over the ontological status of wondrous objects must entail the belief in at least the potential reality of such objects, for one cannot doubt something one has dismissed entirely). Indeed, in wonder there is belief and disbelief at once, just as there is admiration and fear at once.[36] Apprehension of paradox is inherent to the experience of wonder: the root sense of *dubbio* means to look both ways. Puttenham puts the figure of '*Paradoxon*, or the Wonderer' together with '*Aporia*, or the Doubtful,' which he calls 'not much unlike the *Wonderer*.' In the Wonderer, Puttenham says, the poet 'is carried by some occasion to report of a thing that is marvellous, [and] he will seem not to speak it simply but with some sign of admiration'; in the Doubtful the poet will 'seem to cast perils, and make doubt of things when by a plain manner of speech we might affirm or deny him.'[37] Here again, admiration and doubt go together, for that which is so marvellous as to be inappropriable must also be mysterious, inexplicable.[38]

A vivid example of Spenser's characterization of wonder is to be found in canto 11 of book 2, specifically in Arthur's reaction to the realization, which dawns on him with rising horror, that his fellow combatant Maleger is not going to die, even though the knight has just slashed open his guts with a sword. Arthur stares in astonishment:

He doubted, least it were some magicall
Illusion, that did beguile his sense,

Or wandring ghost, that wanted funerall,
Or aery spirite vnder false pretense,
Or hellish feend raysd vp through diuelish science.

His wonder far exceeded reasons reach,
That he began to doubt his dazeled sight,
And oft of error did him selfe appeach.   (2.11.39–40)

It is impossible for Arthur to decide what Maleger is. Paradoxically, the creature has and does not have a body; he seems to be of the earth, yet he behaves like an 'aery spirite' or a demon conjured up by a magician. Maleger's eerie qualities lead Arthur to produce a series of provisional evaluations, each of which posits an identity for Maleger that honors his uncanniness, yet all of which must be abandoned as inadequate: Arthur wonders whether Maleger is 'some magicall illusion ... or wandring ghost ... or aery siprite ... or hellish feend,' but he cannot tell. Maleger's identity exceeds 'reason's reach.' Thus as Arthur wonders, he begins to doubt *himself*, or, rather, 'to doubt his dazeled sight, / And oft of error ... him selfe [to] appeach.' This is not to say that Arthur begins to doubt Maleger's reality – indeed, the knight goes on to assail the creature with his 'naked hands' (2.11.41) in the very next stanza. It is only to say that by repeatedly accusing himself of 'error,' Arthur begins to doubt the truth of what he sees, or to doubt that he is seeing truly; he begins to question the accuracy of his senses as well as his inward responses. Like the phantasms that assailed Redcrosse in his demonic dream, Maleger is a paradox – in Guillory's terms, 'real, but not true.' Arthur's wonder thus illustrates the reaction of Spenser's exemplary subject to the appearance of an ontologically ambiguous representation.

Spenser's instrumental aesthetics depend on the production of this kind of wonder in the reader. For the sixteenth-century reader who believed in the possibility that demons may appear to the mind's eye, to wonder is to inhabit the position of the disciplined subject who, by doubting himself the way that Arthur doubts, performs the kind of self-monitoring that is the very principle of subjection. Maureen Quilligan has suggested that Spenser instructs his reader by asking him to make a moral choice about the images in his imagination, or by leading him on a search for signals that an 'interpretation is right or wrong,' but according to sixteenth-century faculty psychology, in wonder there can be no clear choice between right and wrong.[39] Because the ontological ground of wondrous images is too unstable to allow them to be known, the faculty of the understanding can produce only provisional evaluations about imaginative entities, approaching them with a mixture of extreme curiosity and extreme caution. This interminable, irresolvable suspension of judgment in a shifting multiplicity of provisional evaluations (perhaps a version of 'eterne in mutabilitie') may lead us to feel, as Jonathan Goldberg has ruefully maintained, that the Spenserian subject, 'fashioned by reading, is educated in frustration.'[40] But twenty-first-century readers are trained to see aesthetic effects like the 'suspension of opposites' in paradox as being bound up with New Criticism's notions of aesthetic autonomy or critical disinterest. Yet the sixteenth-century model of disciplined agency that informs *The Faerie Queene* relies on the production of affective states, like desire, which we tend to think we need to put aside to act ethically, and also on the kind of interior doubleness, the suspension of opposites in imagination and understanding, that we assume resists the making of judgments. In other words, *The Faerie Queene*'s model of disciplined agency is analogous to the experience of wonder as an aesthetic effect. This is why wonder is an *instrumental* aesthetic effect for Spenser: in its sixteenth-century cultural context, it seems that it can produce in the reader the habit of mind that enables ideologically minded action.

Yet the key element of wonder's instrumentality in Spenser's era was the belief in the possibility of demonic conjuration, which enabled wonder to overcome the distinction between the poetic and the real (as Arthur's provisional interpretations of Maleger as a 'magicall illusion' or a 'hellish feend raysd vp through diuelish science' all imply). Hence in *The Faerie Queene*, Spenser represents magic using irresolvable verbal ambiguities that permanently keep open the question of whether those images are poetic or demonic or both. He thereby attempts to produce wonder in his readers by casting both admiration for and doubt over the images he invokes in their imaginations. And Spenser's cloud of magical wonder enwraps not only incidental encounters with the poem's more horrifying characters. If Arthur oft accuses himself of error when he is confronted with Maleger, Patricia Parker has noted that Spenser solicits 'the sense of potentially irredeemable "error" even in the poem's central quest,' that of Arthur for Glorianna, the Fairy Queen herself.[41] This quest begins nine months before the present of the poem, after Arthur lies down to sleep on a patch of 'verdant grass' (1.9.13). As Arthur tells Una:

> While euery sence the humour sweet embayd,
> And slombring soft my hart did steale away
> Me seemed, by my side a royall Mayd

Her daintie limbes full softly down did lay:
So fayre a creature yet saw neuer sunny day.

Most goodly glee and louely blandishment
She to me made, and badd me love her deare;
For dearly sure her loue was to me bent,
As when iust time expired should appeare.
But whether dreames delude, or true it were,
Was neuer hart so rauisht with delight,
Ne liuing man like wordes did euer heare,
As she to me deliuered all that night;
And at her parting said, She Queene of Faries hight.

When I awoke, and found her place deuoyd,
And nought but pressed gras where she had lyen,
I sorrowed much as earst I ioyed,
And washed all her place with watry eyen.
From that day forth I lou'd that face diuyne;
From that day forth I cast in carefull mynd,
To seeke her out with labor, and long tyne.   (1.9.13–15)

This episode is notorious for its obscurity. C.S. Lewis first set out the crux,
and his complaint stands unchallenged:

> The episode is peculiar in two ways. First we are not allowed to decide
> whether Arthur's experience was a dream or a reality. At the words 'me
> seemed' it appears to be a dream; the mention of the 'pressed gras where
> she had lyen' sounds as if it were very much more. And secondly, we are
> not given clearly to understand whether, after this night of 'goodly glee and
> lovely blandshiment,' the fairy rose (or was dreamed to rise) with her virgin-
> ity intact. This double obscurity about both the reality and the result of the
> *concubitus* is tolerable only on one condition … that we are being shown the
> sort of experience to which the contrast either between mere 'blandishment'
> and full fruition or between dream and waking does not strictly apply. But
> the soul's new–kindled raptures at its first meeting with a transcendental or at
> least incorporeal object of love, is an experience of that kind.[42]

As Lewis points out, the reader is not allowed to decide what occurred
during Glorianna's nocturnal visitation to Arthur. In Puttenham's terms,
Spenser reports 'a thing that is marvellous' in verse that 'cast[s] perils, and

make[s] doubt of things when by a plaine manner of speech we might affirm or deny him.' Spenser wraps the episode in mysterious obscurity to generate wonder, to make it seem as if 'a thing that is marvellous' has occurred. Characterizing this marvellous thing as 'the soul's new-kindled raptures at its first meeting with a transcendental or at least incorporeal object of love,' Lewis implies that this encounter with transcendence serves to resolve the doubt produced in this episode, as if the ambiguous perils of the verse could find a safe harbour in ideologies of Christian Neoplatonism. But as we have seen, in their own historical context those ideologies were profoundly *un*stable, and the production of wonder here, as in the Maleger episode, fundamentally relies on Spenser's keeping open the question of whether Glorianna is a kind of demon. Parker observes that '"whether dreams delude, or true it were" is the first clear echo of an earlier, more sinister dream,' the dream implanted in Redcrosse's fantasy by Archimago's demon.[43] Indeed, from the very moment the Fairy Queen enters the scene, the episode begins to strike notes that echo the verse in Redcrosse's encounter with the demonic Una. As it seems to Arthur that 'by [his] side a royall Mayd / Her daintie limbes full softly down did lay' (1.9.13), so did it seem to Redcrosse that 'his Lady by him lay' (1.1.47). As Glorianna makes 'most goodly glee and louely blandishment' to Arthur, so did the demon treat Redcrosse with 'gentle blandishment and lovely looke' (1.1.49). And, as Arthur admits that 'whether dreames delude, or true it were, / Was neuer hart so rauisht with delight' (1.9.14), so is Redcrosse said to have dreamt 'of loues and lustfull play, / That nigh his manly hart did melt away' (1.1.47). Finally, 'and most subtly of all,' as Parker observes, 'the final line of the first stanza ("So faire a creature yet saw neuer sunny day") suggests, in the careful inversion of the syntax, the possibility not only that she is the fairest creature ever seen by "sunny day" but that she herself may be one of the creatures of the ambiguous dark' (85).

Although Parker goes on to connect Glorianna with the shades that live in the house of Morpheus and with the figure of Despair, we may also connect Glorianna with the demon who animates the False Florimell, a creature of the ambiguous dark who is yet fairer than the true Florimell. The demonic counterfeit of metaphysical beauty is the problematic that Spenser is keeping alive here (and in this sense Lewis was right to hear a Neoplatonic tone in this episode), for Glorianna does of course represent the transcendent object of love that should inspire ideologically sanctioned action. Indeed, even as *The Faerie Queene* undermines the ethical tenets of Neoplatonic imitation, it also posits an objective, transcendent perfection invisible to the human eye, and it stages heroic behaviour as inspired by ideals which, while not religious per se, always exceed the clayey confines of quotidian existence. For fashioning gentlemen in virtuous and gentle discipline when you are the poet of empire requires at least in part that you orient your readers properly to ideologies of eternal reward for religious war. The poem implies especially in the meeting between Arthur and Glorianna that the disciplined subject will be willing to serve his realm, to kill and die to further its political and ideological goals, only if he believes in a beloved reward that will repay his death (hence the value of the apocalyptic echo in the Fairy Queen's promise to Arthur that 'dearly sure her loue was to [him] bent, / As when iust time expired should appeare' [3.9.14], and hence the importance of the 'monument' to Spenser's ideas of heroism). Spenser posits, then, the reality of an eternal beauty whose ideal existence remains untouched by the contingencies of history, and whose delights reward those who serve power with their lives.

Yet though he posits such a beauty, Spenser never attempts to represent it clearly; he merely suggests it to the reader in 'clowdily enwrapped allegorical deuices,' as he calls them in the 'Letter to Ralegh,' like those that make Glorianna an object of wonder. Of course, to make the reader doubt the provenance of representations of beauty is to ask him to fear the very things in which he is required to be most fully invested. But the poem repeatedly asks the reader to fear the things it makes most compelling. The 1590 *Faerie Queene* ends by enacting this dynamic in its representation of Britomart's journey through Busirane's castle. Busirane is at once a poet and a magician, an artist who produces virtuosic imitations of Ovidian and Petrarchan forms, and a 'vile Enchaunter' who conjures demons with the 'straunge characters of his art' (3.12.31). His very name suggests the complicated and sinister ways his poetry and his magic intertwine. The word 'Busirane' evokes the word 'abuse.' Although this homology has been taken to suggest the abuse of women or marriage,[44] it is also important to remember that 'abuse' was a quasi-technical term in Elizabethan debates over the cultural value of poetry.[45] In those debates, arguments about what constituted poetic abuse often conflated poetry and magic. Even Sidney, attempting to address anti-poetic discourse in his *Defense*, conceded that 'poesy may not only be abused, but being abused, by reason of his sweet charming force, it can do more hurt than any other army of words.'[46] This very symbiosis of poetry and magic is disturbingly embodied in Busirane, who deploys 'a thousand charmes' to compel Amoret to love him 'perforce' (3.12.31). Indeed, Busirane's art attempts to coerce an erotic desire that, among its other negative effects, tortures chaste married women with the temptations of adultery, and it functions by using strategies that are identical to what Scudamore calls 'strong enchauntments and black magic lere' (3.11.16). Yet Spenser represents Busirane as at once poet and magician not only to condemn Busirane's art as magical, but also to *use* the threat of magic instrumentally to his own ends. He does so by representing Busirane's art in language so cunningly ambiguous that it becomes impossible for the reader to decide whether the pictures in his mind's eye are poetic or demonic or both. And Spenser produces this irresolvable doubt in the reader in order to attempt not merely to describe, but above all to enact the summary experience of wonder in his poem.

Busirane attempts to dominate the wills of those who enter his domain by deploying his art to overthrow the discourse of the understanding and to produce erotic desire without outside or end. Hence Busirane's works, his tapestries and his masque, represent the absolute, tyrannous priority of eros over social and political considerations; they rehearse the supposedly successful 'warres' that Cupid has 'wrought / On mighty kings and kesars, into thraldome brought' (3.11.29). They not only imitate the idea of the tyranny of desire, they also attempt instrumentally to produce erotic inclinations in their viewers. In the tapestries are fashioned

> Many faire pourtraicts, and many a faire feate
> And all of loue, and al of lusty-hed,
> As seemed by their semblaunt did entreat.   (3.11.29)

The final two lines of this stanza may of course be read both as 'they seemed to treat love and lust as their whole subject therein' and 'they seemed to beg only love and lust from their viewer.'[47] Along these lines, Katherine Eggert has elegantly detailed the ways the tapestries manifest 'modes of poetic efficacy derived from sensual pleasure.'[48] Such modes of efficacy in Busirane's instrumental aesthetics derive not only from visual pleasure, as in the quasi-pornographic tapestries, but also from aural pleasure, as in the sounds of the masque. Although it will be revealed as a horrifying demonic spectacle, the masque begins with, and proceeds accompanied by, music filled with sensual delight. As Britomart waits in the empty third room,

> A most delitious harmony,
> In full straunge notes was sweetly heard to sound,
> That the rare sweetness of the melody
> The feeble senses wholly did confound,
> And the frayle soule in deepe delight nigh drownd.   (3.12.6)

The effects of this music recall those produced by the atmosphere of the Bower of Bliss, where only Guyon, although he 'much wondred ... at the fayre aspect / Of that sweet place,' is able to suffer 'no delight / To sincke into his sence, nor mind affect' (2.12.53).[49] Like the art in the Bower, which in its subtle grace serves to augment the power of Acrasia's erotic spell, the music in Busirane's castle produces sensuous, delicious delight that practically overwhelms or 'drown[s]' the subject in pleasure. Hence the idol of Cupid, which figures the worship of desire as its own end – or, as Harry Berger phrases it, of 'desire uprooted from any of its functional contexts' – stands as 'an Image all alone / Of massy gold, which with its own light shone' (3.11.47).[50] The end of Busirane's instrumental aesthetics is the deifying of desire alone, a desire that thereby shines with its own light rather than receiving illumination from the various beams of the provisional perspectives of the discourse of the understanding. Such desire cannot motivate labour towards an ethical end, as all the empty armour hanging in Busirane's second chamber eerily confirms (3.11.52).

Of course, as far as Amoret is concerned, the ending end of Busirane's art is not simply the arousal of her desire but also, the episode implies, her capitulation to Busirane's sexual demands. However, being a 'Lodestarre of all chaste affectione' (3.6.52), Amoret does not yield to Busirane. As Scudamore rather brutishly but accurately puts it: 'to yield him loue she doth deny / Once to me yold, not to be yolde againe' (3.11.17). Yet clearly, Amoret does feel the arousing effect of Busirane's instrumental aesthetics. The gaping wound in her breast, horrifically gory as it is, is the very wound of desire, a wound shared by Jove and Mars – who, in love with Venus, bears 'many wide woundes launched through his inner parts' (3.11.44) – and even by Arthur himself, who tells Una that for the Fairy Queen he suffers a 'fresh bleeding wound, which day and night / Whilome doth rankle in [his] riuen brest' (1.11.7). Here, this wound of desire is opened by Busirane: the 'cruell dart' (3.12.31) that wounds Amoret is at once Cupid's cruel arrow and Busirane's 'sharpe steele' (3.11.11), with which he is able Amoret 'so cruelly to pen' (3.11.10). Yet Busirane 'pens' Amoret not only by 'writing' or encoding on her the wound or sign of desire (for in the end this signifies only that Busirane can represent Amoret *as if* she were desiring), but also by kidnapping her and keeping her captive in chains, which suggests that he does in fact dominate her affect with his art. The image of Amoret bound 'with yron bands, / Vnto a brazen pillour' (3.12.30) recalls, decadently, the *Hercules Gallicus*, Alciati's emblem for rhetoric, in which captivated listeners are bound to rhetoric's throne by chains of amber and gold.[51] The image also recalls Giordano Bruno's argument that the magician is most able to bind others magically 'when he commands great persuasion,' for the 'magical bond' consists of 'faith or credibility [and] of love and of strong emotions,' as much as it does of occult 'incantations.'[52]

Yet even though Amoret wishes to be free from Busirane's chains, she also clearly feels affected by the magician's charms and tormented by her desire. But the desire she fears is not the desire she feels for Scudamore, nor even her desire in general, but the *adulterous* desire Busirane's art arouses in her. This desire she attempts to resist even unto death. Hence, her torture is her erotic ambivalence. She undergoes agony from the pain of the 'sharpe steele' that 'doth riue her hart in tway' (3.11.11); from the 'horror' (3.12.19) of being forced to participate in a masque that demonically embodies the 'phantasies / In wavering wemens witt' (3.12.26); from the wrenching contradiction of the fact that, as Spenser insists, a 'thousand charmes could not her steadfast hart remoue' (3.12.31), yet with his 'strong charmes' (3.12.19), Busirane has removed her heart, causing it to be 'drawne forth, and in silver basin layd / Quite through transfixed with a deadly dart' (3.12.21). Of course, as Amoret's resistance implies, the power of Busirane's charms is not absolute. Indeed, Britomart proves that their power comes from their context, for when she frees Amoret the lady's wound closes up 'as it had not been sor'd' (3.12.38) – 'as' implying both '*as if* it had not been opened' and '*because* it had not really been opened.' It is also important that the contextual nature of Busirane's charms is revealed only after Amoret has Britomart force him to undo those charms, as Eggert points out, 'either by reading them backward or by remaking them entirely – "re-versing" (3.12.36) them, as the stanza punningly puts it.'[53] As Amoret seems to understand, Busirane's verses serve instrumentally to produce the arts that have wounded her and kept her bound to his 'brazen pillour' (3.12.30). To neutralize their power, the verses that compose Busirane's instrumental aesthetics must be 'reversed,' erased, or rewritten.

Even Britomart receives a small cut of desire in Busirane's castle, although, of course, for her 'the wound [is] nothing deepe imprest' (3.11.33). In exemplary fashion, Britomart maintains the bi-fold intellectual habit that enables her to respond to Busirane's art at once with desire and with the distantiating suspicion provided by the discourse of the understanding. As she makes her way through the rooms of Busirane's castle, Britomart reacts to the tapestries, to the masque, and to everything else, with neither delight nor ravishment, but with wonder. When she comes upon the statue of Cupid,

That wondrous sight faire Britomart amazd,
Ne seeing could her wonder satisfie,
But euermore and more vpon it gazed,
The whiles the passing brightness her fraile sences dazed.   (3.11.49)

And, as she moves into the second room,

The warlike Mayd beholding earnestly
The goodly ordinaunce of this rich Place,
Did greatly wonder, ne could satisfy
Her greedy eyes with gazing a long space.   (3.11.53)

It is not that Britomart does not feel the arousing effects of Busirane's representations. On the contrary: her 'greedy eyes' seem to want to possess the images of desire they behold and thereby be satisfied. But her wonder tempers her desire by providing her with a frame in which to place it. For what remains also to be satisfied is her curiosity and even her anxiety over the strange context of the beauties that she is seeing. The stanza immediately goes on to tell us that Britomart wonders even 'more … that no footings trace, / Nor wight appear'd, but wastefull emptiness, / And solemne silence ouer all that place' (3.11.53.5–7).

Though Britomart's wonder provides the reader with a clue towards interpretation, the Busirane episode is less a guide for the reader than it is an object lesson, or a test. Spenser renders the tapestries and the masque in not narration but direct address to the reader, who sees the art through Britomart's eyes. The reader's visual field is filled with the images of Busirane's productions invoked so vividly by Spenser's ecphrasic verse.[54] This visual immediacy encourages the reader to consume the spectacle with something like Britomart's optical greed. To be sure, the verse also suggests the need for Britomart's suspicion and anxiety: the empty, tomb-like silence of Busirane's outer chamber reinforces the sense that the liveliness of the tapestries is vaguely ghostly, or demonic, and later, in the masque, the figures Doubt and Daunger enter directly upon, if not along with, Fancy and Desyre (3.12.7–11). Yet Spenser encourages the reader's scopophilic absorption into the scene by presenting, for much of the episode, Busirane's arts as nothing more than forms of court poetry. His tapestries are so many Ovidian imitations, his masque a Petrarchan rehearsal, and the very familiarity of these stock forms serves to discourage the reader's doubt or fear about the ontology of Busirane's representations. However, when Amoret is led into the masque by Despight and Cruelty the reader is forced not just to entertain the possibility of error, but to undergo the very experience of error itself.[55] For at this moment Spenser represents the masque with such irresolvable ambiguity that it becomes impossible for the reader to discern whether Amoret is herself or the Petrarchan figure of cruelty or a demon called up by 'strong charms,' or all these three at once:

> After all these there marcht a most faire Dame,
> Led of two grysie villeins, th'one *Despight*,
> The other cleped *Cruelty* by name:
> She dolefull Lady, like a dreary Spright,
> Cald by strong charmes out of eternall night,
> Had Deathes owne ymage figured in her face ...   (3.12.19)

For a split second, suspended, the verse encourages the identification of the demon Cruelty as the 'she' who is doleful, and until the verse proceeds the reader's understanding cannot determine beyond doubt whether the allegorical vehicle, the phantasm in the imagination, is either the demon Cruelty or Amoret who 'like a dreary Spright' is 'cald by strong charmes out of eternall night.' Like Arthur confronted with the eerie mystery of Maleger, the reader here is compelled to doubt the truth of what he sees in his mind's eye, or, rather, to doubt that he is seeing it truly. Indeed, for the reader who believes in the possibility that demons can implant images into the imagination, this verse enacts the experience of ontological doubt that makes allegorical figures objects of wonder. The poem encourages this wonder by calling into question all the images the reader has imagined by reading the masque. Highlighting the inscrutability of the figures whose contours had seemed so clear, Spenser uses Puttenham's figure *aporia*, or 'The Doubtful,' to end his description:

> There were full many moe like maladies,
> Whose names and natures I note readen well;
> So many moe, as there be phantasies
> In wauering wemens witt, that none can tell,
> Or pains in love, or punishments in hell.   (2.12.26)

The provisional sense that the masque has been personated by the 'punishments in hell' seems to be confirmed and even privileged when Britomart enters the third room and discovers with the reader that Busirane is in fact a magician. But by clarifying that Busirane's art is magic – or, rather, that it is simultaneously poetry and magic – Spenser paradoxically settles a cloud of wondrous doubt retrospectively over the entire episode, for he endows all of the images invoked by Busirane's art, and hence by his own, with a potential objectivity, a ghostly form and pressure. Spenser's magic was thus inextricably tied to his desire to fashion disciplined subjects. In a culture where images in the imagination were potentially demonic, and where poetry and magic shared a discursive field, Spenser was able to blur the ontological distinctions between allegory and demonology in order to train the reader in the bi-fold habit of mind enacted by the effect of wonder. Moreover, by producing an image in the mind's eye that was always at once allegorical vehicle and demon, Spenser made not just his poem but the reader's mind itself an object of wonder. This inward-looking wonder, this admiration for the beauty of mental images coupled with anxious doubt over their ontological provenance, produces the very self-regulation that characterizes the disciplined subject the 1590 *Faerie Queene* is meant to fashion.

3 Why Devils Came When Faustus Called Them

Certainly, even at this time I do most plainly see
The devils to be about me round, which make great preparation,
And keep a stir here in this place which only is for me.
Neither do I conceive these things by vain imagination,
But even as truly as mine eyes behold your shape and fashion.

Nathaniel Woodes, *The Conflict of Conscience*

Like Sidney and Spenser, Marlowe deployed instrumental aesthetics in order to establish his art as a distinct and valued cultural form. Unlike them, however, Marlowe never sought patronage by promising to improve his audiences morally; rather, he attempted to draw people to the Bankside with the charisma of his persona, expanding the market in which theatre arose as an independent institution by staging astonishingly powerful performances whose effects appeared to transcend the disenchanted boundaries that usually frame the experience of a play. Nor did he hesitate to exploit the connection of instrumental aesthetics and magic to achieve his artistic goals. Indeed, in his *Doctor Faustus* Marlowe staged a Protestant conflation of theatrical representation and magical practice that seemed to call devils themselves to the stage. Thus in his 1632 anti-theatrical tract *Histrio-mastix*, the Puritan lawyer William Prynne claimed that a devil had appeared 'on the stage at the Belsavage playhouse, in Queen Elizabeth's days (to the great amazement of both the actors and spectators) while they were there profanely playing the History of Faustus (the truth of which I have heard from many now alive, who well remember it) there being some there distracted with that fearful sight.'[1] Prynne was not the only early modern commentator to repeat this rumour. In a note written on the last page of a sixteenth-century monograph, one G.J.R. recorded the experience of 'certain players at Exeter, acting upon the stage the tragical story of Dr. Faustus the conjurer': 'As a certain number of devils kept every one his circle there, and as Faustus was busy in his magical invocations, on a sudden they were all dashed, every one harkening the other in the ear, for they were all persuaded, there was one devil too many amongst them; and so after a little pause desired the people to pardon them, they could go no further with this matter; the people also understanding the thing as it was, every man hastened to be first out of doors. The players (as I heard it) contrary to their custom spending the night in reading and in prayer got them out of the town the next morning.'[2] These rumours of extra devils appearing on the Faustian stage demonstrate that in early modern England theatre could be imagined to have such theological instrumentality that even *representations* of conjuration could appear to work magic. They thus belie the model of the relationship between the dramatic and the theological in which the theatre 'evacuates' the spiritual content from sacred forms only to stage those forms within a sphere of pure make-believe. In this case, it was 'make-believe' itself that seemed to pose the soteriological danger, and it was precisely this danger that Marlowe used to his aesthetic advantage.

In the late 1580s and early 1590s, just before *Doctor Faustus* was first performed, popular devotional writers such as George Gifford and William Perkins attacked the traditional understanding of conjuration as a ritual in which the magician commands devils by iterating a version of the formula, 'In the name of the divine, I conjure you no more to resist, but to appear and be obedient.' These reformist writers brought remarkably corrosive scepticism to bear on the essentialist linguistic assumptions underlying the belief that devils could be conjured with performative language, while simultaneously maintaining or even buttressing theological justifications for the idea that devils, and Satan in particular, intervened in people's lives via the instrumentality of the magician. What the reformers argued (in the terms we saw Walter Ralegh use in the Introduction) is that magical language has no intrinsic spiritual efficacy – that it cannot control the devil or any other supernatural being. Yet they did not dismiss conjuration as a superstitious fiction. Rather, they placed magic within a providential eschatology, recasting it as evidence that God granted agency to devils to test the faithful. Devils appeared to magicians, the reformers argued, because Satan himself produced conjurations as theatrical spectacles, which he used instrumentally to ensnare people into damnation. In this account of magic, the formula of conjuration functioned as a script which would *cue* devils to appear and behave *as if* they had been commanded, and the magician's participation in this fiendish performance would not only compound his own reprobation, but also produce aesthetic responses in the conjuration's spectators that would anger God and lead him to withdraw his salvific grace.

Marlowe seemed to have realized that this revisionary account of magic had powerful dramatic potential – and that it had circulated widely enough in the cultural imaginary to be recognized on the popular stage – for in *Doctor Faustus* he represented the mechanism of conjuration in precisely the reformers' terms.[3] Marlowe's Faustus is a man so invested in the idea that spiritual efficacy inheres in the material, in bodies and texts, that he believes there is 'virtue' in the 'heavenly words' that seem to conjure Mephistopheles forth (1.3.28).[4] Mephistopheles, however, tells Faustus explicitly that his magical words worked only *'per accidens'* (1.3.47), and that in truth he appeared only in the hope that he could 'get' Faustus's 'glorious soul' (1.3.50). Yet Faustus persists, his misgivings about magic repeatedly overcome by Mephistopheles' ability to stage pageants and dumbshows personated by apparently embodied spirits. These spectacles suggest to Faustus that in hell the individuated personhood supposedly delineated by the body's superficial boundaries will last in a spiritual form that the magician may inhabit and control. But it goes without saying that this occular proof of embodied immortality is only theatrical spectacle, in all its ontological insufficiency. Yet at some performances of *Doctor Faustus* in the last decade of the sixteenth century, this very fact – that the instrument of Faustus's damnation is the very spectacle represented on stage – seemed to produce a mirror effect in spectators who feared that their own interest in Faustus's magic was theologically dangerous. The metatheatrical doubling solicited their terrifying identification with Faustus, whereby their own absorption in the events on stage served as evidence of their own reprobation. At times this evidence seems to have been overwhelming enough to cause collective hysteria, and whole groups of people involved in productions of *Faustus*, like the despairing sinner in *The Conflict of Conscience*, felt suddenly convinced that devils had flown to the scene, as if God had judged them irredeemable for their investment in the play. In *Doctor Faustus*, then, Protestant anxiety about salvation and popular desire for entertainment converged to produce historically contingent aesthetic effects. Marlowe brilliantly exploited the reformist understanding of magic as at once theatrical spectacle and theological instrument in order to produce an *aesthetic* instrumentality, in which onstage performativity – the staging of conjuration – generated effects that offstage conjuration quite obviously could not.

The Protestant attack on the idea of intrinsically magical language was an inflection of the broadly confessional attack on sacramentality. Arguments connecting the formula for conjuration to the Catholic Eucharist began to emerge in Germany and Denmark in the 1560s and '70s and were imported into England by a distinctly heterogeneous group of devotional writers.[5] Gifford and Perkins are often reductively characterized as Puritans, perhaps for their early interest in Presbyterianism, although in fact they both embraced the Elizabethan settlement before they published their major tracts on magic.[6] Other writers who rehearsed the Continental account of conjuration had little association with nonconformity: Henry Holland, for instance, was settled in his London living by the establishment dean of Westminster, and Robert Burton, the author of *The Anatomy of Melancholy*, used the opportunity of his Oxford fellowship to ignore theological controversy almost entirely. James I (then James VI of Scotland) repeated the new Protestant arguments about magic verbatim in his 1597 *Daemonologie*, as did the seventeenth-century physician John Cotta in *The Triall of Witchcraft*.[7] The new reformed discourse of magic was, then, generated in pastoral, academic, royal, commercial, and theatrical spaces to various and divergent ends. Indeed, historians of the English Reformation have generally seen the emergence of a reformist theory of magical language as linked to pastoral attempts to discredit 'cunning' men and women as medical authorities and to reinterpret witchcraft as a form of spiritual affliction.[8] But this model of the pastorate attacking popular practices from above, as it were, in order to consolidate its own spiritual authority against the traditions of the laity tends not to provide for the breadth of perspectives and interests – theological, political, and theatrical – which generated and disseminated the new account of the spiritual instrumentality of representation.

It may at first seem as if the reformers did not allow for the theological instrumentality of signs at all: according to their primary argument, human representation has no performative efficacy in the spiritual realm. The supposedly sacred signs of conjuration – the figures and characters carved into the protective circle, the gestures enacted to awe demons, and the words pronounced in the conjuration itself – are all, according to the reformers' arguments, simply 'natural' or material things, and as such they cannot force supernatural creatures to obey human will. Thus Gifford wonders how the magician could be 'so foolish as to imagine' that spiritual beings are 'affected by the virtue of words, gestures, figures, or such like.'[9] 'All words made and uttered by men,' Perkins elaborates, 'are in their own nature but sounds framed by the tongue, of the breath that comes from the lungs; and that which is only a bare sound, in all reason can have no virtue in it to cause a real work, much less to produce a wonder.'[10] Even the text of scripture itself has no essential efficacy: 'the truth is,' Holland ruefully explains, Satan 'nothing regards the outward letter of the Word [any] more than [magicians'] characters, signs, crosses, figures, &c.'[11]

Although they maintain that the letter of the Word lacks the performative power to conjure devils, the reformers nonetheless argue that biblical texts, as well as signs made sacred by scriptural authorization, do have a kind of spiritual efficacy when deployed properly by preachers. Under the right conditions, such signs can produce or strengthen faith and prepare the believer to receive God's grace, which otherwise might run off, as it were, like rainwater on rocky ground. For the reformers, the Eucharist exemplifies the salvific instrumentality of the letter. 'Though it be a thing above [its] common and natural use,' Perkins explains, eucharistic bread is an efficacious sign that has 'the power and property ... to seal and signify unto every believing receiver the body of Christ, [for] thereupon we have warrant from Christ's own commandment, ordinance, and example to use it.'[12] Such a spiritual impression is not produced automatically, however, but according to the inward attitude and intent of those who participate in the ritual (not *ex opere operato*, that is, but *ex opere operantis*). As Perkins elaborates: 'There is not any such force or efficacy of making us holy inherent or tied unto the external figures'; rather, all such efficacy is 'an inseparable companion of true faith and repentance, and of such as turn unto the Lord.'[13] For Perkins, those who 'turn unto the Lord' do so by using the Eucharist as an allegorical figure for a hermeneutic meditation that increases repentance and faith. The meditation upon the allegorical significance of the sacrament is a special means of eschewing the materiality of the letter and dedicating the inward self and the spiritual soul to God – a dedication that in turn, the reformers argue, readies the believer to feel and know God's saving mercy.

In these instrumentalist eucharistic hermeneutics letter and spirit are not exactly equivalent to vehicle and tenor: the letter does not just signify the spirit in a purely referential sense; rather, if *used* with the proper intention, the letter enables the spirit to enter the soul as a sacred gift to the believer. Thus in his commentary on *Corinthians* Calvin argues that 'these words, LETTER and SPIRIT, pertain nothing to exposition [i.e., typological allegory], but to force and fruit.'[14] Unlike the signs of magic, which supposedly produce the outward embodiment of spirits, the Eucharist functions as a vehicle for an idea that works regeneratively in the inward person, if it is interpreted, or used, with a felicitous spiritual intention. This theory of efficacious allegorical hermeneutics, while sustaining an Aristotelian conception of instrumentality, radically devalues the materiality of the sign, giving it only contingent force. It is this commitment to material contingency that at least partly motivates the reformers' condemnation of the Catholic Eucharist and their identification of conjurers with Catholic priests who attempt to make God present in bread by pronouncing what Reginald Scot calls Latin 'babbles.'[15] Indeed, it is no accident that the prestidigitator's phrase 'hocus-pocus' sounds a lot like *hoc est enim corpus meum*: 'hocus-pocus' finds its genealogical root in the Catholic formula or, more precisely, in the Protestant argument that Catholic priests do the work of the devil in claiming that their articulations have the performative efficacy to invoke the presence of God.[16]

Yet despite their critique of the Catholic Eucharist as an inefficacious conjuration, the reformers take it for granted that the devil does, in fact, come when the magician calls him. Their premise that devils are being conjured all the time is so fundamental to their polemic that it is never debated or even really discussed. With their commitment to providentialism, they assume that an embodied creature called Satan must be using people's desires for efficacy as a weapon of spiritual attack. But even if we accept this premise for the sake of argument, the question still arises: how does the magician's language manage to conjure the devil when it lacks power? Although its essence is merely material, Perkins answers, conjuration nonetheless has 'another nature in regard of its immediate relation to the devil, to whom it is a sign.'[17] In its second nature, conjuration works not by essential performativity but *'per accidens'* (1.3.47), as Mephistopheles says to Faustus. It manifests not the magician's power to command spirits with language, but his inward alienation from the spirit of God. As Perkins insists, although 'signs, characters, and figures [are] no whit effectual in themselves,' they do 'serve for watchwords unto Satan,' revealing that 'the user thereof hath his heart secretly indented ... for the accomplishment of [Satan's] intended works.'[18] Perkins's rhetoric here is of spiritual warfare: 'watchword' is a military term denoting a preconcerted signal to begin an assault. But in this case the devil attacks not with violence but with the apparent satisfaction of desire. As soon as he apprehends his watchwords, he appears and, as Gifford puts it, 'doth ... *feign* himself to be bound.'[19] In other words, Satan attacks the soul of the magician by behaving *as if* he had been conjured by the magician's language. 'In all conjurations,' Perkins goes on to say, 'when [Satan] is raised by the Sorcerer, he is willing to be adjured by all the holy names of God that are in the Scripture, to the end that he may more deeply seduce his own instruments, and make them to think that ... names will bind him & force him to yield unto their desires in the particular, when indeed there is no such matter.'[20] (As Burton reiterates it, 'There is [no] power at all in those spells, charms, characters, and barbarous words, but that the Devil doth use such means to delude them, *ut fideles inde magos* [so that he might keep those magi faithful to him].')[21] To believe that 'names will bind' the devil and force him to yield to desire is, in these writers' accounts, to believe that human beings may rise above their fundamentally wretched place in the cosmos and escape their irreducible dependence on God's grace for any satisfaction that would transcend mortality. And to fail to recognize one's irreducible dependence on God is to fail to see the need to cultivate faith.

If Satan's goal is to ruin the magician's faith, his further goal, according to these preachers, is to use the magician as what Perkins calls 'his own instrument' to undermine the faith of others besides the magician himself. 'As Satan used the serpent in the beginning to seduce our first parents from the obedience of God's word,' Holland argues, 'so is it not to be doubted that after the fall he uses man himself as his instrument by magical arts to withdraw men from faith in the promise of their redemption by Christ.'[22] Satan performs this feat, the reformers warn, by staging his false conjuration as a theatre piece that has the instrumental end of producing aesthetic responses in spectators that incline them towards reprobation. 'The power of this Prince of darkness ... manifests itself herein,' Perkins insists, 'by works of wonder, transcendent in regard of ordinary capacity, and diversely dispensed by his chosen instruments of both sexes ... sometime by enchantment, sometime by rare sleights and delusions ... and all to purchase himself the admiration, fear, and faith of the credulous world, which is usually carried away, with affectation and applause of signs and wonders.'[23] If 'wonder' here is ontological, engendered by a frightening yet awe-inspiring encounter with a supernatural being, it is also theatrical, produced by the aesthetic 'enchantment' and the spectacular 'rare sleights and delusions' that generate precisely the 'admiration' and 'fear' that sixteenth-century literary theory defines as the dual effect of the most elevated dramatic modes. And this wonder, in turn, inspires the 'affectation' – that is, the affection or delight – that leads spectators to offer 'applause.' Such applause expresses, for the reformers, 'faith' in magical power, the very antithesis of the justification that leads to salvation.

The reformers thus imagine that the devil may use theatre to produce an aesthetic delight that leads to sin and damnation. Indeed, they never posit anything approaching a modern model of theatrical experience, in which staged illusions, institutionally marked out as such, are cultivated and consumed as ends in themselves; rather, they assume that forms of theatrical cognition and pleasure undermine the habits of mind that sustain faith and are, therefore, instruments producing disastrous theological effects. The reformers thus warn their readers to avoid participating in spectacles of magic at all costs, or, at least, to monitor their responses to such spectacles very carefully and root out any sources of pleasure they might feel with intensive self-examination and repentance, lest their enjoyment corrupt their faith and undermine their certainty of their own salvation.

In the reformers' accounts, then, faith itself is performative since it has no objective ontological status outside of the acts of consuming representations that either produce or obscure it. The performativity of faith even has a constant witness: God himself, who surveils the subject's invisible sensations very closely. For it turns out that God monitors peoples' aesthetic responses to theatrical representations as well as their thoughts about their responses. These feelings and thoughts at once manifest and transform the quality of one's faith, judged by God when he decides to save or damn one's soul. Indeed, according to the reformers, it is *God* who allows Satan to use the magician instrumentally; more specifically, it is God himself who uses Satan instrumentally, as he did in Job, actively to test the faith of his professed believers, and confirm the declining fortunes of nonbelievers, by indirectly eliciting and directly scrutinizing human beings' inward responses to diabolical spectacle and drama.[24] Holland explicitly argues that God uses Satan's magic both so that he may both 'fatherly forewarn his Saints to pass their dwelling here [on earth] with all diligence, to avoid the contagion of the wicked with whom they have any conversation,' and so that he may 'punish them who would not receive his truth' by sending these reprobates *strong delusions that they may believe lies.*'[25] For Holland, God's active, providential intervention into the world via Satan's theatre of magic is, in a strange way, a blessing that allows the faithful to recognize their own sins and infirmities, giving them the opportunity to repent. In his view, even the magician himself can repent and be saved.[26] For Perkins, by contrast, God's use of Satan in the spectacle of conjuration is less an opportunity for the faithful than an interrogation of the individual subject, whose response to magical 'strong delusions' reveals the predestined fate of his immortal soul. Glorified by his own power above all, Perkins's God uses Satan's magic 'to avenge himself on Man for his ingratitude,' and 'to try and prove his people, whether they will cleave to him and his Word, or seek unto Satan and his wicked Spirits.'[27]

When in his opening soliloquy Faustus resolves to learn the secrets of magic, he articulates a phrase that echoes those used by the reformers to describe the signs that serve as 'watchwords' for Satan: 'lines, circles, schemes, letters and characters!' Faustus cries, 'ay, these are those that Faustus most desires' (1.1.53–4). With this phrase, Faustus signals to the audience that he is the conjurer their ministers have warned them about, the magician who most desires to possess the signs of magic for their purported spiritual power 'to gain a deity' (1.1.65). And at first such signs do seem to have spiritual force, for Faustus manages to conjure up the devil's emissary in Mephistopheles. When the spirit responds obediently to his commands, Faustus, delighted, exclaims: 'I see there's virtue in my heavenly words!' (1.3.28). But Mephistopheles goes on to explain that he appeared not because Faustus's conjuration enforced him to rise, but because he recognized the watchwords that indicate that the enchanter has a relation in his mind to the devil. When Faustus demands to know whether his 'conjuring speeches' (1.3.46) in fact raised him, Mephistopheles replies:

> That was the cause, but yet *per accidens*
> For when we hear one rack the name of God,
> Abjure the Scriptures, and his savior Christ,
> We fly in hope to get his glorious soul,
> Nor will we come, unless he use such means
> Whereby he is in danger to be damned:
> Therefore the shortest cut for conjuring
> Is stoutly to abjure the Trinity,
> And pray devoutly to the prince of hell.   (1.3.47–55)

Dismissing the notion that magical signs have essential spiritual efficacy, Mephistopheles explains that Faustus's language worked performatively in the spiritual realm only by its accidental, contingent qualities, or by its second nature regarding its relation to the devil. It was not any force in the literal instruments of conjuration – the lines, circles, characters, letters – that induced the spirit to appear. Rather, it was the mere fact that Faustus took to conjuring at all that raised the 'hope' in Mephistopheles that the devil might 'get his glorious soul,' and only in this hope did he 'fly' to the scene.[28] Hence, as Mephistopheles goes on to explain, magic is not even the most effective instrument with which to invoke the devil's presence, for it is not the most direct 'means' whereby the magician 'is in danger to be damned.' To conjure the devil, one need just 'stoutly … abjure the Trinity, / And pray devoutly to the prince of hell.' As if disdaining the idea that he neglected to use any tool of magical efficacy, Faustus assures Mephostophiles that he has already taken this shortest of shortcuts: 'So Faustus hath already done, and holds this principle: / There is no chief but only Beelzebub, / To whom Faustus doth dedicate himself' (3.56–9). With this reply, Faustus both performs and confirms what the reformers would call his inward relation to Satan.

But why does Faustus have this relation in his mind to the devil? As the reformers argued about the magician, Faustus inclines to the devil because he rejects faith, which is to say that he refuses to believe that God promises him any immortal happiness. Critics have long since noticed that Faustus has a complete aphasia on the subject of mercy – in his first soliloquy he omits the lines of 1 John that promise forgiveness to those who repent, rather perversely proclaiming instead that the Bible insists 'we must sin, / And so consequently die … an everlasting death' (1.1.46–8).[29] Faustus erases the promise of God's mercy because he disdains the dualistic Christian metaphysics that underlies that very promise. Christian dualism is taken for granted in the play even by Mephostophiles, who makes a clear distinction between body and soul, radically subordinating the value of the former to the latter. When Faustus orders him to attack the Old Man, the devil replies: 'His faith is great / I cannot touch his soul. / But what I may afflict his body with / I will attempt, which is but little worth' (5.1.79–81). In contrast to his conjured companion, Faustus values the body more than the soul, as if for him the truly sacred communion were found not in the valence of symbolic bread, but in the juicy and perfumed grapes he gives to the hugely pregnant duchess who has been longing for fruit through the dearth of winter. His investment in embodiment is less social, though, than epistemological: he implicitly denies the assumption that signification requires dematerialization, and that 'real' meaning should be fundamentally allegorical. Indeed, Faustus eschews allegorical interpretation. He never reads past the letter, as it were, to search for spirit; he never seeks what recedes beyond the textual mark as if it were the invisible, impalpable, transcendent truth. To read in that way is to perform faith. The Old Man, for instance, describes faith as the first step on an unfolding journey to salvation, calling it 'the way of life / By which sweet path thou may'st attain the goal / That shall conduct thee to celestial rest' (5.1.37–9). The striking catachresis of the 'goal' that becomes the boatman or the angel who will 'conduct' the believer to 'celestial rest' – not to mention the pun that makes 'way of life' at once a method and a path with duration – emphasizes the strange requirement that faith places on the believer to seek in thought what is not only absent, but also deferred beyond any end that he can conceive for himself. Faustus refuses this injunction to read the Word and the world allegorically, to perform faith by consuming representation like a Protestant.

Faustus enters into the play with his anti-allegorical habit of mind firmly in place. In his opening soliloquy he not only ignores the scriptural promise of mercy, but also never acknowledges that every profession he considers and abandons resounds as a figure for salvation. In his refusal to read allegorically, Faustus articulates, but does not hear, that the study of each art stands as a metonym for a larger spiritual quest to come to God; he makes visible, but does not see, the eschatological trajectory in which the ends of earthly things are themselves means to move the soul towards an invisible, deferred ending in heaven.[30] Thus Faustus begins with Aristotle, asking whether 'to dispute well' is 'logic's chiefest end' (1.1.8). When he concludes that it is, and that this 'art' affords 'no greater miracle' (1.1.9), he decides to abandon its study since he has already 'attained the end' (1.1.10). This seems fair enough, since merely to dispute well may indeed seem a rather limited goal. In the very next line, however, as Faustus actually renounces the art, he bids '*on kai me on*, farewell' (1.1.12), and the significance of what he is abandoning changes.[31] Faustus is abandoning not just the form of disputation, but the opportunity to study being and non-being, existence itself: he seems to think he understands the mysteries of ontology since he has already mastered the external form of the art that is the vehicle for its study. In the same manner, Faustus renounces the law with an almost Pauline critique, calling it a form of 'external trash' (1.1.35), yet from the perspective of faith even the Justinian rule 'If one and the same thing is bequeathed to two persons, one should have the thing itself, the other the value of the thing,' which Faustus dismisses as a case of 'paltry legacies' (1.1.30), may be seen as a vehicle with which to ruminate on the very problem of having a self split into body and soul, with one part, 'the thing,' going to the earth after death and the other part, 'the value of the thing,' going to the spiritual domain that God judges it deserves.

But Faustus feels little need to read allegorically, to seek the signification that transcends direct presentation, for he never imagines spirit or even presence as anywhere but in signs themselves. Despite striking moments of doubt and panic in which he senses he is deceived, he consistently reads with the belief that spirit is entirely immanent in the letter. That is why he so loves the signs of magic: the lines, circles, schemes, and characters that apparently perform 'the metaphysics of magicians' (1.1.51) by seeming to enact visibly, palpably, and presently that letter and spirit, and matter and soul, are one.[32] The fantasy that objects have spiritual efficacy provides his consolation. Indeed, Faustus seems even more invested in the spiritual power of the materiality of the sign than is the devil himself: when at one point Lucifer warns Faustus to 'not think of God' (2.3.92), Faustus responds by vowing 'never to look to heaven, / Never to name God' (2.3.95–6), as if naming God or performing acts that mark or deal in 'the outside' of things were equivalent to thinking about God – or as if naming and thinking were phenomenologically identical, or produced the same results. For Faustus, naming suffices: for him spirit inheres in surfaces, and being therefore exists only in embodied form. And Faustus manifests this principle in both his epistemology and his very sense of subjectivity itself. When Faustus reflects on his achievements in medicine – his having helped 'whole cities' (1.1.21) to escape plague – he decides that such successes are worthless, and that only by being able to 'make men ... live eternally, / Or, being dead, raise them to life again' (1.1.24–5) were the medical profession 'to be esteemed' (1.1.26). Faustus is not abandoning medicine here to take up divinity, as if he thought that the prolongation of earthly life were less vital than the pastoral care of immortal souls. Rather, Faustus is revealing that he conceives of eternal life itself as something that must entail embodiment, the literal survival or resurrection of the body.

Faustus depends upon fantasies of embodiment because he imagines no being, no self, grounded in the soul at all, neither in the future of salvation nor even in the present, where the identity of the man 'Faustus' might seem to emerge from some invisible core within, something given a sense of itself in the palpable imagination, animated by belief, that in fact something is there. For Faustus, there is simply nothing there: when Faustus refers to himself in the third person, for example ('I charge thee wait upon me whilst I live, / To do what ever Faustus shall command' [1.3.37–8]), or when he addresses himself with his name ('why Faustus, hast thou not attained that end?' [1.1.18]), it often seems as if he were swerving away from speaking from the phantasmatic inward plenitude of an 'I,' or as if he needed to imagine himself as a bounded object, seen from the outside in his mind's eye, in order to articulate himself (and thus could make himself present only by *naming* himself, 'Faustus').[33] Faustus must name himself, conceive of himself from the outside, as it were, because he never identifies with his soul.[34] Faustus finds his soul to be alien to him, so much so that he feels it to be a burden he would be happy to be rid of ('why wert thou not a creature wanting soul?' he cries out desperately at one point [5.2.105]). There is some theological justification for Faustus's dissociation. Perkins, for instance, argues that 'God is the life of the soul' just as 'the soul is the life of the body.'[35] With God residing inwardly as his immortal, animating essence, Faustus views his soul only as an absent, impalpable other for which he knows he is responsible but about which he feels that it is 'not Faustus.' Subject to this vertiginous alienation from his soul, Faustus takes salvation to be a fate that entails the very annihilation of his identity, an annihilation more complete and terrifying to him than that imposed by earthly death itself.

Faustus's rejection of faith is both producer and product of his sense that salvation will entail his own erasure, for it alienates him from his soul by alienating him from God; it is both producer and product of his determination not to read 'past' what is material and embodied to what is intangible, for it gives him the sense that the intangible will turn out to be nothing. Yet Faustus's lack of faith does not enable him to feel that there is in fact nothing after death for him to worry about. On the contrary, Faustus is obsessed with the afterlife and with hell specifically, about which he repeatedly questions Mephistopheles. Not that Faustus believes what Mephistopheles *tells* him about hell, however: he scoffs, 'Come, I think hell's a fable' (2.1.130) when the devil informs him that 'hell hath no limits, nor is circumscribed / In one self place; for where we are is hell, / And where hell is, must we ever be' (2.1.124–6). Faustus will not imagine hell as a universally diffused, Augustinian state of privation; rather, he insists on imagining hell as an extension or reproduction of the university where he currently resides. In response to Mephistopheles' insistence that he himself is 'damned, and ... now in hell' (2.1.140), Faustus impatiently replies, 'How now, in hell? Nay, and this be hell, / I'll willingly be damned here! What, walking, disputing, / etc.' (2.1.141–3). 'Damned here ... walking, disputing, etc.' Faustus reveals how much it matters to him that hell be a place, and not a state of the soul. Faced with a salvation that seems to entail his annihilation in the disappearance or dissolution of his body, Faustus is *comforted* by the idea of a hell where he can walk and dispute, where he can have reading groups with the 'old philosophers' (1.3.62), and where the 'infernal spirits' will 'swarm' (1.1.117) to his lectures. Imagining hell as a continuation of his brilliant academic career, Faustus simply sees damnation as the better choice.

Obsessed with his afterlife yet disdaining to be dissolved into God's heaven, Faustus develops a relation in his mind to the devil as his solution to his dilemma. By adopting the 'metaphysics of magicians,' Faustus finds a way, he thinks, to control the terms of his own death, securing for himself an eternity of continued embodiment, boundedness, lack of self-transcendence. Indeed, at first Faustus passionately catalogues the epicurean marvels that he will command his spirits to procure – the 'orient pearl' (1.1.85), the 'princely delicates' (1.1.87) – but it becomes increasingly clear over the course of the play that whatever *worldly* rewards magic may afford him are secondary. When Valdes promises Faustus that by magic he will gain fame and sex and money if only he will 'be resolute' (1.1.135), Faustus answers in a way that tells more than he knows: 'Valdes,' he says, 'as resolute am I in this / As thou to live' (1.1.136–7). His resolution to live indicates less Faustus's determination to satisfy himself than his determination to *save* himself, to use magic to self-create the materialized afterlife, the embodied end, he most ardently desires. Thus the ability to conjure up and play with spirits is what he wants; only magical personation enables him to face his own death and what is then to come, for it enables him, he believes, to experience being already in hell, where he will not only continue to walk, dispute, eat, and give lectures, but also participate in delightful entertainments that celebrate personation itself. That is why Faustus is so easily distracted from repentance and doubt by the apparently trivial shows that the devil stages for him, or that he thinks he conjures up himself.[36] Far from being inexplicably minor applications of the exalted magical power Faustus supposedly possesses, those pageants and dumbshows are at the very core of the satisfaction that Faustus looks to magic to afford him. The spirits personating poetic figures give Faustus evidence seen that he too may remain embodied after death, perhaps even in a more heroic form than the one he inhabits in earthly life. Of course, this representation of embodied forms by the devil is the very theatrical pretense to which the Protestant witchcraft writers referred. Yet Marlowe makes Mephistopheles' pretense much more subtle than the one imagined even by Perkins in his fierce obsession with Satan's wiles. Whereas the Protestant witchcraft writers assumed that Satan would feign himself to be bound by conjuration, Marlowe has Mephistopheles deceive Faustus not by feigning to be bound (for the spirit clearly defies Faustus's commands at many points along the way) but by feigning hell to be a place where bodies last, in a form more beautiful than those they possess on earth, and where they perform delightful scene after delightful scene that Faustus may not only watch but join as an actor himself.

This dynamic is never more apparent than in Faustus's encounter with the diabolical personification of Helen of Troy, who is spirit made literal or *material* in the 'sweet embracings' (5.1.185) that he/she allows Faustus

to enjoy. Faustus has specifically asked Mephistopheles for these embrac-
ings so that they may 'extinguish clean' the 'thoughts that do dissuade'
him from his satanic 'vow' (5.1.185–6). And when Faustus says 'embrac-
ings,' he means *embracings*: the play suggests one entire sexual act (and,
perhaps, the beginnings of another one) in a mere three lines:

> Sweet Helen, make me immortal with a kiss:
> Her lips suck forth my soul, see where it flies!
> Come, Helen, come, give me my soul again.   (5.1.92–4)

Once erotic union is achieved, or at least implied, the abstraction of 'faith'
has no gravity to counterweight the fullness and depth and pressure that
Faustus believes that he finds now in spirit. By embracing the demonic
Helen, Faustus seems to discover that spirits have interiority, or, rather,
that their gorgeous exteriority and their interiority are one, just as their
bodies and their souls seem to be one. He feels such ecstasy in this discov-
ery because it apparently provides concrete, palpable evidence that spirit is
material – or, rather, that 'spirit' exists as a sort of third term that obviates
the distinction between body and soul. Yet what 'flies' from Faustus does
not necessarily encompass the 'soul'; it may well be 'spirit' in the sense
of 'a waste of spirit in an expense of shame is lust in action' (which itself
is not the kind of spirit that composes devils' shapes).[37] Faustus wants so
much to materialize his soul, in order for it be *his* soul, that the distinc-
tion between his vital spirits, the devil's airy spirits, and his soul is lost on
him. But how could it not be lost? Faustus experiences his embrace of the
demonic Helen as a ravishment that leads to something at once like or-
gasm and like the immolation of one's soul flying to something infinitely
greater than self ('brighter art thou,' Faustus cries to Helen, 'than flaming
Jupiter / When he appeared to hapless Semele!' [5.1.106–8]). Yet Faustus
seems sure that whatever Helen has taken from him returns at once again,
enabling him to 'die' and be resurrected over and over, living perpetually
in a 'heaven' in the 'lips' (12.86) that indeed seem to make him 'immortal
with a kiss' (12.85).

This kind of rapture so transports Faustus because he believes that it
proves magic is making him immortal precisely in the way he wishes to be.
But when Faustus attempts to codify his belief by signing the diabolical
contract that promises he will remain forever an embodied spirit 'in form
and substance' (2.1.72), to his utter horror he discovers that his body re-
mains a disobedient vehicle for the invisible hand that writes '*Homo fuge*'
(2.1.76) on his arm. Yet once again, Mephistopheles manages to distract

Faustus from his dramatic crisis merely by going to 'fetch him somewhat to delight his mind' (2.1.82). The devil exits stage left, then:

> *Enter[s] [again] with devils, giving crowns and rich apparel to Faustus;*
> *they dance, and then depart.*
> *Faustus*: Speak, Mephistopheles, what means this show?
> *Mephistopheles*: Nothing, Faustus, but to delight thy mind withal,
> And to show thee what magic can perform.   (s.d., 2.1.83–5)

In contrast to riddling texts that use Faustus's body and that demand interpretation, 'this show,' although allegorical in the morality tradition, here means 'nothing.' It demands no interpretation, no deferral of significance, no acknowledgment of transcendence. It is all surface. The 'crowns' and the 'rich apparel' that the devils give Faustus emblematize the attention to materials and to outsides that characterizes both life in hell and a certain kind of disinterested aestheticism that in this context functions only to deceive. Over and over Mephistopheles tricks Faustus into believing that the shows conjured up in the theatre of hell's delights find their ends in the enjoyment of their own performance. Perhaps his most telling trick is to seem to make 'music' (2.3.30) with Amphion simply to provide 'sweet pleasure' (2.3.25) to Faustus. Amphion along with Orpheus usually exemplifies the dream of an *instrumental* aesthetics, a beauty that can pacify beasts and even compel rocks and stones to organize themselves into cities with its moving sweetness of song. But Mephistopheles makes this sweet pleasure seem inconsequential, as he makes all magic seem inconsequential, as if magic were a production that celebrated only itself, showed only 'what magic can perform,' or as if the delight inspired by the spirits personated on stage had no effect. But, of course, there will be an effect, no end of effect, just not yet.

Faustus's dilemma, which impels him to adopt the 'metaphysics of magicians' and choose damnation, is based, then, on the Protestant revision of traditional accounts of conjuration. But Marlowe used those accounts not only to develop a compelling dramatic character, but also to stage a play so emotionally powerful that it seemed to invoke, in William Prynne's words, 'the visible apparition of the Devil on the stage' to the 'great amazement of both the actors and spectators ... there being some there distracted with that fearful sight.' The ambiguity of Prynne's final phrase, 'there being some there distracted with that fearful sight,' suggests both that the participants in the performance were distracted by the fearful sight of the devil appearing among them and that the devil appeared among them *because* some participants were already driven to distraction by a fearful sight. And what else was this latter sight but the representation of conjuration itself? If you imagined magic as a spectacle meant to produce thoughts and feelings that would be watched and judged by both devils and God, to feel yourself taking pleasure in the staging of conjuration was to sense yourself being led into reprobation. Let us take, for example, the divertissement just quoted, in which Mephistopheles presents devils who give 'crowns and rich apparel' to Faustus and who 'dance and depart.' Mephistopheles is quite obviously entertaining the audience with this spectacle as much as he is entertaining the magician himself. And he is doing so after having made the audience complicit in his intent to deceive Faustus with his confiding aside: 'I'll fetch him something to delight his mind' (2.1.82). The aside serves to remind the audience that delight is theologically suspect in this context, a fatal distraction from thoughts of God and repentance, and as such something to be resisted. Yet how could the audience not have delighted, at least somewhat, in the unusual sight of jewels and embroidered brocade glittering in the light of the torches, in the sweet sound of the music playing as graceful bodies moved in intricate patterns around, in the very qualities of lightness and harmony that the moving figures exuded into the heavens? To disdain these things would be to disdain the sensuous pleasures of theatre itself. Yet how could spectators not have felt anxious about their delight if they believed that it indicated that they were in spiritual danger? Such anxiety indeed sometimes reached such a pitch of collective tension that audiences became convinced there was 'one devil too many amongst them,' as G.J.R. put it. Of course, the palpable sense that devils had actually appeared in the playhouse was precisely the theatrical effect that Marlowe intended to produce: in order to tie the aesthetic effects of his play to the theological effects of magic, he had Mephistopheles proclaim at the outset that he had been summoned not because there was any 'virtue' (1.3.28) in Faustus's words, but because Faustus's interest in magical language indicated he was 'in danger of being damned' (1.3.52).

It is not only when Mephistopheles first appears and contextualizes his invocation in terms of the reformed understanding of magic that the play attempts to cast its spectators as active participants in a production that has soteriological consequences. Take, for instance, the Knight's refusal to remain on the scene when Faustus conjures at the Duke of Vanholt's palace. The Knight seems like a throwaway character, a mere opportunity for Faustus to perform yet another trivial prank, but he also enacts the reformist doctrine that Marlowe deploys to make the audience anxious about their own interest in magical spectacles. As if assessing everything through a lens of faith (he begins most of his statements with the preface, 'I'faith'), the Knight reacts to Faustus in the exemplary Protestant manner: on the one hand he entirely devalues the magician's abilities (when Faustus promises to 'accomplish' the Duke's request by the 'power' of his 'spirit' [4.1.43, 44], the Knight spits out contemptuously, 'I'faith that's nothing at all' [1.3.45]); on the other hand, he seems to fear the spiritual implications of witnessing Faustus's invocations. Accordingly, he leaves the hall when Faustus begins, as if refusing to risk the danger of being interested in or pleased by a magical sight.

The play implicitly opposes the attitude and behaviour of this doctrinally exemplary character to those of the audience on the ground and in the galleries, who have not only gathered but paid their own coin to watch a staging of a historical magician's courtly spectacles. Indeed, by conflating theatrical and magical shows, and by staging that conflation in ways that implicate the audience in the action, *Doctor Faustus* repeatedly attempts to compel its spectators to identify almost involuntarily with characters who are invested in the effects of magic. When the Scholars ask Faustus to produce Helen, for example, the play positions them as members of the audience who desire to see a conjuration, while it subsumes the audience into the group of scholars by having the boy actor playing Helen move through the paying crowd. (Allardyce Nicoll has convincingly argued that the stage direction 'music sounds, and Helen passeth over the stage' [s.d., 5.1.26] implies that the actor entered from one side of the yard, walked through the audience, and exited at the other side.)[38] And the play stages this scene to attempt to produce the diabolical wonder, the very combination of erotic admiration and fear, that Perkins identified as augmenting the devil's power: as the boy actor makes his way through the close-pressed groundlings, his body becomes tactile and almost invasive, contaminating the visual domain of spectatorship with the presence of materiality. That contaminating presence may well be as frightening as it is erotic, not least because Faustus commands the scholars, and by extension the audience, to 'be silent, for danger is in words' (5.1.24), as if their hushed attention were the only prophylactic against the transformation of this feminine impersonation into a violent diabolical horror.

Yet the structure of theatrical identification changes as the boy actor returns to the stage and Helen and Faustus are swept up into their erotic union. Then it is Faustus who consumes and is ravished by Helen as an impersonation, and insofar as the audience becomes swept up in the high power of Marlowe's heroic verse (and in the actors' ability to project

erotic desire and fulfilment), they too become transported by the plea-
sures of rhetorical and theatrical embodiment. The play increases the ter-
ror of the pleasure of this identification by juxtaposing the celebration
of magical and theatrical mimesis with the theological imperatives of the
Old Man, who appears here specifically in contrast to Helen's conjura-
tion. The Old Man's theological directives ('break heart ... and mingle it
with tears' [5.1.40]) remind the audience of their obligation to attend to
their faith just at the moment when their inclinations are being most sorely
tested by the erotics of the spectacle that they are witnessing. In making
the audience aware of the requirements of faith while ravishing them with
theatrical spectacle, the play lays bare the dangers of identification with
Faustus, whose desire to consider repentance is repeatedly obscured by
his absorption in the shows Mephistopheles stages. Yet again and again the
audience is invited to enjoy Mephistopheles' spectacles while being made
aware that their aesthetic effects serve to bring Faustus ever closer to the
point at which it will be too late for him to repent. Even when Faustus acts
less as a passive consumer of Mephistopheles' theatre pieces, and more as
a jester who seeks to 'delight' his patrons 'with some mirth' (4.1.90), the
audience is encouraged to feel that Faustus represents their interests, as it
were, since even his cheapest tricks stand as forms of the most basic social
wish-fulfilment. If Faustus and Mephistopheles are able to slap around
the Pope and his Friars despite their curses, not only do they confirm the
reformist argument about magic (which of course dismisses any *maledi-
cat Dominus* as entirely ineffective), but they also enact the desire of any
hot-blooded apprentice who would fully enjoy beating up one of his na-
tion's enemies. Or, again, by selling the horse courser a bum steed and then
undoing him by disappearing his leg, Faustus would provide vicarious,
if gruff, satisfaction to any resentful spectator who had been fleeced by,
essentially, the used-car salesman of his day. In both its high and low plea-
sures, then, *Doctor Faustus* solicits identification with its hero, increasing
the audience's queasy sense of sympathy with a magician being led to his
damnation.

Just as the play solicits sympathy with Faustus in its spectacle and its
comedy, so does it invite pity for Faustus in its tragedy. Such pity emerges
from a slightly different kind of theatrical identification, however: rather
than accompanying the spectator's recognition that a character shares his
or her interests, pity may arise when the spectator recognizes the char-
acter's otherness, when he apprehends or infers that the character suffers
inwardly in some extraordinary way. Yet in pity the spectator also identi-
fies in some sense with the tragic character, for he feels psychic pain in his

imagination of the character's suffering (the word 'compassion' derives, of course, from a compound of the Latin *pati*, 'to suffer,' and *com*, 'together'). For Levinas, for instance, pity, as an expression of the subject's irreducibly asymmetrical obligation to the other, is fundamental to ethics.[39] But in *Doctor Faustus*, pity has no salutary ethical or moral value; on the contrary, the play explicitly contrasts the quality of human pity to that of divine mercy, thereby fashioning pity for Faustus as an aesthetic response that undermines the spectator's faith in God. It is the Old Man who thus devalues tragic pity. After Helen leaves the stage for the first time, the Old Man tells Faustus that an 'angel' hovers over his head 'with a vial full of precious grace' to 'pour' into his 'soul' (5.1.54–6), and he urges Faustus to repent – to 'break heart, drop blood, and mingle it with tears' (5.1.40) – warning him that he has endangered his inward soul 'with such flagitious crimes of heinous sins / *As no commiseration may expel* / But mercy, Faustus, of thy Savior sweet, / Whose blood alone must wash away thy guilt' (5.1.43–7, emphasis added). 'Commiseration' is, of course, the contemporaneous word for the pity inspired by tragedy; Sidney uses it as such in *The Defense of Poesy*.[40] The Old Man argues, then, that Faustus is no less damnable for being pitiful, yet his argument, orthodox as it may be, not only makes God seem somehow less compassionate than even the crudest member of the audience moved by Faustus's suffering, but also makes his justice seem all the more inscrutable.

The play's implication that God lacks compassion and, even more capriciously, that he has subjected Faustus to some inexorable, necessary damnation, is concentrated in Faustus's final soliloquy, where the audience witnesses Faustus struggling to save himself:

> O I'll leap up to my God! Who pulls me down?
> See, see where Christ's blood streams in the firmament!
> One drop would save my soul, half a drop: ah my Christ –
> Ah, rend not my heart for naming of my Christ;
> Yet I will call on him – O spare me Lucifer!
> Where is it now? 'Tis gone: and see where God
> Stretcheth out his arm, and bends his ireful brows!   (5.2.77–83)

It is utterly clear that Faustus is being inwardly tortured. The longing and the sense of exile invoked by his cries ('see, see where Christ's blood streams,' 'one drop would save my soul,' 'ah my Christ') are utterly palpable yet horribly answered by sharp internal pain, as if an invisible claw slashed at Faustus's heart for its very longing ('ah, rend not my heart for naming of Christ'). And by this wound Faustus becomes all the more alienated from mercy, as if he were confronted with the hallucination of Christ's blood disappearing ('where is it now? 'Tis gone'), or as if God himself looked down in the sternest, most unforgiving judgment ('see where God / Stretcheth out his arm, and bends his ireful brows!'). But what makes God appear entirely confounding is not merely that he seems to all too ready to squash Faustus, as if Marlowe's hero were nothing more than a scurrying, terrified bug, but also that Faustus himself finally seems horrified by damnation yet remains utterly bereft of any chance of salvation, simply because he manifests the very same habit of mind he displayed in his opening soliloquy. He still feels like he can live only in his body, addressing the earth as if it could hide him from God by hiding his body ('then will I headlong run into the earth: Earth gape! O no, it will not harbor me' [5.2.87]). He still feels like salvation is an annihilation worse than death, and for that very reason he cannot help but prefer either to be in endless pain in hell or to have no soul at all ('O no end is limited to damned souls! / Why wert thou not a creature wanting soul?' [5.2.104–5]). And he still thinks that his soul is flesh and that his flesh will endure forever in hell ('Now body, turn to air, / Or Lucifer will bear thee quick to hell / O soul, be changed into little water drops, / And fall into the ocean, ne'er to be found' [5.2.116–19]). Thus he can do nothing but call on God in a gasping panic ('my God, My God!' he cries, just before the devils enter to drag him away). And yet: is he not performing the Old Man's injunction to 'break heart, drop blood, and mingle it with tears'? But God still rejects him ('my God, my God, look not so fierce on me!' [5.2.120]).

Even if Faustus performs the affects of repentance, he cannot repent and be saved in the strict theological sense, because until the very end he exhibits the inward disposition of the faithless magician who must choose to be duped by Satan. But why does he have such an inward disposition in the first place? Is it indeed that God has predestined Faustus to hell, subjected him to the most miserable necessity? For Paul Ricoeur, the question of 'the scandalous theology of predestination to evil' is the tragic question par excellence, which is why the tragic is always, in Ricoeur's formulation, 'a temptation to despair' in its display of the 'hostile transcendence to which the hero is prey.'[41] But Marlowe's play, as much as it invites the audience to despair, stages something more subtle and finally more wrenching than blank divine vengeance, for in fact it employs the more charitable theology represented by Holland rather than that of Perkins: Faustus may indeed repent, and God may indeed change his mind. The possibility of repentance provides the suspense that makes the play *dramatic* rather than merely iconographical, and that gives force and fear to those apparently trivial spectacles that repeatedly persuade Faustus not to perform his inward penance. Yet at the same time, there does seem to be something fated in the tenacity of Faustus's habit of mind preventing him from taking his given opportunities to repent. *Doctor Faustus* thus brings the audience right up against the non-dialectical, and therefore tragic contradiction of the theology of grace: that an omnipotent and supposedly loving God permits creaturely suffering, or, in terms more specific to the play, that God rejects a man who cries out to him simply because that man thinks like a dramatist rather than an allegorist.[42] Milton, for his part, tries to solve this problem with a theodicy of human insufficiency – the archangel Raphael notoriously tells Adam not to seek to know things above his ken – but Marlowe's play lays bare the ethical poverty of this strategy (not least because it is hard to see what Faustus has done with his magic that is really so evil: Ask some questions about the stars? Put on some shows? Find a pregnant woman some grapes?).

Even to consider these questions, let alone to feel stirred or moved by them, is, it seems, to begin to doubt the goodness of God.[43] And to doubt the goodness of God, even if you still believe in his existence, is to slide into what was generally understood in the period as atheism.[44] Perhaps that is why Prynne accused acting companies of 'prophanely' playing the history of Faustus, despite the fact that the play stages the orthodoxy of the unrepentant magician's damnation. Or perhaps something else was at stake in Prynne's sense that the play was profane. Insofar as Faustus is compelling as a tragic character, the play reveals the inexorable negativity at the heart of Protestant Christianity; it reveals not that damnation is predestined, but that salvation itself entails self-obliteration into the absolute otherness of an inscrutable God. From a humanist perspective such Christianity is fundamentally tragic because the life that it offers universalizes all sensuous particularity, all subjectivity signified or even felt in the material embodiment of persons and texts. But the ultimate effect of Marlowe's play is not simply to provoke the audience to doubt whether they should continue to desire God and salvation; rather, it is for the audience terrifyingly to feel that God is *watching* them doubt, and, bending down his 'ireful brows,' judging their thoughts and feelings and condemning them to the damnation that they are compelled to contemplate. In a context where magic was a theatrical show created by the devil, but permitted by God so he could see whether his subjects would, as Perkins put it, cleave to him or to the devil and his wicked instruments, to cleave in compassion to Faustus was to sense yourself entering into alliance with the devil, alienated from the inscrutable source of your immortal soul.

By characterizing Faustus's magic as efficacious only because his interest in it signified that he was inclined to be damned, Marlowe turned the aesthetic strategies of dramatic forms into instruments that produced effects that seemed to have soteriological consequences. Yet he dramatized the reformers' arguments not because he wrote his play to disciplinary ends (it is hard to imagine Marlowe having an interest in reforming his audience's faith). Rather, Marlowe made the aesthetics of *Doctor Faustus* instrumental to increase the cultural and material power of his art. He knew full well that immediate, popular, and even naive theatrical experiences motivate the distribution of such power; from an ambitious and brilliantly cunning playwright's point of view, they are the means to that very end. In writing *Doctor Faustus*, Marlowe was not just cunning, but fearless. If he argued, as Baines claimed, that 'the first beginning of Religion was only to keep men in awe,' it still could not have been an easy thing, when atheism was a felony and religious discourse structured all of English life, to maintain such a demystifying view of the ideological function of the sacred.[45] Yet Marlowe used belief in the devil and in God himself as his dramatic instrument to wrench the psychic and social force of religious experience away from its dominant institutional contexts and to place it in the peripheral space of the theatre, which he, above all his immediate contemporaries, was creating as a charged, extraordinary, and charismatic social space.

In saying this, I am not arguing that Marlowe 'appropriated' the sacred from its dominant institutional contexts. On the contrary, the rumours of devils appearing on the Faustian stage belie that model of the relationship between the dramatic and the theological in which the theatre 'evacuates' the spiritual content from theological forms only to stage them within the sphere of rational disenchantment that supposedly frames the experience of a play. Such a model relies on a modern, or indeed modernist, understanding of theatre as a compartmentalized zone of experience, where entertainment has no further end than its own production and consumption, and where aesthetic efficacy, if it exists at all, remains limited to art's ability to contain the contradictions of ideology. Theatrical representation clearly had a certain kind of autonomy in Marlowe's England, produced and consumed as it was in its own institutional space, yet at the same time, as I hope I have been able to show, that same representation could be understood by anti-theatrical writers and theatregoers alike as an instrument that had theological ends. To put it another way, theatre was not always understood as a disenchanted product of human agency. When the reformers argued that Satan staged theatre pieces through the instrumentality of the magician, to the end of creating beliefs in the audience that would augment his own power, they were quite capable of imagining that such spectacles were well-crafted illusions without needing to go on to posit that the devil was an ideological fiction. The rumours of the Faustian devils powerfully demonstrate that even representations that announced their own theatricality – even illusions that were institutionally marked out as such – could still be understood as having theological consequences. Those who believed that the devil came when Faustus called him may have been fully invested in their faith, but they were never so gullible as to believe that the actors were anything but players. They were simply subjected to (and by) their own culture just enough to fear that the admiration, grief, and delight the players inspired served as damning evidence of the worth of their souls. It is this spiritual instrumentality of embodied representation that Marlowe exploited to his own dramatic and institutional purposes. That audiences subjected to the power of Marlowe's play feared that devils were flying to the scene to drag their souls to hell resoundingly attests to the success of his theatrical strategy.

4 The End of Magic: Instrumental Aesthetics in *The Tempest*

> The renunciation of musical magic is a decisive moment in that sort of ultimate attempt, so many times deferred, by which the poet sets out, 'late in life' but with a Cartesian boldness, 'to acknowledge through and through the crisis of the ideal and equally the social' that 'tests' him.
>
> Pierre Bourdieu, *The Rules of Art*

Twentieth-century Shakespeare criticism has bequeathed us a picture of *The Tempest* as a document of early British imperialism.[1] Like the interpretations they serve to contest, postcolonial readings of the play usually view Prospero as an analogue of James or his colonial administrator.[2] Such readings, though, ignore the historical fact that in his political writings and his legislation James represented magicians as traitors who should be tortured and executed without pardon. In his 1597 *Daemonologie*, and again in his 1603 *Basilikon Doron*, James explicitly proclaimed that in using powers given to them by devils, magicians undermine the divine sovereignty of the monarch and should in all cases, therefore, receive a sentence of torture and death.[3] Taking this historical reality into account revises our understanding of the political import of *The Tempest*.[4] It becomes clear, then, that Prospero is no analogue of James, but a subject wielding potentially treasonous power over his king. And the epilogue to the play, in which Prospero asks for and receives the 'forgiveness' of applause, emerges as a moment of extreme subversion in which the audience enacts the compassionate pardon James swore he would never admit. And when we imagine James himself in the audience, applauding after the epilogue, *The Tempest* becomes a play that makes the monarch complicit in his own subversion by enticing him playfully, in his expression of theatrical pleasure, to renounce his claim to divine sovereignty and instead acknowledge his common humanity with the repentant magician.

How, then, could *The Tempest* have enjoyed success at court, where it was staged in 1611 and performed again for the wedding celebrations of Princess Elizabeth in 1613? How did it not offend the king? I will argue that the play's success at court evinces Shakespeare's consummate power to produce a drama with a fully efficacious instrumental aesthetics. If works of instrumental aesthetics, as they were defined by Sidney, promise to enact ethical transformations in readers and audiences in order to secure the legitimacy of their own cultural forms, in its own historical context Shakespeare's *Tempest* enacted a performance of sovereign mercy in order to produce and demonstrate the theatre's institutional autonomy and freedom from political law. Over the course of the play, Shakespeare transmutes magic from an instrument of political domination into a form of artistic creation whose only effect is to provide a joyous experience that blessedly, if temporarily, obscures the reality of death. By the epilogue, in which Prospero asks the audience to pardon him by applauding, magic has been so subsumed into exquisite but disinterested art that pardon appears as nothing more than an expression of theatrical delight. Yet when James applauded, *The Tempest* enacted both the ethical and cultural ends of instrumental aesthetics in the English Renaissance. The king's applause-as-pardon, playfully suspending his right to torture and execute the magician, not only enacted an ethical reformation, but produced theatre itself as a culturally sovereign form in which the laws of play triumphed over the laws of the realm. If Shakespeare's predecessors had attempted to use metaphysical entities as instruments in order to establish the literary as a unique and valuable discourse, Shakespeare through Prospero staged magic only to turn it into a metaphor for theatre. Yet in doing so he fulfilled the promise of Renaissance instrumental aesthetics: not only did he script and produce a performance of his own king's ethical transformation, but he also demonstrated that theatre could transcend and thus dominate the sovereign in cultural life.

To see that Prospero has been miscast as an easy analogue to James, it is useful to consider just how deeply James hated and feared magicians. James's antipathy to magic began when he was caught in a tempest. In August of 1589, after a period of indecision during which he considered Catherine de Bourbon for the role of Queen of Scotland, James VI married Anne of Denmark in a proxy ceremony, and set about to wait for his new wife to arrive from Copenhagen. Two months later she had still not arrived. In a letter dated October 7 – a letter which appeared in Scotland, ironically enough, three days after it was sent – James was informed that the Royal Danish fleet had been beset by terrible storms each time it had attempted to cross the North Sea, and that the queen had protested that she could not join her new husband in Scotland until at least spring, having been horribly afflicted by seasickness in the terrible waves and weather that had met their ships. Within hours of receiving this letter, James decided to sail to Denmark and bring his queen home himself; on October 22, with his chief advisor and a retinue of three hundred, he left for Scandinavia. The Scottish fleet met some of the bad weather that had impeded the Danish navy, but James managed to arrive safely and to marry Anne in person. The royal couple spent the winter and much of the spring in Denmark, where James met and had extended conversation with such intellectual northern lights as Tycho Brahe and the Lutheran theologian Niels Hemmingsen, an original and influential expounder of the Protestant witchcraft theory disseminated in England by George Gifford and William Perkins, whom I discussed in the previous chapter.[5] Hemmingsen's *Admonitio de Superstitionibus Magicis Vitandis* (1575), like Gifford's and Perkins's later works in the vernacular, argued that witches and magicians, as well as Catholic priests, were deluded when they believed that human language could command spirits, for Satan and his minions merely pretended to be bound by conjuration, in order both to entice the magician to sign his soul away and to endanger the souls of those who believed erroneously that magic demonstrated the spiritual power of human utterance. Hemmingsen seems to have made an impression on James.[6] Not only did James cite Hemmingsen in his 1597 *Daemonologie* as one of his two chief authorities on magic, but he also repeated nearly verbatim the Dane's Protestant arguments. 'It is,' James wrote, 'no power inherent in the circles, or in the holiness of the names of God blasphemously used: nor in whatsoever rites or ceremonies at that time used, that either can raise any infernal spirit, or yet limit him perforce within or without these circles. For it is he only, the father of all lies, who having first of all prescribed that form of doing, feigning himself to be commanded & restrained thereby ... as likewise to make himself to be trusted in these little things, that he may have the better commodity thereafter, to deceive them in the end with a trick once for all; I mean the everlasting perdition of their soul & body.'[7]

Pointing to the 'dramatic change in the climate of opinion' about magic in Scotland after James's return – a change which 'became apparent during the massive trials for treason by sorcery of 1590–91' – Christina Larner has argued suggestively that Hemmingsen was the catalyst for James's interest in demonology.[8] Yet it was not just Hemmingsen's pastoral influence that made James newly aware of the possibility of 'treason by sorcery' in his realm; evidence of such treason seemed to show itself everywhere in the early years of James's marriage. For example, the awful weather that had impeded Anne's travel to Scotland in 1589 thundered forth again when the royal couple sailed home together in 1590: the storms were so fierce that one vessel of James's flotilla was lost. Within weeks, the Danes began to hold a series of trials prosecuting purported witches for raising tempests in order to prevent the royal alliance from coming to fruition. After the news of these trials reached James's court, Scottish magistrates also began to prosecute purported covens of witches who had supposedly confessed to conjuring tempests meant to drown the king and queen.[9] According to the pamphlet *Newes from Scotland*, which James published in 1591 in part as an apologia for the executions of dozens of women in connection with these storms, the king witnessed these trials himself. Initially sceptical about the witches' own claims to efficacy, he had his mind decisively changed when one Agnes Sampson took him a little aside and, as the narrator relates it, 'declared unto him the very words which passed between the Kings Majesty and his Queen at Vpslo [*sic*] in Norway the first night of their marriage, with their answer each to other: whereat the Kings Majesty wondered greatly, and swore by the living God, that he believed that all the Devils in hell could not have discovered the same.'[10] Once having 'wondered greatly,' James doubted no longer, but rather gave 'credit' (15) to the confessions of the accused; thus, when Sampson claimed that she knew their spells caused to arise 'a tempest in the Sea [which] was the cause of perishing of a Boat of vessel ... wherein was sundry Jewels and rich gifts, which should have been presented to the now Queen,' James openly corroborated these details of the ship's contents, 'which thing was most strange and true, as the King's Majesty acknowledges' (17).

By corroborating the details of the testimony of a woman accused of witchcraft, not to mention by swearing that a witch was able to find out something 'that all the Devils in hell could not have discovered,' James was hardly espousing the strict Protestant argument that the spiritual power of witches and magicians was limited. Indeed, in *Newes from Scotland* James was represented precisely as the kind of believer William Perkins attempted to warn his readers against becoming, which is to say as someone who, in Perkins's words, witnesses the devil's 'works of wonder ... diversely dispensed by his chosen instruments of both sexes' and then credulously affords witches and magicians a dangerous 'admiration, fear, and faith.'[11] Even in his own *Daemonologie*, James afforded magicians much more agency than Perkins or, for that matter, Hemmingsen would admit.[12] James did, however, share the fundamentally Protestant belief that God and Satan were waging eschatological war, one in which magicians and witches were Satan's special instruments. But where the pastoral witchcraft theorists argued that God's primary instrument in earthly battle against Satan's minions was the Spirit mediated by scripture (and perhaps by scripture's preachers), James maintained that God's primary instrument was the *sovereign* and the magistrates who were his proxies. 'The King is the child & servant of God, and they [witches and magicians] but servants to the devil; he is the Lords anointed, and they but vessels of Gods wrath': so proclaimed the author of *Newes*, who goes on to point out that the king had no reluctance to 'hazard himself in the presence of such notorious witches, lest thereby might have ensued great danger to his person and the general state of the land.' As 'the Lords anointed,' James never was 'feared with their enchantments,' but 'resolute in this, that so long as God is with him, he fears not who is against him' (29).

All this suggests that for James, magic was less a religious or doctrinal issue than a *political* issue. But it was so because his politics were spiritually enchanted. The king was 'the Lords anointed,' and as such was never subject to the Satanic enchantments spun forth by the instruments of 'Gods wrath.' Indeed, according to both *Newes from Scotland* and *Daemonologie*, James refused to confine the jurisdiction of magic to the purely pastoral realm. Doing so would have entailed limiting the spiritual power James wanted vested in the monarchy, a power which came especially into view when it constructed, condemned, and punished its magical, diabolical other.[13] Stuart Clark is thus right to argue both that 'demonology was in fact intrinsically related to the presuppositions of godly rule,' and that *Daemonologie* itself 'was not tangential to, let alone aberrant from, [James's] other political writings.'[14] In fact, as Clark maintains, *Daemonologie* elucidates the metaphysics of divine absolutism on which James's political ideas ultimately rested, articulating theoretically what *Newes from Scotland* reported narratively. In *Daemonologie*, James made the magical claim that if the 'apprehending and detention' of witches and magicians 'be by the lawful Magistrate, their power is then no greater than before that ever they meddled with their master [the devil], for where God begins justly to strike by his lawful Lieutenants, it is not in the Devil's power to defraud or bereave him of the office, or effect of his powerful and revenging Scepter' (51).

The king's role as God's magistrate or lieutenant, whose instrumental agency, through which God strikes with a 'revenging Scepter,' disables any power witches and magicians have to charm, was central to James's conception of his monarchy. It was so central that James had it enacted again and again in his masques, which, as Stephen Orgel has maintained, were 'expressions of the age's most profound assumptions about the monarchy.'[15] In *The Masque of Queens*, a coven of witches was banished and bound by sovereign virtue; in *Mercury Vindicated from the Alchemists at Court*, the Alchemists, who had enslaved Mercury in an ill-fated attempt to produce the philosopher's stone, were dispersed once the god invoked the power of James's majesty: 'Vanish with thy insolence,' the deity intones to the alchemists, 'and all mention of you melt before the majesty of this light, whose Mercury I profess to be, and never more the philosophers.'[16] The text of *The Masque of Blackness* even verged on blasphemy in giving James the power to resurrect the dead as 'bright Sol, / Whose beams shine day and night, and are of force / To blanch an Aethiop and revive a corse.'[17] Like his witchcraft pamphlets and his *Daemonologie*, James's masques served as attempts to produce the Stuart fantasy of the absolute, and absolutely efficacious, grace of the Protestant king.[18]

As this concept of the king's absolute grace was essentially a fantasy of political power, it should come as no surprise that James was particularly obsessed with magic that could be practised as policy. In *Daemonologie* James warned that the devil will 'make his scholars to creep in credit with Princes, by fore-telling them many great things, part true, part false ... and he will also make them to please Princes, by faire banquets and dainty dishes, carried in short space from the farthest part of the world' (22). James here rehearsed the belief (also circulated, as we have seen, by Foxe and Marlowe) that the magician could gain 'credit' from his patrons, here 'princes,' by pleasing them with gossipy and gustatory tidbits. Such diabolical 'credit' had the power to weaken the spiritual foundation of the king's authority by turning the king away from God. If magicians could manage to insinuate themselves into royal favour, James fretted, they might then begin to influence the king's will.[19] James also warned that magicians could cozen the king by acting as spies or double agents: magicians, he insisted, could get the devil 'to carry them news from any part of the world [and] to reveal to them the secrets of any persons, so being ... once spoken (for thought none knows but GOD, except so far as you may guess by their countenance)' (21–2).[20] The really powerful magi might even spy by getting the devil to 'enter in a dead body, and there out of to give such answers of the event of battles, of matters concerning the estate of commonwealths, and such like other great questions' (20). That magicians may compel the devil to enter the resurrected body of a dead person in order to have agency on earth is an idea that James returned to again and again.[21] In *Daemonologie*, James discussed magical reanimation repeatedly and at length, warning that if conjured spirits have 'assumed a dead body, whereunto they lodge themselves, they can easily enough open ... any Door or Window' (59). Countering the objection that God would not 'permit these wicked spirits to trouble the rest of a dead body, before the resurrection thereof,' James argued that when the magician prompts the devil to carry a body 'out of the Grave to serve his turn for a space,' he 'may use as well the ministry of the bodies of the faithful in these cases, as of the unfaithful ... for his haunting with their bodies after they are dead, can no-ways defile them: in respect of the soul's absence' (59). The ability of the magician to conjure evil spirits into dead bodies was, for James, centrally related to the question of monarchical power: the king was doubtless unable to reanimate dead bodies, so such powers stood in theory as a disturbing counterexample to James's claim that the monarch enjoyed absolute spiritual as well as temporal dominance.

Of course, in *Daemonologie* James made sure to emphasize that whatever power magicians enjoyed was derived contingently and only temporarily from the devil, who would be repaid at last with interest to eternity. In contrast to this contingent power, the king's power was, James insisted, derived absolutely and permanently from God's revenging sceptre, which always and everywhere disabled the agency of the devil and the derivative force witches and magicians had to charm. This revenging sceptre, James explained, manifested itself above all in the king's responsibility to punish magic absolutely, and without mercy. For James, not to punish magic absolutely was to fail God, and thereby to weaken the divine patronage relationship from which the king derived his sovereignty. Hence James argued that magic being 'the highest point of Idolatry, wherein no exception is admitted by the law of God,' magical practitioners were always – without exception for age, sex, or rank – 'to be put to death according to the Law of God, the civil and imperial law, and municipal law of all Christian nations' (77). James also absolutely condemned to death all those 'that are of the counsel of such crafts,' for 'the consulters, trusters-in, over-seers, entertainers or stirrers-up of these crafts-folks are equally guilty with themselves that are the practicers' (78). 'In the end,' James wrote, 'to spare the life, and not to strike when God bids strike, as so severely punish so odious a fault and treason against God, it is not only unlawful, but doubtless no less sin in that Magistrate, [than] it was in SAULES sparing of AGAG. And so comparable to the sin of Witchcraft itself, as SAMUEL alleged at that time' (78).[22] Even in his 1603 *Basilikon Doron*, a political rather than expressly demonological work, James counselled Prince Henry that while he may grow more lenient once he has established 'the severity of [his] Justice' and has made his subjects 'know [he] can strike,' he must always remember that witchcraft, like 'Incest (especially among degrees of consanguinity)' and 'false coin,' was a crime that he was 'bound in conscience never to forgive.'[23] Magic is unforgivable, James maintained, even if used to benevolent ends: 'The Devil hath never better tidings to tell to any, then he told to *Saul*: neither is it lawful to use so unlawful instruments, were it never for so good a purpose: for that axiom in Theology is most certain and infallible: *Nunquam faciendum est malum vt bonum inde eueniat* [An evil deed is never done so that a good may thence emerge].'[24]

Within a year of becoming king of England, James repealed Elizabeth's witchcraft statutes, which, as we saw in chapter 1, left open the possibility that magicians could conjure up spirits to benevolent ends. James instituted a new act against 'Conjuration, Witchcrafts, and Dealing with evil and wicked Spirits' which made all magical practices capital crimes, for 'the better restraining of said Offenses, and more severe punishing the same.'[25] Although Jesuits began to take the place of witches and magicians as the putatively diabolical agents who most threatened his divine authority, James always sustained his fearful interest in magical practices. Sir John Harington reported that when he received an audience with the king, James, having heard Harington was a learned man, did 'much press for [his] opinion touching the power of Satan in matter of witchcraft.'[26] Interestingly enough, Harington also reported that James told him Queen Mary's death had been predicted in Scotland, 'as he said, "spoken of in secret by those whose power of sight presented to them a bloody head dancing in the air,"' and that he himself 'had sought out of certain books a sure way to attain knowledge of future chances' (viii). Although he advised Harington to avoid 'evil consultations' (viii), James may in fact have been willing to entertain the possibility that magic could help him secure his own political power. He certainly felt it unnecessary in 1615 to execute either the earl or countess of Somerset, even though they had been accused of using magic to murder Thomas Overbury.[27] However, the Overbury trial and the pamphlets that circulated the news of its proceedings were still to come when Shakespeare wrote *The Tempest*. In 1610 James believed firmly, it seems, that magicians who raised tempests, offered banquets to princes, used spirits to spy, or brought dead bodies out of their graves should be tortured and executed without mercy.

Not only does Prospero raise a tempest that seems to threaten the lives of a royal party returning from a wedding, he also offers that shipwrecked party a banquet, and uses Ariel as a kind of double agent, employing the tricksy spirit to inform him of both the plot to kill the king and the clownish conspiracy. Even more scandalously, Prospero almost gratuitously confesses to having opened graves and 'waked their sleepers' by his 'so potent art.'[28] Even Prospero's admitted motivations for practising magic appear to have been modelled on *Daemonologie*. Prospero claims that he turned away from the government of Milan because he was 'transported / And rapt in secret studies' (1.2.76–7); similarly, James had emphasized that '*Magicians,* as allured by *curiosity,* in the most part of their practices, seek principally the satisfying of the same.'[29] Ariel too appeared first in *Daemonologie*. No Neoplatonic daemon, James's airy spirit was the devil playing the role of 'a continual attendant, in form of a Page,' who abuses 'the simplicity of these wretches, that become their scholars,' by making them believe that there are some spirits 'in the air, some in the fire, some in the water, some in the land: in which Elements they still remain' (20). (James also derided the idea that such spirits 'as [are] in the fire, or in the air, are truer then they, who [are] in the water or land, which is all but mere trattles [*sic*], and forged by the author of all deceit' [20].) Most interestingly, Prospero's revenge plot, in which he uses magic to confound his enemies, also enacts James's supposition that the magician may be allured into magical practice by 'thirst of revenge, for some tortes deeply apprehended' (8).

If, then, Prospero is the magician of James's magical imaginations – seeming to attack his enemies with the magic by which James felt most threatened – how does Shakespeare manage to win for him a performance of the forgiveness that James swore he would never bestow? How does the transformation in the King's relationship to Prospero occur? Much of the work of making James thus merciful is done by the play's epilogue, which evacuates the charged content of magic from the form of theatrical spectacle, and under the name of 'make believe' requests and receives the applause that represents forgiveness. But much of it is also done by the story itself – or, rather, by the play itself, which is less a story to be contemplated than an experience to be undergone. As Jan Kott has long since noted, there is a correspondence between 'the inner time of performance and the time of the audience,' which enables 'both the actors and the spectators' to go 'through the same tempest.'[30] This correspondence is marked by Prospero when he notes towards the end of act 1 that 'the time 'twixt six and now' must be spent by him and Ariel 'most preciously' (1.2.239–41), and again when he asks Ariel in the beginning of act 5, 'how's the day?' and the spirit replies: 'On the sixth hour, at which time, my lord, /

you said our work should cease' (5.1.3–5). At the end of the play, the literal quality of the stage time of *The Tempest* is noted by other characters as well, as if to cue the audience to feel that they have witnessed something that 'really happened': Alonso tells Prospero, as if he didn't know, that it was 'three hours since' (5.1.136) he was wrecked upon the shore, and on his restoration the Boatswain also marvels that it was 'but three glasses since we gave out split' (5.1.223). These three hours correspond loosely to the Donatan dramatic structure of protasis, epitasis, and catastrophe, which Shakespeare uses to fashion Prospero's dramatic arc, adding to these a prologue and an epilogue. The prologue – the series of expository conversations in act 1 – establishes Prospero's personality, his power, and his relationships with the other characters on the island. The protasis – the meeting of Ferdinand and Miranda, the introduction of the regicide plot, and the establishment of the clownish conspiracy – moves the action forward and modifies the information the audience learned in the prologue. The epitasis – the banquet scene, the masque, and the resolution of the conspiracy – synthesizes what had been juxtaposed by the prologue and the protasis, and gathers Prospero's project 'to a head' (5.1.1). And the catastrophe – Prospero's decision to pardon his enemies, his renunciation of magic, and the subsequent social reconciliation (or reconstitution, if you prefer) – ties up all the disparate plot lines and completes Prospero's transformation from fearsome magician to supposedly unthreatening poet.

When we meet Prospero in the prologue, he appears unsympathetic, or even repellent. The storm may have been shocking for the audience, as it was for Miranda, and it is hard to see that Prospero has committed this act of violence compassionately, in care of his daughter. As Prospero tells Miranda about her past, it is not clear until the end of his tale that the shipwreck had anything to do with the wrongs once done to them, and his impatient interjections demanding that she listen closely feel both abrasive and oddly disconnected from the attention with which she seems to heed his story. Yet Prospero's interjections serve a double function: they make him seem all the more unsympathetic, but they also ensure that the spectators, who may well be cracking their walnuts or talking among themselves, hear that Prospero had a brother who betrayed him. Almost all the interjections occur when Prospero is talking about Antonio: 'Antonio – I pray thee mark me, that a brother should be so perfidious' (1.2.66) and 'thy false uncle – Dost thou attend me? (1.2.77–8) and 'hence his ambition growing – dost thou hear?' (1.2.105–6) and so on. The one exception occurs when Prospero explicitly marks his statement that he began to practise magic *not* because he wanted to gain political power:

Prospero: – thou attend'st not!
Miranda: O, good sir, I do!
Prospero: I pray thee mark me:
   I thus neglecting all worldly ends, all dedicated
   To closeness and the bettering of my mind
   With that which, but by being so retired,
   O'er-prized all popular rate.   (1.2.87–92)

These pieces of information will be specifically developed by the rest of the play in ways that attempt to change the audience's initial impression of Prospero's character. But here, the prologue continues to represent Prospero as violent, imperious, vengeful, and, at times, even diabolically inspired. When Ariel enters to recount the tempest from his point of view, he represents his work using images of flaming hellfire: 'The fire and cracks of sulphurous roaring the most mighty Neptune / seem to besiege' (1.2.203–5). Further, to Prospero's delight, he gleefully reports that Ferdinand took him to be a devil: 'The King's son Ferdinand ... / Was the first man that leapt, cried, "Hell is empty, / And all the devils are here"' (Prospero replies, 'Why, that's my spirit!') (1.2.212–16). Of course, Prospero will soon ask Ariel whether all the men are safe, but this expression of concern becomes lost in the next phase of their conversation, which recounts the circumstances of Prospero's and Ariel's entering into contract after Prospero's freeing of Ariel from Sycorax. In this phase of the prologue, Prospero and Sycorax appear uncomfortably similar, if not identical. Depending on how Prospero is directed, he too may seem at this point 'with age and envy' to have 'grown into a hoop' (1.2.258–9). Since it is as yet possible to imagine that Antonio, like the Habsburg archdukes, had been merely prudent when he exiled Prospero, Prospero may seem, like Sycorax, 'banished' legitimately, 'for mischiefs manifold and sorceries terrible' (1.2.266, 264). And finally, the torments that Sycorax apparently inflicted on Ariel for his refusal to perform her commands – the torments that Ariel vented in 'groans' which made 'wolves howl' and penetrated 'the breasts of ever-angry bears' (1.2.280) – are reproduced in the torments that Prospero inflicts on Caliban for his refusal, or, rather, for his mere reluctance to perform his commands.

Indeed, Prospero's relationship to Caliban is at first what makes him most despicable. Even Caliban's expression of defiance after Prospero reminds him of his attempted rape ('O ho, O ho! Would't had been done!' [1.2.348–9]) becomes rhetorically overshadowed by Prospero's Sycorax-ian amplification of the tortures he will inflict on Caliban merely for his lack of enthusiasm for enslavement:

> If thou negelct'st, or dost unwillingly
> What I command, I'll rack thee with old cramps,
> Fill all thy bones with aches, make thee roar,
> That beasts shall tremble at thy din. (1.2.366–9)

Even aside from his suffering (which may or may not have affected early modern spectators as it does contemporary readers), Caliban lays claim to the audience's sympathies in the beginning of the play by casting Prospero in the role of usurper. By reminding Prospero (and thus informing the audience) of his hereditary claim to the island, Caliban casts Prospero in the role of Bolingbroke to his Richard II, as if to emphasize that putative superior fitness to rule makes the usurper no more legitimate in the eyes of God (indeed, Prospero himself suggests that in some sense Antonio usurped the dukedom of Milan because the latter enjoyed superior fitness to rule).[31] Moreover, Caliban seems to resist Prospero not, like Antonio, to fulfil some nefarious ambition, but simply to enjoy his freedom to be left alone to dig 'pig-nuts,' find 'a jay's nest,' or 'snare the nimble marmoset' (2.2.162–4). Caliban's desire to explore and forage on the island expresses his autonomy and his understanding of the island as the source of self-sufficient pleasure. That is why he hears Prospero's music as *natural*, a product of the island's quality: 'Be not afeared,' he tells his new friends:

> The isle is full of noises,
> Sounds and sweet airs that delight and hurt not.
> Sometimes a thousand twangling instruments
> Will hum about mine ears; and sometimes voices,
> That if I then had waked after long sleep,
> Will make me sleep again, and then in dreaming
> The clouds methought would open and show riches
> Ready to drop upon me, that when I waked
> I cried to sleep again. (3.2.132–41)

Even though Caliban, like Miranda and Alonso, is so charmed by Prospero's music that he sleeps and dreams, he never views the sweet airs and the visions of riches in the clouds as having any other end but themselves. If his desire for freedom manifests itself in his love for the island's beauty, his response to Prospero's art reinforces his claim to meriting that freedom.

Once he has made Prospero seem very much like a villain, Shakespeare begins to change the lineaments of his character by changing the tone of his magic and by confirming the claims that Prospero made in the prologue. The change of tone is announced by the music that accompanies Ferdinand's entrance on to the stage, the songs 'Come on to These Yellow Sands' and 'Full Fathom Five,' which transform the irritating sounds of conflict into the moving, sweet strains of Ariel's clear voice. Although Prospero continues to seem power-mad and capricious in his treatment of Ferdinand (although one may also plausibly imagine that he is acting, more sympathetically, like an overprotective father), the action goes on to prove Prospero right: the royal party enters, and Sebastian and Antonio reveal themselves to be not only as irritating as Prospero, but also much more murderously selfish and ambitious. Leaving aside Sebastian's uncompassionate and cruel statement to the miserable Alonso, who thinks that Ferdinand has died – 'Sir, you may thank yourself for this great loss' (2.1.121) – even just their cynical jokes about Gonzalo's clumsy attempts to comfort Alonso serve to alienate the sympathies of the audience, especially if the jokes are, as is likely, incomprehensible. (Conversely, if the jokes manage to amuse they may still go on to serve a didactic function, by putting the spectator in the oddly uncomfortable position of having laughed along with fratricidal murderers who have made fun of kindness).

The spectacle of Antonio persuading Sebastian to murder is chilling, and the play ties it directly to Antonio's usurpation of Prospero by having Sebastian take that usurpation as a point in favour of the present murder:

> *Sebastian*: I remember
>   You did supplant your brother Prospero.
> *Antonio*: True;
>   And look how well my garments sit upon me,
>   Much feater than before.   (2.1.168–71)

Not only does Antonio seem to feel no guilt for his crimes against his brother, he also appears unable to sustain the kind of familial attachment that would produce such a sense of guilt in the first place.[32] Indeed, one of the great cruxes of *The Tempest* is the fact that Ferdinand tells Miranda that 'the Duke of Milan, / and his brave son' (1.2.440–1) are two of the men who appeared to perish in the shipwreck, but Antonio never mentions having a son nor behaves as if he had one, and none of the other characters seem to take such a son into account either. Contemporary editors, including Kermode and Orgel, insist that Antonio's son cannot be identified with any of the shipwreck victims. Kermode raises the suggestion that Francisco might be considered Antonio's son, but immediately dismisses it, insisting that Antonio would not contemptuously speak of his son as someone who would, like the other nobles, 'take suggestion' as a 'cat laps milk' (2.1.284). Yet that Antonio would in fact speak indirectly about his son with such contempt seems psychologically consistent with his never directly mentioning his son at all.[33] Not feeling the claims of his blood, not having to fear the pain of loss, Antonio is free to do as he wishes. And so he does, going on to assure Sebastian that the shoe of rule fits so well that it need not pinch the 'kibe' (2.1.274), or sore, of conscience:

Sebastian: But for your conscience?
Antonio: Ay, sir, where lies that? If 'twere a kibe
            'Twould put me to my slipper, but I feel not
            This deity in my bosom. Twenty consciences
            That stand 'twixt me and Milan, candied be they
            And melt ere they molest!   (2.1.273–8)

Antonio seems to hold conscience as a trifle (or a truffle) throughout the play: in response to the spectacle of the disappearing banquet, to which Alonso reacts with guilt and despair, Antonio only rages, rushing off with Sebastian, swords drawn, to fight the spirits and harpies. And, of course, Antonio keeps his silence at the end of the play, never asking Prospero for pardon, strongly suggesting that he remains unrepentant to the end. Thus does the play confirm Prospero's insistence that his brother is utterly perfidious.

But this confirmation is, perhaps, relatively easy to achieve, since the claims of inheritance most often in Shakespeare seem to have right on their side (Prince Hal being a complicated but notable exception). Caliban's claim to the island is, thus, one that is more difficult for Shakespeare to undermine in Prospero's favour, but, as Orgel points out, 'whatever merit the claim has philosophically, it is allowed to have little dramatically,' for 'his immediate attachment to Stephano is sufficient to confirm Prospero's view of him as a natural servant.'[34] Caliban, as Orgel remarks, doesn't just readily toss his freedom aside by taking on a new master, he attaches himself to Stephano, willingly kissing his foot, because he believes Stephano to be a 'brave god' who 'bears celestial liquor' (2.2.111). It turns out that, as Prospero suggested, Caliban *is* subject to a sort of magical compulsion of the will, at least the tawdry magical compulsion of alcohol, which makes him 'ridiculous,' as Trinculo puts it, for making 'a wonder of a poor drunkard' (2.2.159–60). Even Caliban's curses, which seemed to epitomize a kind of Foucauldian resistance to power ('You taught me language, and my profit on't / Is I know how to curse' [1.2.362–3]), turn out to arise from a sort of *inward* compulsion that prevents Caliban from acting, in the scheme of things, in his own best interests: 'His spirits hear me, / And yet I needs must curse' (2.2.3–4), he tells the audience ruefully.

Having represented Prospero as being correct in his initial judgments, *The Tempest* now begins to make Prospero sympathetic or, at least, worthy of mercy. But rather than working on a characterological level, the play makes Prospero appear forgivable by changing the quality of his magic, emptying it of political content and turning it into celebratory spectacle, and thereby transforming the magician into a *playwright* who conjures spirits only for the audience's pleasure. Indeed, in some ways Prospero's personality recedes in the epitasis, and his collaborative relationship with Ariel, and Ariel's joy in his art, and the art itself, comes to the forefront.[35] Moreover, the character of Prospero's art changes as well. Despite the proleptic hint suggested by the fact that the tempest was merely an illusion meant ultimately to produce 'amazement' and touch the 'piteous heart' (1.2.14), in the prologue and the protasis Prospero's art appeared mostly as the diabolical magic of illegitimate politics imagined by James. But in the epitasis, Prospero's art becomes not only mere theatre, but a form of theatre that, in its ideal state, is *disinterested* rather than instrumental, having no other end but to please.

To be sure, the banquet scene, which Ariel performs with what Prospero calls 'grace ... devouring' (3.3.84), has a provisionally devastating instrumental effect on Alonso, as it is meant to. Prospero makes Alonso feel that he is subject to overwhelming cosmic forces, and that he is so specifically because he injured the former Duke of Milan. Once Ariel, dressed as a harpy, makes the banquet vanish, he thunderously informs the royal party not only that 'Destiny ... hath to instrument' the whole 'lower world / And what is in't' (3.3.53–5), but that Destiny has caused them to be shipwrecked on a deserted island, since they among men are 'most unfit to live' (3.3.58). In response to this horrifying apparition, the men naturally draw their swords, but, once again, Prospero paralyses them, making their rapiers seem 'too massy' for their 'strengths' (3.3.67). And, again, Prospero connects their paralysis to their crimes against him: Ariel commands the royal party immediately after their binding to 'remember' (3.3.68) that they 'did supplant good Prospero' (3.3.70), and, shrieking, he insists that their present pain is their punishment.[36] Thus Ariel lashes out at Alonso specifically for his crime:

The powers delaying, not forgetting, have
Incensed the seas and shores, yea all the creatures
Against your peace. Thee of thy son, Alonso,
They have bereft; and do pronounce by me
Ling'ring perdition, worse than any death
Can be all at once, shall step by step attend
You and your ways; whose wraths to guard you from,
Which here, in this most desolate isle, else falls
Upon your heads, is nothing but heart's sorrow,
And a clear life ensuing.   (3.3.73–82)

The repentance that Alonso must perform to expiate his guilt has the structure of a sacred duty, and the need for it seems to resonate cosmically, in the very fibre of the world. Yet Prospero has appropriated those quasi-divine 'powers,' that 'destiny' has 'to instrument the lower world,' by having Ariel claim that those powers caused the tempest and now cry for expiation on Prospero's behalf. And Alonso accepts this fiction, attributing to the thunder the awful harmony of a natural *dies irae* whose theme is Prospero: 'The thunder, / That deep and dreadful organ-pipe, pronounced / The name of Prosper: it did bass my trespass. / Therefore my son i' th'ooze is bedded' (3.3.97–100). This fiction forces Alonso to equate his wrenching loss of Ferdinand with the loss he caused Prospero to bear, readying Alonso to return Prospero's dukedom on sight. Thus his 'high charms work,' Prospero confirms, punning on the function of the epitasis: 'These, mine enemies, are knit up / In their distractions' (3.3.88–90).

The intensely instrumental aesthetics of the banquet quickly give way to the more disinterested beauty of the masque, which Prospero characterizes as merely a 'vanity' (4.1.41) of his art. The masque seems to empty Prospero's art of magical instrumentality, even though Prospero acknowledges it is enacted by 'spirits' (4.1.120). It is clearly not a transitive 'charm' in the way the banquet was: when Ferdinand proclaims the masque to be 'harmonious charmingly' (119), he seems to be using the word *charmingly* simply to describe the manner in which it produces his sensations of pleasure. And the kind of 'distractions' the masque provides differ from the emotional terrors produced by the banquet: they draw attention away from (rather than towards) the political business at hand. The masque is a 'distraction,' a 'vanity,' because it is an expression of Prospero's desire, suggested earlier by his entering into the study of magic to the neglect of all 'worldly ends,' to imagine a poetics that are not instrumental, a delight that is not compulsive, a labour that is not alienated, and a life in which he would be free to make art that does nothing more than celebrate ideal harmony. His masque thus shares features with Gonzalo's utopic commonwealth: Harry Berger calls it 'an artful, sophisticated, and refined ... expression of the same pastoral escapism.'[37]

Yet the masque does more than express Prospero's desire for escapism. It also provides a way for Shakespeare to satisfy *his audience's* desire for escapism, or more precisely, their desire for a sense that there is something in this life that is almost purely beautiful. (Escapism can, after all, be achieved by Stephano's liquor.) Shakespeare satisfies this desire for a fleeting moment only to interrupt it with the absurd reality of the clownish conspiracy. Can it really be the case that no spectators would share in some of Prospero's disappointment at the dissolution of his vision, his grief at the impossibility of enjoying an ideal art? Especially since Shakespeare, with the meta-theatricality that makes all the world the stage, connects the ending of Prospero's vision to the end of time itself:

These our actors,
As I fortold you, were all spirits, and
Are melted into air, into thin air,
And, like the baseless fabric of the vision,
The cloud-capped towers, the gorgeous palaces,
The solemn temples, the great globe itself,
Yea, all which it inherit, shall dissolve,
And, like this insubstantial pageant faded,
Leave not a rack behind. We are such stuff
As dreams are made on, and our little life
Is rounded with a sleep.   (4.1.148–59)

Berger writes brilliantly on this passage, arguing that its crux 'lies in the phrase "the baseless fabric of this vision," especially in the word baseless. Baseless means insubstantial, not firmly based, without proper ground but also not base, not evil, too purely beautiful ... and therefore, once again, without grounds. "We are such stuff / As dreams are made on" – *on* as well as *of*: the evil matter or basis ... on which our nobler works are built, which they deceptively cover over, and from which they rise as an escape ... And man's works are dreams not only in being vanities, fragile illusions, but also in being – as Freud called them – the guardians of sleep protecting the mind in its denial of or flight from reality.'[38] But where Berger sees an ethical failure in this 'flight from reality,' I see almost a necessity. I read the reality from which works of art protect the mind as a too-close knowledge of our coming death. What Berger a bit ironically calls the 'evil matter' on which dreams are made, I would more literally call the body – the body as ground of mortality, as the ever-shifting, ephemeral base, rounded with nothingness just like the insubstantial pageant that leaves not a rack behind.[39] Yet in the revels speech, death also comes to history – the great vanished past constantly invoked in *The Tempest* by the allusions to the *Aeneid* – and all subsequent cycles of time, the great globe itself and 'all which it inherit.' Once the world and all which it inherits passes away, the 'vanity' of Prospero's art becomes the vanity of Ecclesiastes, which reduces everything, even kings, to nothing. Thus does the revels speech serve not only to disenchant monarchical politics, as ultimately of the same ephemeral stuff as beauty itself, but also to suggest that, unlike politics, beauty and its ephemeral spell can protect us from our knowledge of nothingness, at least contingently, or for a time.

Shakespeare has, then, made Prospero's art not magic but theatre, and he has made this theatre both something trivial, an enactment of Prospero's 'present fancies' (122), and something necessary to life, an illusory presence that saves the mind from the madness of Lear. He has offered *this* art as an unexpected gift to the audience, just as Prospero has offered his masque as an unexpected gift to Miranda and Ferdinand. Shakespeare then attempts to resolve the last vestiges of ambivalence about his art by having Prospero explicitly confess and abjure his magical practice. The moment is highly imitative – a citation of Ovid that in its own way confirms Prospero as not only a poet, but an elite poet – yet Shakespeare gives Prospero's recitation of the *Metamorphoses* characterological resonance as well by making it clear how profoundly the magus will miss his magic. When Prospero promises that once he has worked his 'end upon their senses that / This airy charm is for,' he will break his 'staff' and '*deeper than did ever plummet sound*' he'll 'drown' his 'book' (5.1.53–7, emphasis added), he echoes almost exactly the phrase that Alonso used to express his grief, his suicidal despair over his loss of Ferdinand:

> That deep and dreadful organ-pipe, pronounced
> The name of Prosper: it did bass my trespass.
> Therefore my son i'th'ooze is bedded; and
> I'll seek him *deeper than e'er plummet sounded*,
> And with him there lie mudded.   (3.3.98–102, emphasis added)

It is as if in his renunciation of his magic, Prospero exchanges guilt with Alonso; as if in exchanging this guilt, he renounces his right to immortality, as the future, in the book and the son, seems to sink beyond the depth of the plummet. Prospero's 'book,' as Barbara Mowat shows, can be heard to refer to the standard collection of magical instructions, charts, lists of names of the angels, and so on, which magicians used to practise their art.[40] Yet at this point in the play the idea of the 'book' also resonates with the play-book or the prompt-book, or even with a collection of poems ('Not marble nor the gilded monuments / Of princes shall outlive this pow'rful rhyme') whose promise shall not now be fulfilled.

Of course, though the audience sees Prospero give Ariel his freedom with the sore admission that he 'shall miss' his perfect instrument, they never see Prospero drown his book. Yet they do see him set aside his illusions along with his power in order to walk forward a mere man and pardon his enemies. Critics who dislike Prospero have been put off by his proffered forgiveness, specifically by the lack of enthusiasm or even distaste with which Prospero pardons Antonio, but pardon in this political context should not be expected to resemble a 'sincere,' Oprah Winfrey-style reconciliation in which all wrongs are confessed and all resentment purged. Rather, pardon should be understood in this context *as the decision not to execute Antonio and Caliban for treason.* And the power of this decision arises not from its ethical efficacy within the play (for Prospero's forgiveness has no effect on Antonio, who will thenceforth be controlled by blackmail with the clandestine information about the planned regicide that Prospero was able to obtain by magic); rather, the force of Prospero's pardon arises from its metatheatrical exemplarity. When Prospero claims that he will 'take part' with his 'nobler reason' against his 'fury' (5.1.27, 26), performing the 'rarer action' of 'virtue' rather than 'vengeance' (5.1.27–8), he is representing the sovereign power to execute traitors not as the expression of a divine right to rule but as a petty form of 'vengeance' motivated by 'fury.' And he is representing 'virtue,' in contrast, as the compassion to stay death. He is, in short, at once citing and rebuking James's justifications for wielding God's 'revenging Scepter' against the magicians he considers traitors, challenging him to approve a pardon that proves the 'rarer' humanity of the merciful.

This challenge is developed by the epilogue, which goes even further in rebuking the king by implying that mercy should be grounded in the recognition of universal human guilt. 'Now my charms are all o'erthrown,' Prospero proclaims:

And what strength I have's my own,
Which is most faint: now, 'tis true,
I must be here confin'd by you,
Or sent to Naples. Let me not,
Since I have my dukedom got,
And pardoned the deceiver, dwell
In this bare island by your spell;
But release me from my bands
With the help of your good hands:
Gentle breath of yours my sails
Must fill, or else my project fails,
Which was to please. Now I want
Spirits to enforce, art to enchant;
And my ending is despair,
Unless I be relieved by prayer,
Which pierces so, that it assaults
Mercy itself, and frees all faults.
As you from crimes would pardon'd be,
Let your indulgence set me free.   (1–20)

Every member of the audience, including James, has committed 'crimes' from which he would be 'pardoned,' and the proper response to the recognition of this shared guilt is a kind of ecumenical 'indulgence' that sets sinners 'free.' Even the magician, Prospero submits, is worthy of such forgiveness. Thus does the epilogue critique the spiritual premises of Jacobean absolutism. But did this critique offend James? Surely not: *The Tempest* was staged at court not once, but twice. And when James applauded at the end of these performances, his applause not only performed the precept that the rarer action is in mercy rather than in vengeance, but also acknowledged the sovereign's common humanity with the repentant magician, who here, finally, became worthy of forgiveness. Of course, that forgiveness itself, like the play as a whole, was merely a species of make-believe. Prospero even reminds us that his 'project' was meant only 'to please,' and that the pardon for which he longs is found merely in the clapping and 'gentle' cheers that express his audience's pleasure. Indeed, by characterizing Prospero's 'art to enchant' as nothing more than the power to stage plays, Shakespeare finally separates the conjuring of James's magical imaginations from the beauty and drama of theatrical aesthetics. In so doing, Shakespeare neatly turns magic into a metaphor for theatre. Yet at the same time, in his own historical context Shakespeare thereby ful-filled the promise of instrumental aesthetics envisioned by Sidney in his *Defense of Poesy*: using pure play that seemed to have no end beyond pleasure, Shakespeare managed to script and enact a transformation of his own king's Christian ethics and politics. Moreover, Shakespeare demon-strated that his theatre was an utterly autonomous space in which the laws of the realm – specifically the laws requiring the torture and execution of all magicians – were suspended in favour of the laws of make-believe. This suspension, transcending the sovereign, at once relied on and produced the supreme cultural value of poetry. If such value is precisely what Sid-ney marshaled instrumental aesthetics to establish, it emerged fully, thirty years later, in Shakespeare's theatre at the consummate hour of his art.

Epilogue: Kant's Charm

Le poème devient ainsi école de deux manière: d'abord, il amène le désir à trouver les paroles qui le réalisent ... mais en même temps, il enseigne au désir ses limites ... A mon sens, c'est cette double vocation de la poesié qui la distingue du charme.

Thomas Greene, *Poésie et Magie*[1]

The historical relationship between magical spells called 'charms' and literary texts meant to have instrumental effects has emerged repeatedly a leitmotif of this book. The Elizabethan parliament outlawed the practice of charming as a felony in 1563, yet in *The Defense of Poesy*, Sidney characterized poetry's efficacy as its 'sweet, charming force.'[2] A figure for the court poet who attempts to seduce his married beloved with sonnets, Spenser's Busirane deployed 'a thousand charms' to compel Amoret's love 'perforce.'[3] The Protestants whose account of conjuration Marlowe appropriated for *Doctor Faustus* insisted that any signs used to spiritual ends without scriptural authorization were, as Robert Burton put it, nothing but 'charms' employed by the devil to deceive magicians into renouncing God.[4] And Prospero in *The Tempest* attempted to manipulate his enemies into submission with the powerful spectacles that he called his 'high charms.'[5]

By the start of the eighteenth century, long after Prospero had renounced magic and left the stage, the word 'charm' had become a metaphor describing a natural if intangible quality that makes objects or people especially compelling.[6] 'Charm' in this disenchanted sense then emerged in British empiricist aesthetics as a term for beauty, which was characterized as a force that arouses the desire of the subject, attracting him to the aesthetic object and swaying him towards moral sentiment.[7] At the end of the century, however, in his 1790 *Critique of Judgment*, Kant explicitly rejected this concept of beauty's power, denigrating as 'barbaric ... any taste that relies on charms [*Reize*] for its approval.'[8] Having thus separated beauty from charm, Kant went on to theorize aesthetic experience as arising not from the subject's submission to beauty's force, but from his mastery of a style of consumption – a kind of taste – that confirms his autonomy and freedom from compulsion.[9]

In taking up Kant's aesthetics here, I do not mean to trace a historical development that follows from the Renaissance, a task that lies far beyond the scope of this study. I intend merely to revisit the putatively Kantian paradigm underlying New Critical and New Historical assumptions about the literary that I discussed in my Introduction. As I argued there, both New Criticism and New Historicism assume that the autonomy of literary aesthetics relies on the inutility of beauty and the disinterestedness of aesthetic analysis: New Critics by maintaining that literature has no other end than the expression of its own essential core of meaning, and New Historicists by asserting that literature has no essence at all since meaning is constructed by readers and communities to non-literary ends. What I hope to suggest here is that these assumptions need to be re-evaluated on theoretical as well as historical grounds. Kantian aesthetics, I will argue, are not in the end disinterested, but themselves instrumental. Kant expressly requires the cultivated subject 'to use the beautiful as an instrument for our aim regarding the good' (78, Ak. 230–1), and at the conclusion of his writings on the beautiful, he even identifies the origin of this salutary instrumentality as the subject's pleasure in charms. Ending on a theoretical note, then, this coda to *Magical Imaginations* invites a reassessment of the conventional assumptions about Kantian aesthetics underlying both formalist and anti-formalist approaches to literature.

Kant at first dismisses taste that enjoys charms as 'barbaric' because he maintains that charms undermine the autonomous decision making that makes us human. Indeed, Kant implies that pleasure in charms is fundamentally bestial ('agreeableness holds for non-rational animals too' [52, Ak. 210]), as the pleasure of the charm – the feeling of 'agreeableness,' in Kant's term – is sensuous rather than cognitive, satisfying only the longings of the body. Such corporeal longings are outside our control, and as such they are not aspects of our capacity for self-determination, but symptoms of our basic needs. And it is from our needs that our interests arise ('all interest either presupposes a need or gives rise to one,' Kant explains [52, Ak. 210]). Hence any satisfaction we take in things that serve our interests – any sense that such things are agreeable to us – only underscores our lack of freedom. 'Because interest is the basis that determines approval,' Kant maintains, 'the judgment about the object [is] unfree' (52, Ak. 210).[10] That is why, for Kant, our pleasure in charms unduly influences our personal and political dispositions: when a charming object gratifies us, we become 'biased in favor of the thing's existence' (46, Ak. 205), and we develop this bias whatever the social or moral value of the object. Thus Kant attempts to dismiss the aesthetic value of charms precisely because they, like the magical spells from which they descend, influence us instrumentally in ways we never chose, compromising the autonomy that he believes should be confirmed, rather than attenuated, by aesthetic experience.

In contrast to the pleasure produced by charms, pure aesthetic experience, Kant argues, demonstrates that we possess 'the freedom to make an object of pleasure for ourselves out of something or other' (52, Ak. 210). 'The liking involved in taste for the beautiful,' Kant elaborates, 'is disinterested and *free*, since we are not compelled to give our approval by any interest' (52, Ak. 210, emphasis in the original). Unlike the pleasure we feel in charms, the pleasure we take in beauty 'is indifferent to the existence of the object' (51, Ak. 209). Transcending personal desire and political inclination, it bases itself on only the contemplation of pure form.[11] Properly construed, the form that provides pleasure is what Kant calls the object's 'purposiveness' (*Zweckmäßigkeit*). Purposiveness is what allows the mind to identify an object as well as recognize its practical ends (the identity and teleological end of an object being the purpose [*Zweck*] of the object's purposiveness).[12] We understand that a flower, say, is a flower and not a bush by cognizing its purposiveness. But if normally it gives an object its purpose in the world, when purposiveness is contemplated aesthetically it becomes, Kant says, purposiveness *without* purpose (*Zweckmäßigkeit ohne Zweck*). We may know that flowers are coloured and perfumed in order to attract pollinating insects, but generally we do not take aesthetic pleasure in flowers for their instrumental role in the reproduction of plants. By bracketing the purpose of an object's purposiveness, the subject thus chooses to make the object aesthetic by contemplating its form to no other end than the pleasure of that contemplation.[13] Neither the charming nor the good thing may be used in this way: 'Neither an object of inclination, nor one that a law of reason enjoins on us as an object of desire, leaves us the freedom to make an object of pleasure for ourselves out of something or other' (52, Ak. 210). Strictly speaking, then, the Kantian aesthetic object makes no claim on us – it does not compel our desire for it in any way, nor does it produce any inclination transitively; rather, we select it as an occasion for a purely subjective reflection in which the mind is free to play with the presentation of the object's form. Indeed, 'the cognitive powers brought into play by the [aesthetic] presentation are,' Kant affirms, 'in free play' (62, Ak. 217).

Kant's distinction between the subtly coercive force of charm and the liberating potential of beauty corresponds to the opposition he adduces between the value of rhetoric and that of poetry. Rhetoric, or 'oratory' as Kant calls it, has the power of charm: a power that compels our interests and thereby compromises our freedom, turning us into instruments rather than self–determining agents who choose our own purposes. 'Oratory,' he argues, 'insofar as this is taken to mean the art of persuasion (*ars oratoria*),' enables the orator 'to win over people's minds for his own advantage before they judge for themselves, and so make their judgment unfree.' It follows, Kant continues, that oratory cannot be recommended, 'for although this art can at times be employed for aims that are legitimate and laudable intrinsically, it is still made reprehensible by the fact that [it] corrupts the maxims and attitudes of the subjects ... for it is not enough that we do what is right, but we must also perform it solely on the ground that it is right' (197, Ak. 327). Now, Kant is no consequentialist – he takes the motives for action to be much more important than the ends of action – but surely there is something at once more visceral and more ideological in his distaste for rhetoric than his desire to motivate morality with reason. It is as if he feels that by succumbing to the force of persuasion, the subject demonstrates his 'unfree' submission to a tyrannous political machinery.[14] Hence his historical claim that oratory 'came to its peak' in antiquity 'only at a time when the state' – the Roman republican state, that is – 'was hastening to its ruin,' and hence his contemptuous judgment that as 'the art of using people's weaknesses for one's own aims,' oratory 'is unworthy of any *respect* whatsoever' (198, n. 63, emphasis in the original). Rhetoric, like charm, addresses itself to our physical and cognitive 'weaknesses' (our material and affective needs, in other words), 'deceiving' us by means of the 'illusion' (197, Ak. 327) that our desires align with those of the orator and that our assent to his arguments will further our interests.

In contrast to rhetoric, poetry, according to Kant, remains outside immanent networks of desire and interest: it never uses 'illusion' to 'deceive us' (197, Ak. 327). Like beauty itself, poetry sheds its illusory materiality in its presentation to the mind, becoming there in its purely formal arrangement – the internal structure of relationships between sounds and images that harmonize in a multivalent, indeterminate way – an occasion for the free play of the subject's cognitive powers, and for his pleasure in exercising them. And again like beauty itself, poetry has no personal or political purpose: 'Its pursuit,' Kant tells us, 'is mere play' (197, Ak. 327). Yet poetry does more than merely provide us with an occasion to engage in the free play of the mind. It also enables us to enter the kingdom of reason by virtue of its power to invoke 'aesthetic ideas' ('it is actually in the art of poetry,' Kant explains, 'that the power of aesthetic ideas can manifest itself to full extent' [183, Ak. 314]). Aesthetic ideas are *unexpoundable* presentations of the imagination' (217, Ak. 343, emphasis in the original): unexpoundable because they exceed the scope of empirical or even theoretical cognition (the domain of the imagination and the understanding, in Kant's terms). Rather, Kant argues, such ideas 'strive toward something that lies beyond the bounds of experience and hence try to approach an exhibition of rational concepts (intellectual ideas)' (182, Ak. 314). Rational concepts are ideations of the supersensible realm, the realm of the universally true, which we can apprehend only as noumena, things only reason can think. (Which is how Kant would explain, we might speculate, that poetry so resolutely resists satisfying paraphrase: in 'rising aesthetically to ideas,' poetry links its formal 'exhibition' of the world 'with a wealth of thought to which no linguistic expression is completely adequate' [196, Ak. 326].) Poetry thus inspires reason to lift thought into the supersensible realm, where we find our autonomy in our uniquely human ability – 'free, spontaneous, and independent of natural determination' (196–7, Ak. 326) – to contemplate and judge. In Kant's aesthetics, then, we do not merely think about transcendence when we read poetry; instead we think *transcendently*, engaging the power of reason in the play of aesthetic ideas, and thereby confirming our freedom in the power of our cognition to escape 'natural determination.'

Yet in Kant, the experience of our freedom paradoxically entails its opposite: the acceptance of our *duty*. For our ability to think the universal of the supersensible realm leads us to cognize the ideal moral action not governed by natural, mechanistic laws, nor mandated by culture, but simply legislated by reason as what is always and everywhere right. That is why Kant ultimately argues that aesthetics *are* instrumental to moral action – why, although poetry tells us 'that its pursuit is mere play, this play can still be used purposively' (197, Ak. 327) to achieve moral ends in the world. Because we cognize moral ideas by reflecting on aesthetic ideas, poetry has the practical purpose, for Kant, of introducing the will to the legislation of reason. Of course, Kant usually maintains that nothing in aesthetic experience compels us to submit to such legislation; he insists, on the contrary, that we remain free to choose to make poetry an instrument to the good. Yet at the same time, he argues that we *must* do so: 'Unless we connect the fine arts, closely or remotely, with moral action,' Kant warns, 'the aim is merely enjoyment, which leaves nothing behind as an idea and makes the spirit dull, the object gradually disgusting, and the mind dissatisfied with itself' (195–6, Ak. 326). The play of aesthetic ideas in the fine arts has an 'aim,' then: not 'merely enjoyment,' but 'moral action.'

This requirement that we connect art with moral action duly informs Kant's criteria for having taste. For taste in Kant is based not only on our power to chose to use objects aesthetically – to see their purposiveness without purpose, 'leaving out as much as possible whatever is matter, i.e., sensation, in the presentational state, and by paying attention to purely formal features' (160, Ak. 294) – but also on our ability to recognize aesthetic ideas and the moral ideas to which they lead. Indeed, Kant argues that we have fully refined our taste only when we have learned the 'rules for uniting taste with Reason, i.e., the beautiful with the good,' for this union 'enables us to use the beautiful as an instrument for our aim regarding the good, so that the [aesthetic] mental attunement ... may serve as a basis for that other [moral] way of thinking that can be sustained only by laborious resolve, but that is universally valid objectively' (78, Ak. 230–1).[15] Moral thinking, the manifestation of reason, gives human beings their worth, according to Kant, and aesthetics earn their value only insofar as they serve instrumentally to this practical end. In fact, Kant so prioritizes reason that he ultimately claims the judgment of taste is universal only because it expresses a *morality* that bears an objective and thus necessary claim to unanimous agreement: 'Now I maintain that the beautiful is the symbol of the morally good; and only because we refer [*Rücksicht*] the beautiful to the morally good ... does our liking for it include a claim to everyone else's assent, [and] while the mind is also conscious of being ennobled by this reference ... it assesses the value of other people too on the basis of their having a similar maxim in their power of judgment' (228, Ak. 353). In short, then, Kantian aesthetics, in their very claim to theorizing a universal subjective judgment of beauty, are *instrumental* aesthetics. If they do not promise that we will be transformed by beauty without our consent – if they do the opposite and require us to learn the rules uniting taste and reason – Kant still bases the value of aesthetic experience on its instrumentality to moral ends.

Moreover, even without theorizing aesthetic experience as having the ability to transform our dispositions without our consent, Kant still suggests that its instrumentality is grounded in the aesthetic object's charm.

Indeed, in the summary statement of his aesthetics – quite literally in its very last sentences – Kant represents not beauty, but charm as what symbolizes morality, as what sensuously and palpably transmits morality to us from the supersensible realm: 'Beautiful objects of nature or of art are often called by names that seem to presuppose that we are judging [these objects] morally. We call buildings or trees majestic and magnificent, or landscapes cheerful and gay; even colors are called innocent, humble, or tender, because they arouse sensations in us that are somehow analogous to the consciousness we have in a mental state produced by moral judgments. Taste enables us, as it were, to make the transition from sensible charm to a habitual moral interest without making too violent a leap; for ... it teaches us to like even objects of sense freely, apart from sensible charm' (230, Ak. 354). Here is it not beauty, but charm that introduces us to morality, in that the sensation of being charmed is 'somehow analogous to the consciousness we have in a mental state produced by moral judgments,' showing us that we can feel pleasure when our will harmonizes with an objective good. Taste indeed works on that pleasure with the labour that abstracts beauty from charm and connects beauty to reason, yet the foundational moment of this refining (and refined) labour remains the sensation of being charmed. Charm provides the aesthetic experience, and taste provides the lesson that instrumentalizes that experience to moral ends.

Further, Kant argues that charm makes us interested in developing taste and morality in the first place. Since charms 'may offer the mind more than that dry liking' that we experience in a pure, utterly formalized judgment of taste, charms may, Kant submits, 'commend us to taste and its cultivation' (71, Ak. 225). For example, although 'composition' and 'design' – the purely formal elements of music and painting – 'constitute the proper object[s] of a pure judgment of taste,' the 'agreeable tone of an instrument' and the 'charm of the colors' in a landscape supplement those objects and make them attractive to contemplate: 'they enliven the presentation by means of their charm, by arousing and sustaining the attention we direct toward the object itself' (72, Ak. 225–6). Without the educated will's resolute orientation to the eternal (and, for that reason, slightly dead) realm of the supersensible, the mind needs something to adorn and 'enliven' the pure presentation of form. Hence, Kant proposes, 'charms ... may be granted admittance when taste is still weak and unpracticed, and only insofar as they don't interfere with the beautiful form' (71, Ak. 225). And lest we think that only individual subjects might have 'weak' or 'unpracticed' taste, Kant argues that whole cultures celebrate charms before they are civilized: 'Initially, it is true, only charms ... become important in society and become connected with great interest, e.g., the dyes people use to paint themselves (roucou among the Caribs and cinnabar among the Iroquois), or the flowers, sea shells, beautifully colored feathers, but eventually also beautiful forms (as in canoes, clothes, etc.) that involve no gratification whatsoever, i.e., no liking of enjoyment. But in the end, when civilization has reached its peak, it makes [the pure judgment of taste] almost the principal activity of refined inclination, and sensations are valued only to the extent that they are universally communicable' (164, Ak. 297). This racially charged progressive history of taste imagines that people eschew their interest in charms over time until they have refined themselves so thoroughly that they like the beautiful exclusively as a symbol of the morally good, and in so doing manifest, in the world and not just in theory, the universal communicability of aesthetic approval that the harmony of subjective pleasure with objective reason enables. In other words, Kant's history of taste ends in a future society in which each subject is equivalent to all others in value. Although there is something rather chilling in the distaste for sensuousness and difference that underlies Kant's vision of universal equivalence, there is also something benevolent in the liberalism that motivates it: the utopian hope that one day the pleasure we take in the things of this world will express our identities as beings who make our ends for ourselves, and who bend to no other law than that which is legislated to all humans equally by their own volition.

Hence Kant fears charms, although he cannot for all purposes dispense with them, because he sees that they might serve to turn us into instruments, bound to the ends of power by our own needs and determinations. This dehumanizing potential in the charm remains left over, we might say, from the historical moment when charms were understood as soul-killing magical spells. We have seen that it was precisely as magical spells that charms anticipated Kant's fears in the instrumental aesthetics of the English Renaissance: Spenser represented poor Amoret suffering terribly from her own arousal, bound to a phallic pillar by Busirane's strong charms; Marlowe had Faustus gladly become the devil's tool in return for the false promise that he could save his own flesh with charms; Shakespeare manipulated his king into betraying his own law by giving him a supposedly pure pleasure in the play of Prospero's charms. Insofar as beautiful representations move us in ways we do not choose, they seem tied to a coercive magic that turns us into its victims. Yet by virtue of that same charming power, beautiful representations can also invoke a more benevolent magical imagination, one that calls down by the force of human will a more complete, more intense form of life that remains invisible to us in our habitual, quotidian existence. This form of life appears to us in the sweetness and brilliance that attracts and arouses us, that gratifies our longings even as it compels us to want to know more, and to live more exquisitely. And this magical imagination also animates Kant's charm; it must do so, after all, or else his continuum of aesthetic experience would not arc all the way from earthly pleasure to the transcendent reconciliation of means and ends in the kingdom of reason. Even in Kant's aesthetics, then, the charm of beauty is a magnetic force that at once drags us to places we never sought to find and points us in the direction of our highest aspirations.

Notes

Introduction

1 The commonplace derives, of course, from Horace's *Ars Poetica*, where Horace argues that the best poet blends profit with pleasure, at once delighting and instructing his reader (see Horace, *Ars Poetica*, 343–4: 'omne tulit punctum qui miscuit utile dulci, lectorem delectando pariterque monendo').

2 In their *Dialectic of Enlightenment*, Horkheimer and Adorno characterize instrumental reason as the enlightenment principle behind modern technologies that exploit labour in producing the abstract equivalences of capitalist exchange, and they identify Francis Bacon's 'scientific temper' (2) as an early version of such reason. In the recent *Humanism, Machinery, and Renaissance Literature*, Jessica Wolfe has similarly argued that early modern attitudes towards instrumentality began to shift in response to sixteenth- and seventeenth-century developments in mechanics. I should note, however, that instrumental reason in Renaissance humanism generally derives not from the new science, but from Aristotelian and Protestant ethics. In the former, each human activity both enjoys its own end and serves a higher, more complex activity (as saddle making, for example, serves horsemanship); in the latter, all worldly endeavours are framed as instruments through which to serve God. As Horkheimer and Adorno acknowledge, Bacon's instrumental 'credo would have smacked of metaphysics,' because 'for Bacon as for Luther, "knowledge that tendeth but to satisfaction is but as a courtesan, which is for pleasure, and not for fruit"' (2).

3 See Thomas, *Religion and the Decline of Magic*.

4 For the *locus classicus* of this account of magic, see Yates, *Giordano Bruno and the Hermetic Tradition*.

5 See, e.g., Shumaker, *The Occult Sciences in the Renaissance*; Webster, *From*

Paracelsus to Newton; Vickers, 'Analogy versus Identity'; Copenhaver, 'Natural Magic, Hermeticism, and Occultism in Early Modern Science'; Merkel and Debus, *Hermeticism and the Renaissance*; Clulee, *John Dee's Natural Philosophy*; Gatti, *Giordano Bruno and Renaissance Science*; and Harkness, *John Dee's Conversations with Angels*.

6 Thus, for example, in *Renaissance Magic and the Return to the Golden Age*, John Mebane argues that *Doctor Faustus* dramatizes 'the emotional and intellectual conflicts of those who sought to liberate themselves from excessive authoritarianism' (xiii). For Yates's own readings of the relationship between magic and English literature, which anticipate Mebane's, see part 2 of *The Occult Philosophy in the Elizabethan Age* and *Shakespeare's Last Plays*.

7 See Tomlinson, *Music and Renaissance Magic*; Maggi, *Satan's Rhetoric* and *In the Company of Demons*; and Lehrich, *The Occult Mind*.

8 Burke, *A Rhetoric of Motives*, 43 (emphasis in the original), 44.

9 Ibid., 42 (emphasis in the original).

10 On the social construction and force of charisma, see Mauss, *A General Theory of Magic*, and Bourdieu, 'Le couturier et sa griffe.'

11 Tambiah, 'Form and Meaning of Magical Acts,' 12, 26. In 'A Performative Approach to Ritual,' Tambiah exfoliates his basic account of magic as performative. He characterizes magic as performative in 'three senses: in the Austinian sense of performative wherein saying something is also doing something as a conventional act; in the quite different sense of a staged performance that uses multiple media by which the participants experience the event intensively; and in the third sense of indexical values [such as the referent of the pronoun "I," which changes according to the context of enunciation] ... being attached to and inferred by actors during the performance' (119).

12 See Clark, *Thinking with Demons*; Lake and Questier, *The Antichrist's Lewd Hat*, 40–53; Walsham, *Providence in Early Modern England*, and as ed. with Marshall, *Angels in the Early Modern World*.

13 Foxe, *The Seconde Volume of the Ecclesiastical Historie*, 1079–80.

14 Ralegh, *The History of the World*, 2:167. I should note here that Ralegh's statements about magic tend to contradict each other. Elsewhere, contrasting angels to devils, he claims that by virtue of their own servitude to sin, devils may in fact be commanded by magic: 'So seeing [that angels] are most free spirits, there is no man so absurd to think (except the devil have corrupted his understanding) that they can be constrained or commanded out of heaven by threats ... for good spirits or angels cannot be constrained, and the rest are devils which willingly obey' (169). Ralegh's ambivalence about the efficacy of diabolical conjuration may well arise from his divided intentions: on the one hand he seems to desire not to appear credulous where magic is concerned,

and on the other he evidently hopes to please or at least placate James I, who, as we shall see in chapter 4, fervently argues in his *Daemonologie* that magicians can in fact control devils (Ralegh defers to James's text at multiple points in his own: see *The History of the World*, 2:152, 167–8, and 169, for examples). Of course, Ralegh also harbours his own dream of magical power, maintaining that 'herbs, drugs, minerals, and excrements' (2:161) have spiritual virtues, which the art of natural magic draws 'out of nature's hidden bosom to human use' (2:155). This 'art of magic,' Ralegh insists, is good: 'the art of worshipping God' (2:151). On the distinctions between 'good' and 'bad' magic in the Renaissance, see Walker, *Spiritual and Demonic Magic*.

15 See Wimsatt and Brooks, *Literary Criticism*, 727.

16 Ransom, 'Criticism, Inc,' 1115.

17 Wimsatt, *The Verbal Icon*, 87.

18 Ransom, 'Criticism, Inc.,' 1115.

19 Wimsatt and Beardsley, 'The Affective Fallacy,' 1402 (emphasis added). This sense that poetry fixes emotion is played out in Cleanth Brooks's arguments in 'The Heresy of Paraphrase' that poetry imitates life by '*being* an experience rather than any mere statement of experience' (1365, emphasis in the original).

20 Wimsatt and Beardsley, 'The Affective Fallacy,' 1398–9.

21 Gallagher and Greenblatt, *Practicing New Historicism*, 2. I should point out that as the practice of New Historicism matured, its rejection of New Critical methods became less categorical: in the same essay Gallagher and Greenblatt reveal that after they had disparaged the value of 'the formal analysis of the inner structure of literary works,' they found themselves wanting 'to take back' what they had been 'rather too hasty to give away' (3). Their justification for practising New Historicism seems to evolve as well: where it once identified subversion only to reveal how power contained that subversion, now New Historicist practice traces the circulation of social energy in order to augment rather than attenuate the rich experience of reading works of literature. Thus, in *Practicing New Historicism* we find an aesthetic rather than a political rationale for New Historical critical practice: 'To wall off for aesthetic appreciation only a tiny portion of the expressive range of a culture is to diminish its individuality and to limit one's understanding even of that tiny portion, since its significance can be fully grasped only in relation to the other expressive possibilities with which it interacts and from which it differentiates itself' (13). But art appreciation is where New Historicism arrived at last, not from where it set out at first.

22 Greenblatt, 'Introduction to *The Power of Forms in the English Renaissance*,' 2253.

23 Louis Montrose in fact proposed just that in *The Purpose of Playing*: 'The Essex conspirators subscribed to the belief that drama has the capacity to imitate action and, by example, to impel its audience to action – an understanding they shared with the theatre's most vocal defenders and detractors' (71).

24 Nashe, *Pierce Pennilesse*, D3v.

25 Kastan, 'Humphrey Moseley and the Invention of English Literature,' 110.

1 Conjuration and *The Defense of Poesy*

1 Sidney, *Defense of Poesy*, 141–2. I should note that I use the title *The Defense of Poesy* throughout even though I quote from Geoffrey Shepherd's edition, which is based on the Olney *Apology*. I have chosen Shepherd's edition for its extraordinary apparatus, but I have been persuaded by Albert Feuillerat's argument that the Ponsonby *Defense* is the more authoritative of the two published texts (not only was it entered into the Stationer's Register first, and preferred by the Countess of Pembroke when she prepared the Folio of 1598, but at points it is clearly superior in sense). I will quote from the Feuillerat edition if it seems necessary to do so. For further bibliographical details, see Sidney, ed. Feuillerat, *Prose Works*, 3:vi. For the five-part forensic structure of the *Defense*, see Myrick, *Sir Philip Sidney as a Literary Craftsman*, 46–83.

2 See Margaret Ferguson, *Trials of Desire* ('from an epistemological point of view, there is no exit from the circle of irony Sidney draws around his "I" and his oration' [154]), and Ronald Levao, *Renaissance Minds and Their Fictions* ('if the only choice is between those who unconsciously live fictions and those who act their own, then Sidney, as the speaker of the *Apology*, makes it clear that he thinks of himself as one of the latter' [150]). These readings draw perhaps on Catherine Barnes, who in 'Hidden Persuader' argues that Sidney 'dissociates himself from his own endeavour' by demonstrating that he has 'stepped back to a critical perspective on his own artifice' in order to display an 'amused perspective on poets' and 'on the subject of poetry' (426).

3 See also BL Sloane MS 3824, art. 3. For late medieval predecessors to such formulae, see 'Formulas for Commanding Spirits,' in Kieckhefer, *Forbidden Rites*, 126–53.

4 Agrippa, *Three Books of Occult Philosophy*, 3, 657. We might say that this move serves as a cunning way to explain the irreproducibility of magical claims, since it suggests that those who cannot master the 'art' of magic and command spirits to appear are those who have been too imprudent and unintelligent, not to mention 'wicked and incredulous,' to have correctly interpreted Agrippa's narrative and understood the 'mysteries' of his 'secrets.' See also Perez Zagorin, *Ways of Lying*, esp. 261, where Zagorin reads the

magician's deployment of allegory as his attempt to construct an elite, coterie readership for his occult texts.

5 See Bernard Weinberg, *History of Literary Criticism in the Italian Renaissance*, esp. 'Platonism: I, The Defense of Poetry' (1:250–96) and 'Conclusions of Poetic Theory' (1:797–818). Weinberg proposes that Plato established the debate over the cultural status of poetry in terms of the value of its instrumental effects (terms into which Aristotle's account of the salutary effects of tragic pity and fear, as well as Horatian *dolce et utile*, were easily assimilated). See also Spingarn, *History of Literary Criticism in the Renaissance*. For the intellectual history of arguments against poetry through and beyond the early modern period, see Barish, *Antitheatrical Prejudice*, and Herman, *Squitter-wits and Muse Haters*. It might also be worth noting here how Plato concludes the discussion about poetry in Book 10 of the *Republic*. Having proposed that 'poetry should return from exile when it has successfully defended itself,' Socrates proclaims that we should 'allow [poetry's] defenders ... to speak in prose on its behalf and to show that it not only gives pleasure but is beneficial both to constitutions and to human life.' See *Republic*, 607d–e, in *Complete Works*.

6 Quoted in Weinberg, *History of Literary Criticism*, 1:737.

7 Quoted in ibid., 1:748. Scaliger is by no means always cynical about poetry. See note 24, below.

8 Chris Nealon has suggested that Sidney addressed the *Defense* not to his peers, but to the queen, promising her that poetry could transform her louche aristocrats into proper princes, for whom the model is Xenophon's Cyrus. See his 'Poetic Case,' 872. Nealon draws on Robert Matz, who argues in his *Defending Literature* that Sidney represents poetry as inspiring aristocrats to 'martial service' (62) and thereby as justifying 'the profitability of the elite to the rest of the body politic' (65). See also Montrose, 'Celebration and Insinuation,' for a broad reading of Sidney's literary productions as forms of counsel to the queen. It seems to me that in the *Defense* Sidney imagines multiple audiences for poetry: not just his own social group, but also the un-landed 'who think virtue a school-name' (114).

9 Sidney delimits philosophy and history as the two human sciences that most 'deal in the consideration of men's manners' (106), making them poetry's closest competitors for the title of monarch of the human sciences. It is important to note, however, that Sidney considers all humanistic discourses to be instrumental endeavours, or 'serving sciences,' as he calls them. He sees them as both having autonomy, a 'private end in themselves,' and leading to 'the highest end of mistress-knowledge, by the Greeks called *architectonike*, which stands ... in the ethic and politic consideration, with the end of well-

doing and not well-knowing only' (104). For Aristotle's discussion the hierarchy of arts and sciences, in which each human activity both has its own end and serves a 'higher' activity to which it is subordinate – as bridle-making serves the art of riding, and riding serves the art of warfare, and warfare serves the 'master' art of politics – see the *Nicomachean Ethics*, book 1, 1–2, in *Complete Works*.

10 Although he does posit a 'mistress' as the reader of 'such writings as come under the banner of unresistible love' (137), Sidney clearly imagines the reader subjected to the ideological effects of poetry as a male reader, so for that reason I will use the male third-person pronoun in this chapter.

11 Coxe, *A Shorte Treatise*, 5v.

12 Agrippa, *Of the Vanitie*, 57v, 58r. In 'Sidney and Agrippa,' A.C. Hamilton argues that Sidney took much from Agrippa's *Of the Vanitie* when he was writing the *Defense*: not only the figure of the astronomer who, as Agrippa puts it, 'wente out of his house to beholde ye starres, and ... fell into a diche,' but also the designation of Cyrus as the paragon of exemplars. For the relationship between *Of the Vanitie* and Agrippa's *Occult Philosophy*, see Nauert Jr, *Agrippa and the Crisis of Renaissance Thought*, and Keefer, 'Agrippa's Dilemma.'

13 Bruno, *Cause, Principle and Unity*, 130. As Ioan Couliano has pointed out in *Eros and Magic in the Renaissance*, for Bruno persuasion is a form of 'directed hypnosis ... whose rules of production trace those of spontaneous love' (107).

14 See Alciati, 'Eloquentia fortitudine praestantior,' in *Emblemata*, 97. On this emblem, see Wind, '"Hercules" and "Orpheus,"' and Rebhorn, *The Emperor of Men's Minds*, 23–80.

15 See Plato, *Republic*, book 10, 605b (also 596–7.e), in *Complete Works*. I am not claiming that Sidney read Plato, or even any Neoplatonist for that matter. I assume he absorbed the Neoplatonic justification for poetry from his reading of Italian critics, particularly Scaliger (whom Sidney ranks with the 'learned philosophers' [131]). For fuller discussions of these issues, see Weinberg, *The History of Literary Criticism*; Hathaway, 'Platonism, Love, Beauty, and Florence,' in *The Age of Criticism*, 341–8; and Shepherd, 'The Other Nature,' in *An Apology for Poetry*, 61–6. Useful information on Sidney's Neoplatonism may be found within the twentieth-century debate over Sidney's classical influences. See, e.g., Krouse, 'Plato and Sidney's *Defense of Poesie*,' which argues that Sidney marshalled Platonic ideas about poetry's ethical effects and Aristotelian ones about form and genre; MacIntyre, 'Sidney's "Golden World,"' which attempts to connect the *Defense* to Florentine Neoplatonism; and Morriss, 'Sir Philip Sidney and the Renaissance Knowledge of Plato,' which helpfully catalogues references to Plato in the *Defense*. See also

Ulreich, "'The Poets Only Deliver": Sidney's Conception of Mimesis'; Devereux, 'The Meaning of Delight in Sidney's *Defence of Poesy*'; and Robinson, *The Shape of Things Known* for interpretations relying on the assumption that Sidney knew Neoplatonism. For the argument that Sidney's greatest influence was Philip Melanchthon, see Stillman, *Philip Sidney and the Poetics of Renaissance Cosmopolitanism*. And finally, for the still-definitive discussion of Neoplatonism in English Renaissance aesthetics, see Ellrodt, *Neoplatonism in the Poetry of Spenser*.

16 Hooker, *Of the Laws of Ecclesiastical Polity*, 1:65.

17 Plato, *Timaeus*, 49a, in *Complete Works*.

18 Although I have summarized the basic structure of the Platonic cosmos, there were actually multiple versions of this cosmos in circulation in the 1580s. Marsilio Ficino, for example, used two very different cosmological constructs. In his 'Platonic Theology,' Ficino lays out a tripartite cosmos, much like the one I've outlined here, in which metaphysical Ideas are connected to matter by the Soul of the World. This cosmos may be traced to Plotinus, whom Ficino translated for the Medicis. See Plotinus, *Enneads*, 2.1–8, 5.1–4, 6.1–5. By contrast, in his *Commentary on Plato's 'Symposium,'* Ficino adopts the elaborate cosmological architecture of Proclus, who amplifies multiple levels of gods, daemons, and human heroes existing in between the One and the mass of humanity. See Proclus, *Elements of Theology*, esp. chaps. L–M. This hierarchy is Christianized by Pseudo-Dionysius in the third century. See Pseudo-Dionysius Areopagita, *The Divine Names and Mystical Theology*. For analysis of the evolving character of the cosmos in Ficino's philosophy, see Kristeller, *The Philosophy of Marsillio Ficino.* For the classic discussion of the intellectual history of Platonic cosmology, see Lovejoy, *The Great Chain of Being.*

19 Montaigne, *Essays*, 2:225.

20 Bacon, *The Advancement of Learning*, in *Francis Bacon*, 186.

21 Plotinus, *Enneads*, 411.

22 See Panofsky, *Idea*, esp. 26, and Abrams, 'The Transcendental Ideal,' in *The Mirror and the Lamp*, 42–7.

23 Quoted in Robinson, *The Shape of Things Known*, 108.

24 Here Sidney is adapting a passage from Scaliger's *Poetices*, which I will provide below, followed by the Latin from the 5th edition. I have modified the spelling of the Latin to accord with contemporary usage. 'Only poetry embraces all these techniques [i.e., rhetorical techniques used by philosophy and history], which makes it the most excellent of these arts, and even more so because, as we were saying above, where all the others represent things as they are, the poet, as if with a sort of speaking picture, makes quite another nature and even multiple forms of life, and in short, therefore, makes himself as it were another god. For the other sciences are servants of all those things

the Maker fashioned; but the poet sets forth the appearance of both things
that are, making them more beautiful than they are, and things that are not.
Poetry therefore really seems like a unique discourse. It is not like the others,
such as history, which simply narrates – rather, like another god, the poet cre-
ates. Hence, by virtue of this fact, it appears that his common name was given
not by the consensus of men, but by the providence of nature. Whence the
wisdom of the Greeks most fittingly fashioned that name, *maker*.' [Sola poe-
sis haec omnia complexa est, tanto quam artes illae excellentias, quod caeterae
[*sic*] (ut dicebamus) res ipsas, uti sunt, repraesentant, veluti aurium pictura
quadam. At poeta et naturam alteram et fortunas plures etiam ac demum
sese isthoc ipso periende ac Deum alterum efficit. Nam quae omnium opifex
condidit, eorum relique scientiae tamquam actores sunt. Poetica vero, quem
et speciosius quae sunt et quae non sunt, eorum speciem ponit. Videtur sane
res ipsas, non ut aliae, quasi Histrio, narrare, sed velut alter deus condere:
unde cum eo commune nomen ipsi non a consensu hominum, sed a naturae
providentia inditum videatur. Quod nomen Graeci sapientes ubi commodis-
sime effinxissent.] For another example of the maker-as-god leitmotif in
Neoplatonic thought, see Ficino, 'Platonic Theology,' 233: 'Man imitates all
the works of the divine nature, and perfects, corrects, and improves the works
of the lower nature. Therefore the power of man is almost similar to that of
the divine nature, for man acts this way through himself and through his own
wit.'

25 Adorno, *Aesthetic Theory*, 78.
26 Bruno, *Cause, Principle and Unity*, 112.
27 Agrippa, *Three Books of Occult Philosophy*, 1.
28 Quoted in French, *John Dee*, 94. For the theological difficulty this confla-
    tion of Ideas and angels raised for Neoplatonists who considered themselves
    Christians, see Walker, *Spiritual and Demonic Magic*. For medieval anteced-
    ents of this conflation, see Clucas, 'John Dee's Angelic Conversations and the
    Ars Notoria.'
29 Harsnett, *A Declaration of Egregious Popish Impostures*, 159.
30 Calvin, *Institution of the Christian Religion*, 29. For Calvin's full discussion
    of Neoplatonism and the angelology accruing to it, see also the following sec-
    tions of the *Institution*: 1.9.29, 1.14.4, and 1.14.19.
31 Scot, *The Discoverie of Witchcraft*, 421, 427.
32 Sidney, *The Defense of Poesy*, 101.
33 Scot, *The Discoverie of Witchcraft*, 420
34 Gosson, *The School of Abuse*, A6r.
35 Hocus Pocus Junior, *The Anatomie of Legerdemaine*, Dr, E4v.
36 Perkins, *A Golden Chaine*, 65.

37 Willet, *Hexapla in Danielem*, 190 (emphasis added).

38 Milton, *Mask*, 756–7, 154, in *Complete Poems and Major Prose*.

39 For more about the slippery connotations of the word 'juggler' in the period, see Butterworth, *Magic on the Early English Stage*, chaps. 1 and 9.

40 Dering, *A Briefe Catachiseme*, Aiiv, Aiiir–v. For more on Dering's career see Lake, *Moderate Puritans*, chap. 2, and McCullough, *Sermons at Court*, 36–7; for more on his anti-poetic arguments, see Herman, *Squitter-wits and Muse Haters*, 48–9.

41 5 Eliz 1, c. 16. See *Statutes at Large*, 1:806. I will return to this law later in this chapter.

42 Dering, *A Briefe Catachiseme*, Aiiiv.

43 Bruno, *The Ash Wednesday Supper*, 84.

44 Bruno, *The Heroic Frenzies*, 163.

45 See Sherman, *John Dee*, 130.

46 For an extended examination of Sidney's close friendship with Dyer, see the excellent biography of Sidney by Alan Stewart, *Sir Philip Sidney.*

47 On the astrological determination of Elizabeth's coronation, see Montrose, *The Subject of Elizabeth*, 176.

48 These debates turned out to be embarrassing for Bruno, who was exposed as having taken many of his arguments out of Ficino's *De vita coelitus comparanda.* See Yates, *Giordano Bruno*, 208–9; Feingold, 'The Occult Tradition' and 'Giordano Bruno in England, Revisited'; and Rowland, *Giordano Bruno*, 139–48. It should be noted that the Oxfordians took objection, among other things, to Bruno's advocacy of heliocentricism, complaining, as did one student George Abbott, that he 'undertook among very many other matters to set on foot the opinion of Copernicus, that the earth did go round, and the heavens did stand still; whereas in truth it was his own head which rather did run round, & his brains did not stand still' (quoted in Feingold, 'Occult Tradition,' 76).

49 For a detailed account of this episode in Dee's career, see Charlotte Fell-Smith, *John Dee*, 98. According to Fell-Smith, Laski was so eager to meet Dee that even before the Oxford trip he had summoned him to Leicester's London residence, and had in turn visited him at Mortlake, attended by only two men. Whatever the details, it is clear that Laski's visit set in motion Dee's subsequent sojourn on the Continent.

50 33 HV 8, c. 8. See *Statutes at Large*, 1:734.

51 Thomas, *Religion and the Decline of Magic*, 442.

52 The exchange is discussed in Fell-Smith, *John Dee*, 202–7; and Knapp, *An Empire Nowhere*, 74–5.

53 Susan Bassnet has recently suggested that Dee and Kelly fell out after they

unsuccessfully attempted to share their wives in common. See her 'Absent Presences.'

54 I might note here that Burghley seemed to have had a long-standing interest in securing revenue for the Elizabethan regime by magical means. In a letter of 1574, Dee wrote to Burghley asking to be put on stipend so that he could use his hermetic ability to discover where treasure might be buried in the realm. 'If,' Dee posits, '(besides all books, dreams, visions, reports, and *virgula diuina* [divining by rod]) by any other natural means and Likely Demonstrations of *Sympathia* and *antipathia rerum*: or by Attraction and repulsion, the places may be descried or discovered, where Gold, Silver, or better matter doth lie hid, within a certain distance: how great a commodity should it be for the Queen's Majesty and the commonweal of the Kingdom.' See BL Lansdowne MS 19, 82r.

55 Strype, *Annals of the Reformation*, 3:620.

56 BL Lansdowne MS 103, 210. Also quoted in Fell-Smith, *John Dee*, 206. In an amusing addition, Fell-Smith reports that Burghley was also trying to get Kelly to send him some elixir of life in order to vanquish his 'old enemy, the gout' before the winter came again.

57 As we might well imagine, Kelly never returned to England, and was soon after this exchange exposed as a fraud and thrown into prison on the Continent.

58 See Lhuid, *Britanniae Descriptionis Fragmentum*.

59 Languet to Sidney, 28 Jan. 1574, Sidney, *The Correspondence of Sidney and Languet*.

60 Sidney to Languet, 11 Feb. 1574, *The Correspondence of Sidney and Languet*. I have amended Stuart Pears's translation of 'deum ignotum' ('deus ignotus' in indirect discourse) from 'unknown saint' to 'unknown god.'

61 The *Monas* is a visual figure, an image, that is supposed to embody all the spiritual and, in Dee's scheme, mechanical principles of the universe. The text that accompanies the *Monas* is an extended exegesis of the allegorical significance of the shapes of its parts. For the classic discussion of this symbol, see Yates, *Occult Philosophy*, 83–4; for a recent interdisciplinary reading of it by way of the ritualizations of Noh drama, see Lehrich, *The Occult Mind*, 48–81.

62 Sidney made an official visit both to Gabriel Harvey and to Dee in preparation for his embassy to Germany on the deaths of Maximilian and the Elector Palatine. Sidney visited Harvey in order to study in Livy what Harvey called 'the forms of states, the conditions of person, and the qualities of actions' (quoted in Jardine and Grafton, 'Studied for Action,' 36), or, in other words, historical lessons that Sidney could apply once on the Continent. On Sidney's visit to Dee, see Stewart, *Sir Philip Sidney*, 169. Stewart speculates that Sidney's visit to Dee had a comparably studious purpose. It is possible to

imagine that the purpose of his visit was supernatural (perhaps, at the instiga-
tion of Leicester, to have the horoscope for his trip cast), but it could very
well have been simply to gather information about Maximilian's son, and the
German court, where Dee had resided. The traditional line in Dee scholarship
holds Dee had a tremendous influence on Sidney. In *Giordano Bruno*, Yates
claims that Sidney chose Dee as his 'teacher in philosophy' (188), and that his
'group of courtiers' was regularly 'studying number in the three worlds with
John Dee' (187). In *The Occult Philosophy*, Yates calls Dee the 'mentor of
Philip Sidney' (92). In his *John Dee*, Peter French argues that Sidney took his
ideas for the *Defense of Poesy* directly from Dee (126–60).

63 See Jacqueline de Romilly, *Magic and Rhetoric in Ancient Greece*, chap. 1.
    As de Romilly notes, Gorgias, in his *Encomium of Helen*, used the idea that
    charms had a magical effect on the souls of auditors to argue that Helen had
    been ravished not with physical violence but with the power of speech. See
    also Jacques Derrida, 'Plato's Pharmacy,' in *Dissemination*, on the significance
    for writing of the Gorgian power of persuasive eloquence to 'ravish invisibly,'
    (116) with 'its spellbinding powers of enchantment, mesmerizing fascination,
    and alchemical transformation, which make it kin to witchcraft and magic'
    (115) (as well as the fact that 'the technique of imitation, along with the re-
    production of the simulacrum, has always been in Plato's eyes manifestly
    magical, thaumaturgical' [139]).

64 Mason, *The Anatomie of Sorcerie*, 62.

65 See note 41, above. As Keith Thomas points out in *Religion and the Decline
    of Magic*, 'In the ecclesiastical courts such terms as "witch," "sorcerer,"
    "charmer," and "blesser" were used almost interchangeably' (257).

66 Shakespeare, in his prophetic way, maps the transition from early to modern
    usage in *The Merry Wives of Windsor*. Mistress Quickly says to Falstaff, 'I
    never knew a woman so dote upon a man; surely I think you have charms, la;
    yes in truth,' to which he replies, 'Not I, I assure thee. Setting the attraction
    of my good parts aside, I have no other charms' (2.2.102–6).

67 Coleridge, *Biographia Literaria*, 107 (emphasis in the original).

68 Berger, *Second World and Green World*, 8. I should note here that in his sub-
    sequent work 'Second World Prosthetics,' Berger revises his assumption that
    imaginative language is disjoined from the field of 'actual' experience, arguing
    instead that second-world discourse has 'subtly corrosive influence on atti-
    tudes in the first world' (8).

69 Hammill, *Sexuality and Form*, 98.

70 Levao, *Renaissance Minds and Their Fictions*, 146. Margreta de Grazia has
    already taken issue with Levao's claim that Sidney eschews the theory of po-
    etry's metaphysical objectivity. See her rather devastating 'Sidney's *Apology*.'

2 The Demonology of Spenserian Discipline

1 All quotations of *The Faerie Queene* are taken from the second A.C. Hamilton edition; all citations of book, canto, and stanza will be parenthetical.

2 Giamatti, *Play of Double Senses,* 119. Claiming in *The Analogy of 'The Faerie Queene'* that Archimago conjures 'to feign, in Sidney's language about the poet, notable images of virtues and vices,' James Nohrnberg proposes that 'such an analogy offers to equate Archimago's activity with the imagination concurrently shaping Spenser's poem' (105). In 'Spenser's Merlin,' William Blackburn points out not only that Merlin 'is one of Spenser's most powerful images of the true, god-like poet,' but that 'the "diuelish arts" of Archimago are primarily the arts of language – and the poet' (190, 189). And in 'Archimago and Amoret,' David Quint argues similarly that by introducing a 'split' between 'Una and her eroticized, demonic double at the opening' of book 1, Archimago 'has already invented the structure and method of Spenser's poem' (32).

3 This assumption seems to underlie even Harry Berger's claim in 'Archimago: Between Text and Countertext' that Archimago's power 'resides in his laying bare the unavoidably idolatrous basis' of Spenser's 'allegorical project' (35). Here Berger too implicitly reads magic in terms of an allegory that mimetically refers, although for him the point is that allegorical referral to transcendent truth is self-critically exposed by the doubling magician as an idolatrous fiction.

4 Critics writing on magic in *The Faerie Queene* tend to notice the instrumentality of magic in passing. Giamatti, for example, observes in *Play of Double Senses* at one point that both Archimago and Merlin 'are able, through their control of language, to project and shape the destinies of others' (120). In *Spenser's Allegory*, Isabel MacCaffrey alludes to 'the sinister power of Busirane's fiction to metamorphose those whom it constrains' (110). And in 'Archimago: Between Text and Countertext,' Berger, while reading more resistantly than his predecessors, also considers the ways that magic works instrumentally when he argues that Archimago's enchantments 'seem co-optive rather than coercive' (35). I would like to bring the implications of these considerations to the front and centre of our understanding of the relationship between magic and Spenser's poetry.

5 Spenser, 'Letter to Ralegh,' in *The Faerie Queene*, ed. Hamilton, 714; Teskey, *Allegory and Violence*, 78. I should note here that there has been some controversy over the status of the 'Letter' as a statement of Spenser's poetics. For an excellent summary of the debate and a cogent explanation for the contradictory nature of the document's relationship to the poem, see

Erikson, 'Spenser's "Letter to Ralegh."' In my view, the important thing to keep in mind is that the 'Letter' was appended only to the 1590 edition of the poem, which suggests that its application remains limited to that particular text placed in its own historical context. My discussion of the relationship between magic and Spenser's poetry, and the claims I make about Spenser's instrumental aesthetics, should therefore be understood as literary historical claims pertaining only to books 1–3, since only these books were explicitly advertised by the 'Letter' as having the general end of fashioning a gentleman or noble person.

6 See Helgerson, *Self-Crowned Laureates*, 55–96 (esp. 60–7).

7 Sidney, *An Apology for Poetry; or, The Defense of Poesy*, 114, 104.

8 5 Eliz 1, c. 16. See *Statutes at Large*, 1:806, and chapter 1, n. 41, above.

9 Sidney, *An Apology for Poetry*, 101 (emphasis in the original).

10 Calvin, *Institution of the Christian Religion*, 72.

11 Guillory, *Poetic Authority*, 181, n. 38. Ironically enough, this note appears, like the return of the historical repressed, in the middle of Guillory's attempt to argue that the imagination as generator of fictions (rather than as receiver of inspirations or external notions) actually emerges in the Renaissance, not the Romantic period.

12 Quoted in Fletcher, *Allegory*, 42.

13 Hutchins, *On Specters*, G2v. In a similar voice in *The Discoverie of Witchcraft*, Reginald Scot insists that there is not 'so noble an argument to dispute upon, as this of devils and spirits; for that being confessed or doubted of, the eternity of the soul is either affirmed or denied' (411).

14 Calvin, *Institution*, 67, 72. For the way ideas about angels intersected early modern theological discourses and debates, see Marshall and Walsham, *Angels in the Early Modern World*, in particular Walsham's chapter, 'Angels and Idols in England's Long Reformation,' 134–67.

15 Hooker, *Of the Laws of Ecclesiastical Polity*, 1:72.

16 Although I will discuss the demonology of the imagination in terms of early modern faculty psychology, such a demonology also, of course, had a long history in philosophy and theology. In his *Theory of Imagination in Classical and Medieval Thought*, Murray Wright Bundy locates Plato's *Timaeus* as the origin of the idea that the imagination is the nexus for the subjective and the superlunary, and he traces 'the evolution of the Platonic view that the supernatural may implant phantasms in the phantasy of man' (222) through Augustine, Aquinas, and the medieval mystical tradition. Aquinas, for example, assumes that 'both a good and a bad angel by their own natural power can move the human imagination,' and he provides a syllogistic explanation for this assumption that is, within its own discursive terms, remarkably naturalis-

tic. See *Summa Theologiae*, 1:545 (vol. 1, pt. 1, q. 111, art. 3): on the premises that 'it is manifest that imaginative apparitions are sometimes caused in us by the local movement of animal spirits and humours' and that 'the local movement of bodies is subject to the natural power of the angels,' it follows for Aquinas that angels can move the imagination by affecting the animal spirits and humours.

17 Burton, *The Anatomy of Melancholy*, 173.

18 Reynolds, *A Treatise of the Passions and Faculties*, E2r, p. 27. Reynolds's imagery of demons casting species 'into the Fancie' with such subtlety that they would gain 'admittance' raises the point that the imagination in early modern faculty psychology is by and large a *receptive* faculty, which receives pictures and impressions from the external world rather than from its own 'creative' impulse. Thus in *The Proficience and Advancement of Learning*, Francis Bacon gives the imagination its autonomy not because it can create objects *ex nihilo*, but because it 'may at pleasure join that which nature hath severed, and sever that which nature hath joined, and so make unlawful matches and divorces of things' (see *Francis Bacon*, 186). In this view, feigning, or imagining things that exist nowhere in visible nature, proceeds by piecework, so that one would feign a unicorn, say, by adding a pearly cast to an extended ram's horn and then adding it to the body of a white horse. See also William Rossky, 'Imagination in the English Renaissance.' In recovering much important intellectual history, Rossky aptly observes that the early modern treatment for madness (which faculty psychology understood as the most extreme case of the imagination usurping the governance of the mind) involved putting the sufferer in a dark room, so as to prevent further phantasms from coming in and stimulating the already overactive imagination (52).

19 Wright, *The Passions of the Minde in Generall*, 330. By 'former part of our brain,' Wright means the front chamber of the brain. Faculty psychology divides the brain into three chambers, or compartments, with imagination or phantasy in the front, reason or understanding in the middle, and memory in the rear. Spenser reproduces this scheme in the turret of Alma's castle, where Guyon and Arthur find three rooms occupied by allegorical personifications representing the three mental faculties: Phantastes; an unnamed 'right wise' (2.9.54) middle-aged man; and finally Eumnestes and his assistant Anamnestes.

20 Reynolds, *A Treatise of the Passions and Faculties*, D2r, p. 17.

21 Coffeteau, *A Table of Human Passions*, A6r (emphasis in the original).

22 Bacon, *Francis Bacon*, 217.

23 Coffeteau, *A Table of Human Passions*, A6v.

24 Wright, *A Treatise of the Passions of the Minde*, 51.

25 Coffeteau, *A Table of Human Passions*, A5r.

26 Alpers, *The Poetry of 'The Faerie Queene,'* 288.

27 Fletcher, *Allegory*, 40, 65.

28 In *The Analogy of 'The Faerie Queene,'* James Nohrnberg reads Malbecco as being 'overtaken by his own allegorical other – an 'aery Spright' that is not only Malbecco's jealousy, but his particular evil genius, or demon' (49). In his 'Postures of Allegory,' Kenneth Gross also sees Malbecco as embodying the half-life of the demonic, since his transformation into a personification, in Gross's terms, allows Malbecco to 'accomplish yet put off his own death' by sublating his complex and contingent humanity into a 'fixity' that belongs at once to allegory and to the demon of Jealousy itself (175).

29 In 'Daemon Lovers,' Andrew Escobedo usefully points out that the 'oratorical and neoplatonic traditions ... allow us to think of the daemon as a figure of *either* obsession *or* inspiration' (215, emphasis in the original), and he argues that Spenser deploys these traditions to represent a 'daemonic love' that 'does inspire' Arthur's and Britomart's 'intentions, encouraging them to will' (216).

30 See, e.g., BL Add. MS 36674, art. 4.

31 In '"Secret Powre Unseene,"' Patrick Cheney argues that Spenser presents Merlin's mirror with the simile of the princess Phao emprisoned in a glass tower so that the simile can reveal 'the danger of Merlin's mirror without his accompanying prophecy'; in other words, the simile 'forecasts what would happen to Britomart if she were to misunderstand her vision: like Phao, she would become imprisoned in her own glass world of imaginative desire' (18).

32 Bynum, *Metamorphosis and Identity*, 51.

33 Quoted in Bynum, *Metamorphosis and Identity*, 41.

34 Campbell, *Wonder and Science*, 8.

35 Bynum, *Metamorphosis and Identity*, 69.

36 In book 1, Spenser implicates Christian faith itself in this paradoxical believing disbelief. Describing her instruction of Redcrosse in the House of Holinesse, Spenser represents Fidelia as preaching

> Of God, of grace, of iustice, of free will,
> That wonder was to heare her goodly speach:
> For she was able, with her words to kill,
> And rayse againe to life the hart, that she did thrill. (1.10.19)

Fidelia's speech produces 'wonder' not only because it reveals unearthly truths that humanity's weaker wit cannot grasp without the revelation of faith, but also because the revelation of faith is at once hopeful and frightening. Fidelia's speech 'thrill[s]' – pierces, excites, and terrifies – the sinful heart that may be 'kill[ed]' by law as much as 'rayse[ed] againe to life' by grace. Moreover, as an allegorical figure Fidelia herself provokes wonder, because she is, mysteriously, both the exemplar of Christian belief and an ambiguous figure of doubt. As A.C. Hamilton has noted in his gloss to the poem, Spenser represents Fidelia's spiritual power and Merlin's demonic power in almost identical terms (compare 1.10.20 and 3.3.12). This troubling doubling of the signs of spiritual and demonic power suggests that the reader should doubt the ontology even of the signs of faith itself.

37 Puttenham, *The Art of English Poesy*, 311.
38 For more on wonder in the early modern period, see Daston and Park, *Wonders and the Order of Nature*. See also Daston's 'Marvelous Facts and Miraculous Evidence' and Platt's introduction to *Wonders, Marvels, and Monsters in Early Modern Culture*. For histories of wonder from antiquity to early modernity, see Platt, *Reason Diminished*, chap. 1. For wonder as experienced by early modern colonizers, see Greenblatt, *Marvelous Posessions*. For accounts of modern forms of wonder, see Fisher, *Wonder, the Rainbow, and the Aesthetics of Rare Experiences*, which reads wonder as an aesthetic phenomenon, in *contrast* to fear, which influences the development of modern science, and Fuller, *Wonder: From Emotion to Spirituality*, which discusses wonder as a sensation that leads to compassion and empathy. For a discussion of the way that the devil was thought to use visual wonders to trick the senses, see Clark, *Vanities of the Eye*, chap. 4.
39 Quilligan, 'Reader,' 586.
40 Goldberg, *Endlesse Worke*, 29.
41 Parker, *Inescapable Romance*, 84.
42 Lewis, *Studies in Medieval and Renaissance Literature*, 159.
43 Parker, *Inescapable Romance*, 84.
44 See Roche, *The Kindly Flame*, 82–3.
45 See, e.g., Stephen Gosson's 1579 anti-poetical tract *The School of Abuse*. In 'Busirane's Place' Judith Anderson also glosses Busirane as suggesting poetic abuse, specifically as evoking *abusio*, or catachresis, the figure embodying 'the violent (mis)use of language' (141).
46 Sidney, *An Apology for Poetry*, 125.
47 In *Spenser's Allegory*, Isabel MacCaffrey observes that the tapestries '"entreat" the observer's participation in and assent to [their] pleasures' (108). More recently, in *Transforming Desire* Lauren Silberman has argued that the pun on 'entreat' suggests 'that what might seem straightforward mimesis can be rhetorical manipulation' (59).
48 See Eggert, 'Spenser's Ravishment,' esp. 11–12.
49 I owe this point to Mike Farry.
50 Berger, *Revisionary Play*, 177. Berger further argues that the worship of Cupid in Busirane's castle suggests the perversion of 'sexual desire … conscious-

ly deified by minds locked into a purely erotic universe from which all other functions and all non-erotic concerns have been purged' (177).

51 See chap. 1, n. 14, above. Anderson, in 'Busirane's Place,' also notices Spenser's iconographic allusion to this emblem and its 'identification of rhetoric with spellbound enchainment' (142).

52 Bruno, *Cause*, 130. See chap. 1, p. 23.

53 Eggert, 'Spenser's Ravishment,' 14.

54 See Alpers, *The Poetry of 'The Faerie Queene*,' 15–16.

55 Not coincidentally, this is also the moment in which the horror forced on Amoret by Busirane's art begins to become apparent.

3 Why Devils Came when Faustus Called Them

1 Prynne, *Histrio-mastix*, 556r.

2 Quoted in E.K. Chambers, *The Elizabethan Stage*, 3:424. Chambers cites other rumours of the same kind, such as the incident to which Thomas Middleton referred in his 1604 *Black Book* when he attempted to describe someone's unruly coif: 'He had a head of hair like one of my devils in Dr. Faustus when the old Theater cracked and frightened the audience' (424). Samuel Rowland also liked to say that Edward Alleyn would wear a cross on his surplice when he played Faustus for fear that he might be in the presence of devils. See Roberts, 'Necromantic Books,' 157. These rumours of extra devils appearing on the Faustian stage have long intrigued critics of Renaissance drama. See, e.g., Marcus, *Unediting the Renaissance*, 42; Levin, *The Overreacher*, 121; Goldman, 'Marlowe and the Histrionics of Ravishment,' 40; Halpern, 'Marlowe's Theater of Night,' 472; and Cox, *The Devil and The Sacred in English Drama*, 125. For Halpern the extra devils exemplify Marlowe's ability to transform theatre's internal ontological lack into a generative force.

3 Paul Kocher in 'The Witchcraft Bias in Marlowe's "*Faustus*"' and Barbara Traister in '*Doctor Faustus*: Master of Self-Delusion' have noted that Marlowe used the reformist theory of magic in *Doctor Faustus*, although both critics have elided the reformers' emphasis on the theatrical nature of conjuration and its relevance to the play's dramatic effects. David Hawkes in *The Faust Myth* has noticed the logic of the theology at work in Marlowe's text (see page 58, in particular), but without attributing it to a historical source.

4 All quotations of Marlowe's play are taken from *Doctor Faustus, A- and B-Texts (1604, 1616)*, edited by David Bevington and Eric Rasmussen. Because I am interested in Marlowe's use of Protestant attacks on magic I shall read the A-text of the play, which consistently manifests the theology underlying reformist polemics. For the theologies of the A- and B-texts, see Keefer, 'Verbal

Magic and the Problem of the A and B Texts of *Doctor Faustus*' and Marcus, *Unediting the Renaissance*, chap. 2.

5 See Platz, *Kurtzer, Nottwendiger, unnd Wollgegrundter Bericht* and Hemmingsen, *Admonitio de Superstitionibus Magicis Vitandis*. On Platz, and the German case more broadly, see Scribner, 'The Reformation, Popular Magic, and the '"Disenchantment of the World"' and Clark, 'Protestant Demonology' and *Thinking with Demons*, 435–526.

6 In 1590 and 1591, Gifford wrote two pamphlets arguing against schism, and preached from the established pulpit of St Paul's Cross; he published his longest work on magic, *A Dialogue Concerning Witches and Witchcraftes*, in 1593. In his 1595 *An Exposition of the Symbole or Creed of the Apostles*, Perkins invoked the Thirty-Nine Articles – or, as he called it, 'the Booke of the articles of faith agreed upon in open Parliament' – as expressing what he called the 'true faith' (501). For the scope of Gifford's pamphleteering, see Macfarlane, 'A Tudor Anthropologist,' and Haigh, 'The Taming of the Reformation.' For Perkins as defender of the Elizabethan settlement, see Patterson, 'William Perkins as Apologist for the Church of England.'

7 See also Roberts, *A Treatise of Witchcraft*, and Cooper, *The Mystery of Witchcraft* and *Sathan Transformed into an Angel of Light*. In the interests of concision, I will confine my discussion to the tracts on magic published in England around the time *Doctor Faustus* was first performed.

8 For the narrative of the Protestant pastorate attempting to discredit cunning men and women, see Thomas, *Religion and the Decline of Magic*; Clark, 'Protestant Demonology' and *Thinking with Demons*, 457–71; and McGinnis, '"Subtiltie" Exposed.' For the pastoral reinterpretation of witchcraft as spiritual affliction, see Clark, *Thinking with Demons*, 438–71; Walsham, *Providence in Early Modern England*, esp. 25–8; and Johnstone, *The Devil and Demonism in Early Modern England*, chaps. 3 and 4.

9 Gifford, *A Discourse of the Subtle Practice of Deuilles*, Biiv.

10 Perkins, *A Discourse of the Damned Art of Witchcraft*, 134–5.

11 Holland, *A Treatise Against Witchcraft*, 5, I3r.

12 Perkins, *A Discourse of the Damned Art of Witchcraft*, 137–8.

13 Perkins, *A Golden Chaine*, 127.

14 Calvin, *A Commentarie upon S. Paule's Epistles to the Corinthians*, 226, Ggiiv.

15 Scot, *The Discoverie of Witchcraft*, 234.

16 In the first chapter of *Duessa as Theological Satire*, D. Douglas Waters provides a comprehensive discussion of the Protestant characterization of the Catholic priest as a conjurer.

17 Perkins, *A Discourse of the Damned Art of Witchcraft*, 132.

18 Perkins, *A Discourse of the Damned Art of Witchcraft*, 53–4.

19 Gifford, *A Discourse of the Subtle Practice of Deuilles*, F4v (emphasis added).

20 Perkins, *A Discourse of the Damned Art of Witchcraft*, 151.

21 Burton, *The Anatomy of Melancholy*, 1:205.

22 Holland, *A Treatise Against Witchcraft*, B3v.

23 Perkins, *A Discourse of the Damned Art of Witchcraft*, 'Epis. Ded.,' 2v.

24 For accounts of how God uses Satan in various providential schema, see Russell, *Mephistopheles*, 25–58; Walsham, *Providence*, 8–15; and Johnstone, *The Devil and Demonism*. See also Peter Lake's interesting discussion of early modern representations of diabolical agency in Lake and Questier, *The Antichrist's Lewd Hat*, 40–53.

25 Holland, *A Treatise Against Witchcraft*, G4r (emphasis in the original).

26 'If any such be sorry and begin to show any tokens of true repentance, which either have sought unto or practiced any sorcery ... they must be wisely informed and comforted, for Jesus Christ can and will cast forth an unclean spirit, if in truth of heart with weeping and fasting, and mourning, he be sought unto by repentance.' Holland, *A Short Discourse*, 15, K4r.

27 Perkins, *A Discourse of the Damned Art of Witchcraft*, 'Epis. Ded.,' 5r–v.

28 The fact that Rafe and Robin are able to conjure Mephistopheles from Constantinople, making him 'vexed' with their 'charms' (3.2.32), may seem to contradict the reformist doctrine that the devil articulates here, and indeed the use of magical signs seems always to raise the hope in devils that they might get the souls of those who attempt to conjure. But Mephistopheles does not really perform conjuration for the clowns – he not only declines to feign to enter into their service but even translates them into an ape and a dog – because Rafe and Robin are not really in danger of being damned, having no real desire to commit themselves to the devil.

29 In 'Forme of Faustus' Fortunes Good or Bad,' for instance, C.L. Barber argues that Faustus suffers from the theological condition of despair.

30 In 'Marlowe's *Doctor Faustus* and the Ends of Desire,' Edward Snow argues that Faustus uses the word 'end' in his opening soliloquy to mean not 'an opening upon immanent horizons,' but a 'termination,' so that 'having "attained" [an] end means that he has arrived at the end of it, used it up, finished with it' (54).

31 *On kai me on* is the transliteration of the Greek for 'being and not being.' As Bevington and Rasmussen note, the phrase is not in fact Aristotelian but from Gorgias.

32 As Graham Hammill argues in *Sexuality and Form*, 'When Faustus chooses necromantic books [he] unwittingly chooses signifiers whose materiality mark his desire for a signified as his own ontological insufficiency' (316).

33 Whereas someone like Tamburlaine, for example, almost exclusively uses the third person in the self-aggrandizing style of Julius Caesar, Faustus, although he shares some of Tamburlaine's mighty bombast, uses the third person even, or especially, in his most wretched moments: 'Ah Christ my savior, seek to save / Distressed Faustus's soul' (2.3.82–3).

34 Snow has already marked this in 'Marlowe's *Doctor Faustus* and the Ends of Desire': 'When the possibility of the transmigration of souls is envisioned,' Snow writes, 'the "I" identifies not with the soul ... but with what remains behind when it is gone' (67).

35 Perkins, *A Salve for a Sick Man*, 7. In *Myths of Modern Individualism*, Ian Watt has remarked that in *Doctor Faustus* the soul seems to be 'an invisible but immortal stranger within, God's hostage' (45).

36 The theatrical 'triviality' of Faustus's magic has long since exercised critics of the play. See, e.g., Harry Levin, who in *The Overreacher* descries the 'incongruity between the ... seemingly endless possibilities envisioned by Faustus's speeches and their all too concretely vulgar realization in the stage business' (120–1); and Richard Halpern, who in 'Marlowe's Theater of Night' laments more broadly that the play stages an 'aesthetics of disappointment' (467).

37 For fascinating and deeply strange inquisitorial accounts of sex with devils, see Stephens, *Demon Lovers*, chap. 3.

38 See Nicoll, 'Passing over the Stage.' For details on the layout of the Bell Savage theatre, see Barry, 'The Bell Savage Inn and Playhouse in London.'

39 See especially Levinas's *Otherwise than Being*. For a critique of this ethical basis as eliding the potential for monstrosity or inhumanity in the other, see Žižek, 'Neighbors and Other Monsters.' Žižek refrains from entirely discarding pity as an ethical category; instead, he requires that it be supplemented to counterbalance its excess.

40 See Sidney, *An Apology for Poetry, or The Defense of Poesy*, 35.

41 See Ricoeur, *The Symbolism of Evil*, 212, 323.

42 As Jonathan Dollimore has argued in *Radical Tragedy*, the play implicitly stages the question 'How is evil possible in a world created by an omnipotent God?' (117).

43 Alan Sinfield has made a similar point: see *Faultlines*, 230–7.

44 See Riggs, *The World of Christopher Marlowe*, 30–1. See also the classic study on the construction of atheism in the period, Febvre, *The Problem of Unbelief in the Sixteenth Century*; as well as Wootton, 'New Histories of Atheism.'

45 Reprinted in Kocher, 'Marlowe's Atheist Lecture,' 160. Nicholas Davidson has argued, by contrast, that the opinions attributed to Marlowe in the Bains libel were unexceptional in the period. See his 'Christopher Marlowe and Atheism.'

4 The End of Magic

1 For the classic postcolonial readings of the play, see Barker and Hulme, 'Nymphs and Reapers Heavily Vanish'; Hulme, 'Hurricanes in the Caribbees'; and Skura, 'Discourse and the Individual.' Richard Halpern, Richard Strier, and David Kastan have all recently questioned the utility of the postcolonial paradigm. In 'The Picture of Nobody,' Halpern points out that insofar as Prospero is a colonizer, he is one '*malgré lui,* and he and the other Italians desert their island at the first opportunity' (267). And Strier in 'I am Power,' even as he reads Prospero's 'magical politics' as an allegory for the politics of colonial administration, observes as well that Prospero is not, 'by the English definition, a colonizer at all,' since the *True Declaration of the State of Virginia* (1610) defined colonizers as people who develop new land agriculturally. Finally, after providing a lengthy demonstration of how 'thin is the thread on which the play's relation to the new world hangs,' in '"Duke of Milan,"' Kastan goes on to offer another, very intriguing tenor for the allegory of *The Tempest*: the fact that in 1606 the Holy Roman Emperor, Rudolf II, was stripped of administrative control over the empire by the Habsburg archdukes, who reassigned authority to his brother Matthias, because, as the archdukes themselves proclaimed, 'his majesty is interested only in wizards, alchemists, Kabbalists, and the like, sparing no expense to find all kinds of treasure, learn secrets, and use scandalous ways of harming his enemies' (quoted in '"Duke of Milan,"' 192). (As Kastan acknowledges, Michael Srigley first noticed the similarities between Prospero and Rudolf in his *Images of Regeneration*, 122–31.)

2 Thus in his introduction to his edition of *The Tempest*, Frank Kermode posits that 'like James I in the flattering description, [Prospero] "stands invested with that triplicity which in great veneration was ascribed to the ancient *Hermes*, the power and fortune of a *King*, the knowledge and illumination of a Priest, and the Learning and universality of a Philosopher"' (xlix–l). In '"This Thing of Darkness,"' Paul Brown also sees an analogy not only between Prospero and the colonizer, but between Prospero and James as well, arguing that Prospero uses his magical music 'to charm, punish, and restore his various subjects, employing it like James I in a harmonics of power' (225). The implicit assumption of the equivalence of Prospero's rule and the British monarchy is what enables Barker and Hulme to argue in 'Nymphs and Reapers' that Prospero's rule exposes the discursive strategies of 'European colonial regimes' (239). The same assumption allows Stephen Orgel to argue in the introduction to his edition of the play that 'the philosophical and legal aspects of [Caliban's] claim to the island ... bear not only on the question

of Caliban's rights but even more significantly on the nature and sources of Prospero's – or of any ruler's – authority' (24). And if David Kastan sees a 'damning parallel' between Prospero and Rudolf, in that they both renounce the 'responsibilities of rule' to remain rapt in secret studies, he also views Prospero's renunciation of magic as allowing him to 'escape' the damning parallel with Rudolf and 'achieve a saving one with James' (193).

3 On the monarch's use of torture in Elizabethan and Jacobean England, and on the relation of torture to *The Tempest*, see Curt Breight, '"Treason Never Doth Prosper."' Breight argues that Shakespeare's play demystifies the workings of power by exposing the degree to which the Jacobean sovereign deployed torture as a method of control. But his analysis takes the panopticon for the scaffold: James, at least, never attempted to hide the fact that he used torture, nor did he try to hide its ugliness. James Carmichael's pamphlet *Newes from Scotland*, whose publication James explicitly authorized, goes into lurid detail about the tortures inflicted on Doctor Fian, a captured magician: 'His nails upon all his fingers were riven and pulled off with an instrument called in Scottish a *Turkas*, which in England wee call a pair of pincers, and under every nail there was thrust in two needles over even up to the heads' (27). The sovereign performed his domination in the very spectacle of his right to wrack the bodies of those he designated traitors.

4 And perhaps the debate over whether Prospero is a 'white' or 'black' magician becomes moot. For the traditional arguments that Prospero is a white magician, see Curry, *Shakespeare's Philosophical Patterns*; Kermode, Introduction to *The Tempest*; Sisson, 'The Magic of Prospero'; Yates, *Shakespeare's Last Plays*; Egan, 'This Rough Magic'; and Mebane, *Renaissance Magic and the Return to the Golden Age*. For an account that acknowledges the ambivalence of Prospero's magic, see Mowat, 'Prospero, Agrippa, and Hocus Pocus.' For the crucial point that Prospero's powers are indistinguishable from those of Sycorax, see Orgel, *The Authentic Shakespeare*, 183, and Greenblatt, *Shakespearean Negotiations*, 157. Neither Orgel nor Greenblatt contextualizes his point by citing James's fear of and hatred for magicians.

5 On Hemmingsen, see Clark, 'Protestant Demonology.'

6 In *Cradle King* Alan Stewart, James's latest biographer, cites James's comment that meeting Hemmingsen, along with 'witnessing the Danish churches free of idolatry,' was the highlight of his stay in Denmark (114).

7 James I, *Daemonologie*, xv, 17.

8 Larner, 'James VI and I and Witchcraft,' 79, 81.

9 See Clark, 'King James's *Daemonologie*,' 158; Larner, 'James VI,' 80; and Stewart, *Cradle King*, 124. Oddly enough, Henry IV and VI were also particularly afraid of the purported ability of the magician to conjure life-threatening storms. See Kelly, 'English Kings and the Fear of Sorcery.'

10 Carmichael, *Newes from Scotland*, 15.

11 Perkins, *A Discourse of the Damned Art of Witchcraft*, 'Epis. Ded.,' 2v.

12 For example, displaying full belief in the power of human practitioners of magic, Epistemon, James's mouthpiece in *Daemonologie*, says explicitly that the 'quality' of magical 'forms and effects is less or greater, according to the skill and art of the Magician' (19). James also affords magical signs full efficacy: he warns that if the magician's 'feet once slide over the circle though terror of his fearful apparition, [the devil] pays himself at that time in his own hand, of that due debt which they ought [sic] him, and otherwise would have delayed longer to have paid him : I mean he carries them with him body and soul' (18).

13 As Larner puts it in 'James VI,' James 'was the Lord's Anointed; therefore he was the greatest enemy in Scotland the devil could have' (83).

14 Clark, 'King James's *Daemonologie*,' 166.

15 Orgel, *The Illusion of Power*, 8. In *James I and the Politics of Literature*, Jonathan Goldberg calls the masque 'the form that mirrors the royal mind' (55). This form consistently enacted magical reversals: as Enid Welsford pointed out long ago in her *Court Masque*, the usual occasion for the 'discovery' of the masquers at the end of the entertainment was that 'the masquers had been hidden as a result of adverse spells, and had been freed from enchantment by the beneficent power of the sovereign' (339).

16 Jonson, 'Mercury Vindicated,' 190–3, quoted in Orgel, *The Illusion of Power*, 54.

17 Quoted in Welsford, *Court Masque*, 175.

18 For a series of revisionary readings showing that Jacobean court masques were not merely contests over the power of the sovereign, but also venues for complicated negotiations of policy, see Bevington and Holbrook, eds., *The Politics of the Stuart Court Masque*.

19 In *Religion and the Decline of Magic*, Keith Thomas recounts a case brought to trial in 1620 in which a schoolmaster named Peacock was examined and tortured for practising magic in order to, as Thomas puts it, 'infatuate James I's judgment' (288).

20 I might note here that the Habsburg archdukes who stripped Rudolf II of authority for being 'interested only in wizards, alchemists, Kabbalists, and the like, [and for] sparing no expense to find all kinds of treasure, learn secrets, and use scandalous ways of harming his enemies' were in part accusing him of attempting to practise espionage through magic.

21 It may also be an idea that James either invented or imported into England himself, since, to the best of my knowledge, it appears in no English text on magic written before *Daemonologie*, although it seems to have become commonplace by the time of Jonson's 1616 *The Devil is an Ass*, in which the devil

gives the demon Pug the body of a newly hanged cutpurse to wear during his day in London.

22 James took his duty seriously. In 1591, for example, James heard from a woman accused of witchcraft that one Francis, earl of Bothwell, had hired a coven of witches to curse the king with a spell to waste his body. In response to this news, James imprisoned Bothwell in Edinburgh Castle, after which other accusers came forward to claim that Bothwell had hired a magician to prognosticate the date of the King's death. Throughout this surge of rumour Bothwell maintained his innocence, even challenging his accusers to settle the matter in hand-to-hand combat which would, he claimed, prove that God was on his side. Before the matter could come to this ancient form of resolution, however, Bothwell escaped from the castle. Three days later the Privy Council issued a proclamation calling for Bothwell's death, saying that the earl had 'had consultation with necromancers, witches, and other wicked and ungodly persons' and had given himself 'over altogether in[to] the hands of Satan, heaping treason upon treason against God, his Majesty, and this his native country' (quoted in Stewart, *Cradle King*, 126).

23 James I, *Basilikon Doron*, 22, 23.

24 James I, *Daemonologie*, 26.

25 1 Jac. 1, c. 12, *Statutes at Large*, 2:966.

26 James I, introduction to *Daemonologie*, vii.

27 For an interesting account of the Overbury scandal and the pamphleteering that sustained it in the public's imagination, see Bellany, *The Politics of Court Scandal*.

28 Shakespeare, *The Tempest*, 5.1.49, 50.

29 James I, *Daemonologie*, 34. It should be noted that in *Daemonologie* James never allowed his reader to assume that this curiosity was either morally or theologically neutral. Magicians are, James claimed, 'so allured thereby, that finding their practice to prove true in sundry things, they study to know the cause thereof: and so mounting from degree to degree, upon the slippery and uncertain scale of curiosity, they are at last enticed, that where lawful arts or sciences fail, to satisfy their restless minds, even to seek to that black and un-lawful science of *Magic*' (10, emphasis in the original).

30 Kott, *Shakespeare, Our Contemporary*, 257.

31 On Prospero as Bolingbroke, see Willis, 'Shakespeare's *Tempest*,' 265.

32 As Deborah Willis points out in 'Shakespeare's *Tempest*,' Prospero can 'in-duce repentance in Alonso by making use of Alonso's feelings for his son Ferdinand; we cannot imagine Antonio capable of feeling any tie intensely enough to make him responsive to such a maneuver' (262).

33 It actually also makes dramatic sense that none of the other characters refer to him either: filial loss is represented as more personal than political in

the play, and Antonio's son has no other role in the drama except that of the (non) figure for Antonio's inability to feel such loss. He has no public role, not being in line for the Duchy of Milan. (Alonso calls Ferdinand 'mine heir / Of Naples and Milan' [2.1.110], which makes it clear that Antonio's progeny was, for whatever reason, never in line to inherit the duchy to begin with.)

34 Orgel, introduction to *The Tempest*, 24.

35 It may be well to note here that although Ariel would rather be free from obligation to Prospero, having submitted to command only because Prospero threatens him with a worse confinement than his twelve-year service, he also appears to take so much pleasure in acting as Prospero's instrument that his labors seem less like the drudgery of a servant and more like the spontaneous play of the totally unalienated producer. Strier, who notes in '"I am Power"' that Prospero loves Ariel as 'the perfect instrument' (152), and Berger, who in *Second World and Green World* calls Ariel 'a self-delighting spirit whose art and magic are forms of pure play' (152), are thus both right in their claims.

36 Indeed, *The Tempest* makes it clear that psychological control alone – even in the form of pleasure – is not transformative; those in power must also control the movements of bodies in order to enforce their disciplinary regime. (In 'I am Power,' Strier makes an excellent point in this regard: 'Shakespeare recognized that magic … was the Renaissance name for what we would now think of as the Foucauldian "power-knowledge"; but Shakespeare was explicit, as Michel Foucault is not, that the ultimate meaning of power is physical coercion' [25]). Yet it is also important, I think, that Antonio and Sebastian are the characters in the play who express contempt for the idea of Amphion's harp: the play connects their dismissal of the idea that beauty may transform the subject to their willingness to murder for their own gain.

37 Berger, *Second World and Green World*, 166.

38 Ibid., 174.

39 As Jeffrey Knapp has argued in *An Empire Nowhere*, in 'disrupting the masque and expatiating on his mortality, [Prospero] not only figures such art as distracting him from the real bodily properties of his spirit – a "brain," for instance, that has grown "old" [4.1.159] – but also exchanges the false purity of spiritual enactments for a performances in which "vex'd" [4.1.158] humans like himself take part' (230–1).

40 See Mowat, 'Prospero's Book.'

Epilogue

1 [The poem thus becomes instructive in two ways: first, it allows desire to find a language that expresses it … but at the same time, it teaches desire its limits

... In my opinion, it is this very double vocation that distinguishes the poem from the charm.]

2 Sidney, *An Apology for Poetry*, 125.

3 Spenser, *The Faerie Queen*, 3.12.31.

4 Burton, *The Anatomy of Melancholy*, 1:205.

5 Shakespeare, *The Tempest*, 3.3.88.

6 See the *OED*, *charm* n. 1. When in 1735 the Crown and Parliament repealed the Jacobean Act against magic, the new law did not even cite 'charming' as a crime. The seventeenth-century statute had mandated execution without benefit of clergy for anyone who used or practised 'witchcraft, enchantment, charm, or sorcery' (Ruffhead, *Statutes at Large*, 2:966), but the new act proclaimed 'that no Prosecution, Suit or Proceeding, shall be commenced or carried on against any Person or Persons for Witchcraft, Sorcery, Enchantment or Conjuration ... in any Court whatsoever in *Great Britain*' (Ruffhead, *Statutes at Large*, 6:206). In the text of the law, 'charm' as a magical practice, not to mention a capital felony, simply disappeared. If the word 'enchantment' still invoked the memory of spell casting or invocation, 'charm' no longer signified something literally magical.

7 See, e.g., the Earl of Shaftesbury, *Characteristicks of Men*, in which he discusses how the objects of 'Reason's Culture ... attract and charm' the virtuous mind that seeks to 'contend for Beauty' (2:425); and Frances Hutcheson, *An Inquiry into the Original of our Ideas of Beauty and Virtue*, where he considers 'how Men are charm'd with the Beauty of [scientific] Knowledge ... and how this sets them upon deducing the Properties of each Figure from one Genesis' (34–5). In *A Philosophical Enquiry into the Origin of our Ideas of the Sublime and Beautiful*, Edmund Burke strongly implies that beauty functions as a charm, calling it 'a quality in bodies acting mechanically upon the human mind by the intervention of the senses' (210). Burke also explicitly characterizes the aesthetic experience of reading poetry as that of being charmed. Attempting to account for differences in literary taste, he points out 'that one man is charmed with Don Bellianis, and reads Virgil coldly; whilst another is transported with the Aeneid, and leaves Don Bellianis to children' (20). In *Four Dissertations*, Hume likewise associates the aesthetic pleasure of reading poetry with the sensation of being charmed: Ariosto, Hume claims, 'charms by the force and clearness of his expressions [and] the readiness and variety of his inventions' (211). Hume connects this charm in poetry to the exercise of moral sentiments: 'A generous and noble character affords a satisfaction even in the survey,' he argues, 'and when presented to us, though only in a poem or fable, never fails to charm and delight us' (139). On aesthetics and moral sentimentality in Shaftesbury and Hutcheson, among others, see Guyer, 'Beauty and Utility in Eighteenth-Century Aesthetics.'

8 Kant, *The Critique of Judgment*, 69, Ak. 223. I am providing references to both page and *Akademie* edition line numbers. According to the Grimm and Grimm *Deutsches Wörterbuch*, *der Reiz* ('charm') entered the German in the early eighteenth century as a derivation from the earlier composite *der Anreiz*. *Anreiz* translates as 'conjuration' or 'instigation or incitement in a magical sense' (i.e., 'by means of conjuring devils') [*durch anreiz des teufels*] (1:426). *Reiz* itself first signifies 'charm' with respect to femininity, as 'an enticement with the admixture of sexual or sensual elements' [*erregungen mit beimischung eines geschlechtlich–sinnlichen elementes*], or as 'the sensually exciting effect of feminine beauty and grace' [*der sinnlich erregenden wirkung weiblicher schönheit und anmuth*]. Later it denotes the quality that produces attraction via sensual pleasure more broadly: 'without the sexual element, the pleasurable excitement that one experiences through sensation, as in the charm of nature' [*ohne das geschlechtliche element von wohlgefälliger erregung durch sinneseindruck: die reize der natur*] (8:792). In contemporary German, *der Reiz* has kept its magical connotation: while primarily defining the word as 'charm, attraction, attractiveness, appeal,' *Cassell's German-English Dictionary* also offers *Reiz* as a figurative translation for the English 'spell.' I am grateful to Damion Searls for help with these translations.

9 I might note here that if any early modern poet anticipated Kant's rejection of charm, it was most certainly Milton. In his *A Mask Presented at Ludlow Castle*, Milton clearly distinguishes between affective and intellectual responses to poetry, representing the former, mired in 'gums of glutinous heat' (line 917) as existing outside the subject's control, and the latter as arising from a self-determined freedom that transcends material determinations. ('Thou canst not touch the freedom of my mind / With all thy charms,' the Lady insists to Comus, 'although this corporal rind / Thou hast immanacl'd, while Heav'n sees good' [663–5].) The way the subject chooses to 'taste,' Milton suggests, directly correlates with her degree of autonomy. Moreover, although it conflates poetry and magic (the Lady accuses her enchanter of seeking 'to charm [her] judgment' as he does 'her eyes' with his *carpe diem* verse as much as his spells [758]), *A Mask* in fact rejects the Renaissance tradition of instrumental aesthetics that it seems to engage. Instrumental aesthetics were meant to transform the dispositions of readers and audiences by giving them aesthetic pleasure, and the further purpose of these aesthetics was to augment the cultural value of poetry and theatre. But Milton's *Mask* does not seek to augment the cultural power of literature in this way; rather, it valorizes the power of the 'upright heart and pure' to maintain its commitment to the virtues of deferred gratification, evaluative judgment, and intellectual autonomy in the face of worldly (and otherworldly) charms. And insofar as the Lady appears as an ideal Christian subject who proves her chastity in her confrontation

with Comus, she serves only problematically as an example conveyed by aesthetic pleasure to the reader, for her very renunciation of pleasure grounds her virtue and wins her divine protection. It is as if the Lady triumphs in spite of, not thanks to, the literary form that represents her.

10 It should be immediately clarified that interest is not always bad in Kant: insofar as our reason directs our desire to produce or maintain the existence of the good, the good will be an object of our interest. Thus 'the good always contains the content of a purpose, consequently a relation of reason to volition ... and hence a liking for the existence of an object or action. In other words, it contains some interest or another' (49, Ak. 207). But for Kant there is a crucial difference between the interest we take in the good and that which we take in the agreeable: the former is presented to our desires 'under principles of reason' (49, Ak. 207), which exist in the transcendental realm of freedom, and not 'under principles of sense' (49, Ak. 207), which emerge in the corporeal and historical domains.

11 As Henry Allison has argued in *Kant's Theory of Taste*, Kant's 'fateful shift to a new notion of form, one which supposedly functions as the sole determinant of aesthetic worth' occurs precisely at the moment in the third *Critique* when Kant 'defines a pure judgment of taste negatively as one that is not influenced by charm' (133).

12 Kant defines 'purposiveness' technically as 'the causality that a *concept* has with regard to its *object* (*forma finalis*) [final form]' (65, Ak. 220, emphasis in the original).

13 When we engage in this contemplation, we think about the 'presentation' (*Vorstellen*) of the object's purposiveness to the mind. 'Purposiveness,' Kant clarifies, is 'not a characteristic of the object' (29, Ak. 189); rather, it is found 'in the presentation by which an object is *given* us' (66, Ak. 211, emphasis in the original). ('Presentations' are ideational objects or, as Werner Pluhar puts it, 'objects of our direct awareness,' such as 'sensations, intuitions, perceptions, concepts, cognitions, ideas, and schemata' [44, n. 4].) On the cognitive basis of aesthetic judgment (and its resultant universal communicability), see Ginsborg, 'Reflective Judgment and Taste,' esp. 70–5.

14 Kant suggests as much in a footnote striking for its autobiographical candour: 'I must confess that a beautiful poem has always given me pure delight [*Vergnügen*], whereas reading the best speech of a Roman public orator, or of a contemporary parliamentary speaker or preacher, has always been mingled with the disagreeable feeling of disapproval of an insidious art, an art that knows how, in important matters, to move people like machines to a judgment' (198, n. 63). In this regard, see Jacques Derrida, 'Economimesis,' 17: 'The poet and the orator meet one another and exchange their masks, masks

of an *as if*. Both pretend, but the *as if* of one is more and better than the *as if* of the other. In the service of truth, of loyalty, of sincerity, of productive freedom is the *as if* of the poet ... the orator's *as if* deceives and machinates. It is precisely a machine or rather a "deceitful art" which manipulates men "like machines."'

15 In his *Ideology of the Aesthetic*, Terry Eagleton has described this laborious resolve as the will's 'resolute orientation to [an] organic totality of ends and to the requirement of their harmonious unity,' an orientation which ideally enables the subject to move 'in a sphere where all instrumental adaptation of means to ends has been transmuted into purposive or expressive activity,' producing by 'this reconciliation of ends and means in the kingdom of Reason ... the construction of a noumenal community of free subjects, a realm of norms and persons rather than of objects and desires' (81–2). In other words, the ending end of Kant's instrumental aesthetics is to produce a community in which instrumentality may be eschewed entirely.

Bibliography

Primary Sources

BL Additional MS 36674
BL Lansdowne MS 19
BL Lansdowne MS 103
BL Sloane MS 3824

Agrippa, Henry Cornelius. *Of the Vanitie and Uncertaintie of Artes and Sciences.* Trans. James Sandford. London, 1569.
– *Three Books of Occult Philosophy.* Trans. J.F. London, 1651.
Alciati, Andrea. *Emblemata.* Augsburg, 1531.
Aquinas, Saint Thomas. *Summa Theologiae.* Trans. Fathers of the English Dominican Province. 3 vols. New York: Benziger Bros., 1947–8.
Aristotle. *The Complete Works of Aristotle.* Ed. Jonathan Barnes. Bollingen Series 71. 2 vols. Princeton: Princeton University Press, 1984.
Bacon, Francis. *Francis Bacon.* Ed. Brian Vickers. Oxford: Oxford University Press, 1996.
Bacon, Roger. *The Mirror of Alchimy ... Also a Most Excellent and Learned Discourse of the Admirable Force and Efficacie of Art and Nature.* London, 1597.
Bruno, Giordano. *The Ash Wednesday Supper.* Ed. and trans. Stanley Jaki. The Hague: Mouton, 1975.
– *Cause, Principle and Unity: And Essays on Magic.* Ed. and trans. Richard Blackwell. *Cambridge Texts in the History of Philosophy.* Cambridge: Cambridge University Press, 1998.
– *The Heroic Frenzies.* Trans. Paul Memmo. Chapel Hill: University of North Carolina Press, 1965.
Burke, Edmund. *A Philosophical Enquiry into the Origin of our Ideas of the Sub-*

lime and Beautiful. The Second Edition. With an Introductory Discourse Concerning Taste, and Several Other Additions. London, 1759.

Burton, Robert. *The Anatomy of Melancholy.* Ed. Holbrook Jackson. 4 vols. New York: New York Review Books, 2001.

Calvin, Jean. *A Commentarie vpon S. Paules Epistles to the Corinthians.* Trans. Thomas Tymme. London, 1577.

– *Institution of the Christian Religion.* Trans. Thomas Norton. London, 1611.

Carmichael, James. *Newes from Scotland, Declaring the Damnable Life and Death of Doctor Fian a Notable Sorcerer.* Ed. G.B. Harrison. London: John Lane, 1924.

Coffeteau, Nicholas. *A Table of Human Passions, With their Causes and Effects.* Trans. E. Grimeston. London, 1630.

Coleridge, Samuel Taylor. *Biographia Literaria.* Ed. James Engell and Jackson Bate. Bollingen Series 75. Princeton: Princeton University Press, 1983.

Cooper, Thomas. *The Mystery of Witchcraft.* London, 1617.

– *Sathan Transformed into an Angel of Light ... Emplified [sic] Specially in the Doctrine of Witchcraft.* London, 1622.

Cotta, John. *The Triall of Witchcraft.* London, 1616.

Coxe, Francis. *A Short Treatise Declaringe the Detestable Wickednesse of Magicall Sciences.* London, 1561.

Dering, Edward. *A Briefe and Necessary Catachiseme or Instruction.* London, 1572.

Ficino, Marsilio. *Marsilio Ficino's Commentary on Plato's 'Symposium.'* Trans. Sears Jayne. Columbia: University of Missouri Press, 1944.

– 'Platonic Theology.' Trans. Josephine Burroughs. *Journal of the History of Ideas* 5, no. 2 (April 1944): 227–42.

Foxe, John. *The Seconde Volume of the Ecclesiastical Historie, Conteining the Acts and Monuments of Martyrs.* London, 1583.

Gifford, George. *A Dialogue Concerning Witches and Witchcraftes.* London, 1593.

– *A Discourse of the Subtle Practice of Deuilles by Witches and Sorcerers.* London, 1587.

Gosson, Stephen. *The School of Abuse.* London, 1579.

Grimm, Jacob, and Wilhelm Grimm. *Deutsches Wörterbuch.* 1785–1863. Reprint, Leipzig: S. Hirzel, 1971.

Harsnett, Samuel. *A Declaration of Egregious Popish Impostures to Withdraw the Harts of her Maiesties Subiects from their Allegeance, and from the Truth of Christian Religion Professed in England, vnder the Pretence of Casting out Deuils.* London, 1603.

Hemmingsen, Niels. *Admonitio de Superstitionibus Magicis Vitandis.* Copenhagen, 1575.

Hocus Pocus Junior. *The Anatomie of Legerdemaine, or the Arte of Juggling.* London, 1634.

Holland, Henry. *A Treatise Against Witchcraft; [and] A Short Discourse Shewing the Most Certain and Principal Means Ordeined of God to Discover, Expell, and to Confound all the Sathanicall Inventions of Witchcraft and Sorcierie.* London, 1590.

Hooker, Richard. *Of the Laws of Ecclesiastical Polity. The Folger Library Edition of the Works of Richard Hooker,* ed. Georges Edelen et al. 7 vols. Cambridge, MA: Belknap Press of Harvard University Press, 1977–82.

Horace. *Satires, Epistles, Ars Poetica.* Trans. H. Rushton Fairclough. Loeb Classical Library 194. Cambridge, MA: Harvard University Press, 1926.

Hume, David. *Four Dissertations: I. the Natural History of Religion; II. Of the Passions; III. Of Tragedy; IV. Of the Standard of Taste.* London, 1757.

Hutcheson, Frances. *An Inquiry into the Original of our Ideas of Beauty and Virtue; in Two Treatises ... the Second Edition, Corrected and Enlarg'd.* London, 1726.

Hutchins, Randall. *On Specters.* London, 1593.

James I, of England. *Basilikon Doron.* 1603. In *Political Writings: King James VI and I,* ed. Johann P. Sommerville, 1–61. Cambridge: Cambridge University Press, 1994.

– *Daemonologie.* 1597. Ed. G.B. Harrison. London: John Lane, 1924.

Jonson, Ben. *Ben Jonson.* Ed. C.H. Herford and Percy Simpson. 11 vols. Oxford: Clarendon Press, 1925–63.

Kant, Immanuel. *Critique of Judgment.* Trans. Werner S. Pluhar. Indianapolis: Hackett, 1987.

Lhuid, Humfrey. *Britanniae Descriptionis Fragmentum.* Cologne, 1572.

Marlowe, Christopher. *Doctor Faustus, A- and B-Texts (1604, 1616).* Ed. David Bevington and Eric Rasmussen. Manchester: Manchester University Press, 1993.

Mason, James. *The Anatomie of Sorcerie.* Cambridge, 1612.

Milton, John. *A Mask Presented at Ludlow Castle (Comus).* In *Complete Poems and Major Prose,* ed. Merritt Y. Hughes, 86–113. 1957. Reprint, Indianapolis: Hackett, 2003.

Montaigne, Michel de. *Essays.* Trans. John Florio. 2 vols. London: J.M. Dent and Sons, 1938.

Nash (Nashe), Thomas. *Pierce Pennilesse his Supplication to the Diuell.* London, 1592.

Perkins, William. *The Combat between Christ and the Devil Displayed.* London, 1606.

– *A Discourse of the Damned Art of Witchcraft.* London, 1608.

– *An Exposition of the Symbole or Creed of the Apostles.* Cambridge, 1595.
– *A Golden Chaine, or The Description of Theology* (1591). Trans. R.H. Cambridge, 1597.
– *A Salve for a Sicke Man.* Cambridge, 1595.
Plato. *Complete Works.* Ed. John Cooper. Indianapolis: Hackett, 1997.
Platz, Conrad. *Kurtzer, Nottwendiger, und Wollgegrundter Bericht.* n.p., 1565.
Plotinus. *Enneads.* Trans. Stephen Mackenna. 3rd ed. London: Faber and Faber, 1962.
Proclus. *Elements of Theology.* Ed. and trans. E.R. Dodds. 2nd ed. Oxford: Clarendon, 1977.
Prynne, William. *Histriomastix: The Player's Scourge, Or Actor's Tragedy.* London, 1633.
Pseudo-Dionysius Areopagita. *The Divine Names and Mystical Theology.* Trans. John D. Jones. Milwaukee: Marquette University Press, 1980.
Puttenham, George. *The Art of English Poesy: A Critical Edition.* Ed. Frank Whigham and Wayne A. Rebhorn. Ithaca, NY: Cornell University Press, 2007.
Ralegh, Sir Walter. *The History of the World in Five Books.* 6 vols. Edinburgh, 1820.
Reynolds, Edward. *A Treatise of the Passions and Faculties of the Soule of Man.* London, 1650.
Roberts, Alexander. *A Treatise of Witchcraft.* London, 1616.
Ruffhead, Owen. *The Statutes at Large; from Magna Charta, to the End of the Last Parliament, 1761.* 8 vols. London, 1763–4.
Scaliger, Julius Caesar. *Poetices Libri Septem.* 5th ed. Heidelberg, 1617.
Scot, Reginald. *The Discoverie of Witchcraft.* Ed. Montague Summers. London: J. Rodker, 1930.
Shaftesbury, Anthony Ashley Cooper, Earl of. *Characteristicks of Men, Manners, Opinions, Times. In Three Volumes. The Second Edition Corrected.* London, 1714.
Shakespeare, William. *The Riverside Shakespeare.* Ed. G. Blakemore Evans. 2nd ed. New York: Houghton Mifflin, 1997.
– *The Tempest.* Ed. Stephen Orgel. *The Oxford Shakespeare.* Oxford: Oxford University Press, 1987.
Sidney, Sir Philip. *An Apology for Poetry, or The Defense of Poesy.* Ed. Geoffrey Shepherd. London: Thomas Nelson, 1965.
– *The Correspondence of Sir Philip Sidney and Hubert Languet.* Trans. Stuart A. Pears. London, 1845.
– *The Prose Works of Sir Philip Sidney.* Ed. Albert Feuillerat. 4 vols. Cambridge: Cambridge University Press, 1962.

Spenser, Edmund. *The Faerie Queene*. Ed. A.C. Hamilton. 2nd ed. London: Longman, 2001.

Statutes at Large, The … from Magna Charta, to the End of the Session of Parliament, March 14. 1704. 4 vols. London, 1706.

Willet, Andrew. *Hexapla in Danielem: that is, A Six-fold Commentaire Upon the Most Divine Prophesie of Daniel*. London, 1610.

Woodes, Nathaniel. *An Excellent New Commedie Intitutled, the Conflict of Conscience*. London, 1581.

Wright, Thomas. *The Passions of the Minde in Generall. In Six Bookes*. London, 1630.

Secondary Sources

Abrams, M.H. *The Mirror and the Lamp*. Oxford: Oxford University Press, 1953.

Adorno, Theodor. *Aesthetic Theory*. Ed. and trans. Robert Hullot-Kentor. Theory and History of Literature 88. Minneapolis: University of Minnesota Press, 1997.

Allison, Henry. *Kant's Theory of Taste: A Reading of the 'Critique of Aesthetic Judgment.'* Cambridge: Cambridge University Press, 2001.

Alpers, Paul. *The Poetry of 'The Faerie Queene.'* Princeton: Princeton University Press, 1967.

Anderson, Judith. 'Busirane's Place: The House of Rhetoric.' *Spenser Studies* 17 (2003): 133–50.

Barber, C.L. 'The Forme of Faustus' Fortunes Good or Bad.' In *Creating Elizabethan Tragedy: The Theater of Marlowe and Kyd*, ed. Richard Wheeler, 87–130. Chicago: University of Chicago Press, 1988.

Barish, Jonas. *The Antitheatrical Prejudice*. Berkeley: University of California Press, 1981.

Barker, Francis, and Peter Hulme, 'Nymphs and Reapers Heavily Vanish: The Discursive Con-texts of *The Tempest*.' In *Case Studies in Critical Controversy: 'The Tempest,'* ed. Gerald Graff and James Phelan, 229–45. Boston: Bedford/St Martin, 2000.

Barnes, Catherine. 'The Hidden Persuader: The Complex Speaking Voice of Sidney's *Defence of Poetry*.' *PMLA* 86 (May 1971): 422–7.

Barry, Herbert. 'The Bell Savage Inn and Playhouse in London.' *Medieval and Renaissance Drama in England* 19 (2006): 121–43.

Bassnett, Susan. 'Absent Presences: Edward Kelly's Family in the Writings of John Dee.' In *John Dee: Interdisciplinary Studies in English Renaissance Thought*, ed. Stephen Clucas, 285–94. Dordrecht, the Netherlands: Springer, 2006.

Bellany, Alastair. *The Politics of Court Scandal in Early Modern England: News Culture and the Overbury Affair, 1603–1660*. Cambridge: Cambridge University Press, 2002.

Berger, Harry, Jr. 'Archimago: Between Text and Countertext,' *Studies in English Literature 1500–1900* 43, no. 1 (Winter, 2003): 19–64.

– *Revisionary Play: Studies in the Spenserian Dynamics*. Berkeley: University of California Press, 1988.

– *Second World and Green World: Studies in Renaissance Fiction-making*. Berkeley: University of California Press, 1988.

– 'Second-World Prosthetics: Supplying Deficiencies of Nature in Renaissance Italy.' In *Early Modern Visual Culture: Representation, Race, and Empire in Renaissance England*, ed. Peter Erickson and Clark Hulse, 98–147. Philadelphia: University of Pennsylvania Press, 2000.

Bevington, David, and Peter Holbrook, eds. *The Politics of the Stuart Court Masque*. Cambridge: Cambridge University Press, 1998.

Blackburn, William. 'Spenser's Merlin.' *Renaissance and Reformation* 4 (1980): 179–98.

Bourdieu, Pierre. 'Le couturier et sa griffe: Contribution à une théorie de la magie.' *Actes de la Recherche en Sciences Sociales* 1 (1975): 7–36.

– *The Rules of Art: Genesis and Structure of the Literary Field*. Stanford: Stanford University Press, 1996.

Breight, Curt. '"Treason Doth Never Prosper": *The Tempest* and the Discourse of Treason.' *Shakespeare Quarterly* 41 (1990): 1–28.

Brooks, Cleanth. 'The Heresy of Paraphrase.' In *The Norton Anthology of Theory and Criticism*, ed. Vincent B. Leitch et al., 1353–65. New York: Norton, 2001.

Brown, Paul. '"This Thing of Darkness I Acknowledge Mine": *The Tempest* and the Discourse of Colonialism.' In *Case Studies in Critical Controversy: 'The Tempest,'* ed. Gerald Graff and James Phelan, 205–28. Boston: Bedford/St Martin, 2000.

Bundy, Murray Wright. *The Theory of Imagination in Classical and Medieval Thought*. University of Illinois Studies in Language and Literature, 12, no. 2. Urbana: University of Illinois Press, 1927.

Burke, Kenneth. *A Rhetoric of Motives*. Berkeley: University of California Press, 1969.

Butterworth, Philip. *Magic on the Early English Stage*. Cambridge: Cambridge University Press, 2005.

Bynum, Caroline Walker. *Metamorphosis and Identity*. New York: Zone Books, 2001.

Campbell, Mary Baine. *Wonder and Science: Imagining Worlds in Early Modern Europe*. Ithaca: Cornell University Press, 1999.

Chambers, E.K. *The Elizabethan Stage*. 4 vols. Oxford: Oxford University Press, 1923.

Cheney, Patrick Gerard. '"Secret Powre Unseene": Good Magic in Spenser's Legend of Britomart.' *Studies in Philology* 85, no. 1 (Winter, 1988): 1–28.

Clark, Stuart. 'King James's *Daemonologie*: Witchcraft and Kingship.' In *The Damned Art: Essays in the Literature of Witchcraft*, ed. Sydney Anglo, 156–81. London: Routledge, 1977.

– 'Protestant Demonology: Sin, Superstition, Society (c. 1520 – c. 1630).' In *Early Modern European Withcraft*, ed. Bengt Ankarloo and Gustav Henningsen, 45–81. Oxford: Oxford University Press, 1990.

– *Thinking with Demons*. Oxford: Oxford University Press, 1997.

– *Vanities of the Eye: Vision in Early Modern European Culture*. Oxford: Oxford University Press, 2007.

Clucas, Stephen. 'John Dee's Angelic Conversations and the *Ars Notoria*: Renaissance Magic and Mediaeval Theurgy.' *International Archives of the History of Ideas* 193 (2006): 231–74.

Clulee, Nicholas. *John Dee's Natural Philosophy: Between Science and Religion*. London: Routledge, 1988.

Copenhaver, Brian P. 'Natural Magic, Hermeticism, and Occultism in Early Modern Science.' In *Reappraisals of the Scientific Revolution*, ed. David C. Linberg and Robert S Westman, 51– 72. Cambridge: Cambridge University Press, 1990.

Couliano, Ioan. *Eros and Magic in the Renaissance*. Chicago: University of Chicago Press, 1987.

Cox, John. *The Devil and the Sacred in English Drama*. Cambridge: Cambridge University Press, 2000.

Curry, Walter Clyde. *Shakespeare's Philosophical Patterns*. Baton Rouge: Louisiana State University Press, 1937.

Daston, Lorraine. 'Marvelous Facts and Miraculous Evidence in Early Modern Europe.' In *Wonders, Marvels, and Monsters in Early Modern Culture*, ed. Peter Platt, 76–104. Cranbury: Associated University Presses, 1999.

Daston, Lorraine, and Katherine Park. *Wonders and the Order of Nature, 1150–1750*. New York: Zone Books, 1998.

Davidson, Nicholas. 'Christopher Marlowe and Atheism.' In *Christopher Marlowe and English Renaissance Culture*, ed. Darryll Grantley and Peter Roberts, 129–47. London: Scolar Press, 1996.

Derrida, Jacques. *Dissemination*. Trans. Barbara Johnson. Chicago: University of Chicago Press, 1981.

– 'Economimesis.' *Diacritics: The Ghost of Theology; Readings of Kant and Hegel* 11, no. 2 (Summer 1981): 3–25.

Devereux, James. 'The Meaning of Delight in Sidney's *Defence of Poesy*.' *Studies in the Literary Imagination* 15, no. 1 (1982): 85–97.

Dollimore, Jonathan. *Radical Tragedy: Religion, Ideology, and Power in the Drama of Shakespeare and His Contemporaries*. 3rd ed. Durham: Duke University Press, 2004.

Eagleton, Terry. *The Ideology of the Aesthetic*. Oxford: Blackwell, 1990.

Egan, Robert. '"This Rough Magic": Perspectives of Art and Morality in *The Tempest*.' *Shakespeare Quarterly* 23 (1972): 171–82.

Eggert, Katherine. 'Spenser's Ravishment: Rape and Rapture in *The Faerie Queene*.' *Representations* 70 (Spring 2000): 1–26.

Ellrodt, Robert. *Neoplatonism in the Poetry of Spenser*. Geneva: E. Droz, 1960.

Erikson, Wayne. 'Spenser's "Letter to Ralegh" and the Literary Politics of *The Faerie Queene*'s 1590 Publication.' *Spenser Studies* 10 (1992): 139–74.

Escobedo, Andrew. "Daemon Lovers: Will, Personification, and Character." *Spenser Studies* 22 (2007): 203–25.

Febvre, Lucien. *The Problem of Unbelief in the Sixteenth Century: The Religion of Rabelais*. Trans. Beatrice Gottlieb. Cambridge, MA: Harvard University Press, 1982.

Feingold, Mordechai. 'Giordano Bruno in England, Revisited.' *The Huntington Library Quarterly* 67.3 (2004): 329–46.

– 'The Occult Tradition in the English Universities of the Renaissance: A Reassessment.' In *Occult and Scientific Mentalities in the Renaissance*, ed. Brian Vickers, 64–79. Cambridge: Cambridge University Press, 1984.

Fell-Smith, Charlotte. *John Dee (1527–1608)*. London: Constable, 1909.

Ferguson, Margaret. *Trials of Desire: Renaissance Defenses of Poetry*. New Haven: Yale University Press, 1983.

Fisher, Philip. *Wonder, the Rainbow, and the Aesthetics of Rare Experiences*. Cambridge, MA: Harvard University Press, 1998.

Fletcher, Angus. *Allegory: The Theory of a Symbolic Mode*. Ithaca: Cornell University Press, 1964.

French, Peter. *John Dee: The World of an Elizabethan Magus*. London: Routledge, 1972.

Freud, Sigmund. *The Standard Edition of the Complete Psychological Works of Sigmund Freud*. Ed. and trans. James Strachey. 24 vols. London: The Hogarth Press, 1953–74.

Fuller, Robert. *Wonder: From Emotion to Spirituality*. Chapel Hill: University of North Carolina Press, 2006.

Gallagher, Catherine, and Stephen Greenblatt. *Practicing New Historicism*. Chicago: University of Chicago Press, 2000.

Gatti, Hilary. *Giordano Bruno and Renaissance Science*. Ithaca: Cornell University Press, 1999.

Giamatti, A. Bartlett. *Play of Double Senses: Spenser's 'Faerie Queene.'* Englewood Cliffs, NJ: Prentice-Hall, 1975.

Ginsborg, Hannah. 'Reflective Judgment and Taste.' *Noûs* 24, no. 1 (March 1990): 63–78.

Goldberg, Jonathan. *Endlesse Worke: Spenser and the Structures of Discourse.* Baltimore: Johns Hopkins University Press, 1981.

– *James I and the Politics of Literature: Jonson, Shakespeare, Donne, and Their Contemporaries.* Stanford: Stanford University Press, 1989.

Goldman, Michael. 'Marlowe and the Histrionics of Ravishment.' In *Two Renaissance Mythmakers: Christopher Marlowe and Ben Jonson*, ed. Alvin Kernan, 22–40. Baltimore: Johns Hopkins University Press, 1977.

Grazia, Margreta de. 'Sidney's *Apology.*' *PMLA* 94 (1979): 953–4.

Greenblatt, Stephen. 'Introduction to *The Power of Forms in the English Renaissance.*' In *The Norton Anthology of Theory and Criticism*, ed. Vincent B. Leitch et al., 2251–4. New York: Norton, 2001.

– *Marvelous Posessions: The Wonder of the New World.* Chicago: University of Chicago Press, 1991.

– *Shakespearean Negotiations: The Circulation of Social Energy in Renaissance England.* Berkeley: University of California Press, 1988.

Greene, Thomas M. *Poésie et Magie.* Paris: Julliard, 1991.

Gross, Kenneth. 'Postures of Allegory.' In *Edmund Spenser: Essays on Culture and Allegory*, ed. Jennifer Morrison and Matthew Greenfield, 167–79. Aldershot, UK: Ashgate, 2000.

Guillory, John. *Poetic Authority: Spenser, Milton, and Literary History.* New York: Columbia University Press, 1983.

Guyer, Paul. 'Beauty and Utility.' In *Values of Beauty: Historical Essays in Aesthetics*, 110–28. Cambridge: Cambridge University Press, 2005.

Haigh, Christopher. 'The Taming of the Reformation: Preachers, Pastors, and Parishioners in Elizabethan and Early Stuart England.' *History* 85 (2000): 572–88.

Halpern, Richard. 'Marlowe's Theater of Night: *Doctor Faustus* and Capital.' *ELH* 71, no. 2 (Summer, 2004): 455–95.

– '"The Picture of Nobody": White Cannibalism in *The Tempest.*' In *The Production of English Renaissance Culture*, ed. David Lee Miller et al. Ithaca: Cornell University Press, 1994.

Hamilton, A.C. 'Sidney and Agrippa.' *Review of English Studies* 7, no. 26 (1956): 151–7.

Hammill, Graham. *Sexuality and Form: Caravaggio, Marlowe, and Bacon.* Chicago: University of Chicago Press, 2000.

Harkness, Deborah. *John Dee's Conversations with Angels: Cabala, Alchemy, and the End of Nature.* Cambridge: Cambridge University Press, 1999.

Hathaway, Baxter. *The Age of Criticism.* Ithaca: Cornell University Press, 1962.

Hawkes, David. *The Faust Myth: Religion and the Rise of Representation.* New York: Palgrave Macmillan, 2007.

Helgerson, Richard. *Self-Crowned Laureates: Spenser, Jonson, Milton, and the Literary System*. Berkeley: University of California Press, 1983.

Herman, Peter. *Squitter-wits and Muse Haters: Sidney, Spenser, Milton, and Antipoetic Sentiment*. Detroit: Wayne State University Press, 1996.

Horkheimer, Max, and Theodor Adorno. *Dialectic of Enlightenment: Philosophical Fragments*. Ed. Gunzelin Schmid Noerr. Trans. Edmund Jephcott. Stanford: Stanford University Press, 2002.

Hulme, Peter. 'Hurricanes in the Caribbees: The Constitution of the Discourse of English Colonialism.' In *1642: Literature and Power in the Seventeenth Century; Proceedings of the Essex Conference on the Sociology of Literature*, ed. Francis Barker et al., 55–83. Colchester, UK: University of Essex Press, 1981.

Jardine, Lisa, and Anthony Grafton, '"Studied for Action": How Gabriel Harvey Read His Livy.' *Past and Present* 129 (1990): 30–78.

Johnstone, Nathan. *The Devil and Demonism in Early Modern England*. Cambridge: Cambridge University Press, 2006.

Kastan, David Scott. '"The Duke of Milan / And His Brave Son": Old Histories and New in *The Tempest*.' In *Shakespeare after Theory*, 183–200. New York: Routledge, 1999.

– 'Humphrey Moseley and the Invention of English Literature.' In *Agent of Change: Print Culture Studies after Elizabeth L. Eisenstein*, ed. Sabrina Alcorn Baron, Eric N. Lindquist, and Eleanor Shevlin, 105–39. Amherst: University of Massachusetts Press, 2007.

Keefer, Michael. '"Agrippa's Dilemma": Hermetic "Rebirth" and the Ambivalences of *De vanitate* and *De occulta philosophia*.' *Renaissance Quarterly* 41, no. 4 (1988): 614–53.

– 'Verbal Magic and the Problem of the A and B Texts of *Doctor Faustus*.' *Journal of English and Germanic Philology* 82, no. 3 (July 1983): 324–46.

Kelly, H.A. 'English Kings and the Fear of Sorcery.' *Medieval Studies* 39 (1977): 206–38.

Kermode, Frank. Introduction to *The Tempest*, ed. Frank Kermode, xi–xciii. *The Arden Shakespeare*. 1954. Reprint, London: Thomas Nelson, 1998.

Kieckhefer, Richard. *Forbidden Rites: A Necromancer's Manual of the Fifteenth Century*. University Park: Pennsylvania State University Press, 1998.

Knapp, Jeffrey. *An Empire Nowhere: England, America, and Literature from 'Utopia' to 'The Tempest'*. Berkeley: University of California Press, 1992.

– *Shakespeare's Tribe: Church, Nation, and Theater in Renaissance England*. Chicago: University of Chicago Press, 2002.

Kocher, Paul H. 'Marlowe's Atheist Lecture.' In *Marlowe: A Collection of Critical Essays*, ed. Clifford Leech, 159–66. Englewood Cliffs: Prentice Hall, 1964.

– 'The Witchcraft Bias in Marlowe's "Faustus".' *Modern Philology* 38, no. 1 (1940): 9–36.

Kott, Jan. *Shakespeare, Our Contemporary*. Trans. Boleslaw Taborski. New York: Doubleday, 1964.

Kristeller, Paul Oskar. *The Philosophy of Marsillio Ficino*. Trans. Virginia Conant. Columbia Studies in Philosophy 6. New York: Columbia University Press, 1943.

Krouse, F. Michael. 'Plato and Sidney's *Defense of Poesie*.' *Comparative Literature* 6 (1954): 138–47.

Lake, Peter. *Moderate Puritans and the Elizabethan Church*. Cambridge: Cambridge University Press, 1982.

Lake, Peter, and Michael Questier. *The Antichrist's Lewd Hat: Protestants, Papists, and Players in Post-Reformation England*. New Haven: Yale University Press, 2002.

Larner, Christina. 'James VI and I and Witchcraft.' In *The Reign of James VI and I*, ed. Alan Smith, 74–90. New York: St Martin's, 1973.

Lehrich, Christopher. *The Occult Mind: Magic in Theory and Practice*. Ithaca: Cornell University Press, 2007.

Levao, Ronald. *Renaissance Minds and Their Fictions*. Berkeley: University of California Press, 1985.

Levin, Harry. *The Overreacher: A Study of Christopher Marlowe*. Cambridge, MA: Harvard University Press, 1952.

Levinas, Emmanuel. *Otherwise than Being; or, Beyond Essence*. Trans. Alphonso Lingis. Pittsburgh: Duquesne University Press, 1999.

Lewis, C.S. *Studies in Medieval and Renaissance Literature*. Cambridge: Cambridge University Press, 1959.

Lovejoy, Arthur O. *The Great Chain of Being: A Study of the History of an Idea*. Cambridge, MA: Harvard University Press, 1964.

MacCaffrey, Isabel. *Spenser's Allegory: The Anatomy of Imagination*. Princeton: Princeton University Press, 1976.

Macfarlane, Alan. 'A Tudor Anthropologist: George Gifford's *Discourse* and *Dialogue*.' In *The Damned Art: Essays in the Literature of Witchcraft*, ed. Sydney Anglo, 140–55. New York and London: Routledge, 1977.

MacIntyre, John P. 'Sidney's "Golden World."' *Comparative Literature* 14 (1962): 356–65.

Maggi, Armando. *In the Company of Demons: Unnatural Beings, Love, and Identity in the Italian Renaissance*. Chicago: University of Chicago Press, 2006.

– *Satan's Rhetoric: A Study in Renaissance Demonology*. Chicago: University of Chicago Press, 2001.

Marcus, Leah. *Unediting the Renaissance: Shakespeare, Marlowe, Milton.* New York and London: Routledge, 1996.

Marshall, Peter, and Alexandra Walsham, eds. *Angels in the Early Modern World.* Cambridge: Cambridge University Press, 2006.

Matz, Robert. *Defending Literature in Early Modern England: Renaissance Literary Theory in Social Context.* Cambridge: Cambridge University Press, 2000.

Mauss, Marcel. *A General Theory of Magic.* Trans. Robert Brain. London: Routledge, 1972.

McCullough, Peter. *Sermons at Court: Politics and Religion in Elizabethan and Jacobean Preaching.* Cambridge: Cambridge University Press, 1998.

McGinnis, Scott. '"Subtiltie" Exposed: Pastoral Perspectives on Witch Belief in the Thought of George Gifford.' *Sixteenth Century Journal* 33, no. 3 (Autumn 2002): 665–86.

Mebane, John. *Renaissance Magic and the Return to the Golden Age: The Occult Tradition and Marlowe, Jonson, and Shakespeare.* Lincoln: University of Nebraska Press, 1989.

Merkel, Ingrid, and Alan Debus, eds. *Hermeticism and the Renaissance: Intellectual History and the Occult in Early Modern Europe.* Washington: Folger Shakespeare Library Press, 1988.

Montrose, Louis Adrian. 'Celebration and Insinuation: Sir Philip Sidney and the Motives of Elizabethan Courtship.' *Renaissance Drama* 8 (1977): 3–35.

– *The Purpose of Playing: Shakespeare and the Cultural Politics of the Elizabethan Theater.* Chicago: University of Chicago Press, 1996.

– *The Subject of Elizabeth: Authority, Gender, and Representation.* Chicago: University of Chicago Press, 2006.

Morriss, Henry Partee. 'Sir Philip Sidney and the Renaissance Knowledge of Plato.' *English Studies* 51 (1971): 411–24.

Mowat, Barbara. 'Prospero, Agrippa, and Hocus Pocus.' *English Literary Renaissance* 11, no. 3 (Autumn 1981): 281–303.

– 'Prospero's Book.' *Shakespeare Quarterly* 52 (Spring 2001): 1–33.

Myrick, K.O. *Sir Philip Sidney as a Literary Craftsman.* Cambridge, MA: Harvard University Press, 1935.

Nauert, Charles, Jr. *Agrippa and the Crisis of Renaissance Thought.* Illinois Studies in the Social Sciences 55. Urbana: University of Illinois Press, 1965.

Nealon, Chris. 'The Poetic Case.' *Critical Inquiry* 33, no. 4 (Summer 2007): 865–6.

Nicoll, Allardyce. 'Passing over the Stage.' *Shakespeare Survey* 12 (1959): 47–55.

Nohrnberg, James. *The Analogy of 'The Faerie Queene.'* Princeton: Princeton University Press, 1976.

Orgel, Stephen. *The Authentic Shakespeare, and Other Problems of the Early Modern Stage*. New York: Routledge, 2002.

– *The Illusion of Power: Political Theater in the English Renaissance*. Berkeley: University of California Press, 1975.

– Introduction to *The Tempest*, ed. Stephen Orgel. Oxford: Oxford University Press, 1987.

Panofsky, Erwin. *Idea: A Concept in Art Theory*. Trans. Joseph Peake. New York: Harper and Row, 1968.

Parker, Patricia. *Inescapable Romance: Studies in the Poetics of a Mode*. Princeton: Princeton University Press, 1979.

Patterson, W.B. 'William Perkins as Apologist for the Church of England.' *Journal of Ecclesiastical History* 57, no. 2 (April 2006): 252–69.

Platt, Peter. *Reason Diminished: Shakespeare and the Marvelous*. Lincoln: University of Nebraska Press, 1997.

– ed. *Wonders, Marvels, and Monsters in Early Modern Culture*. Cranbury: Associated University Presses, 1999.

Pye, Christopher. 'Froth in the Mirror: Demonism, Sexuality, and the Early Modern Subject.' In *Repossessions: Psychoanalysis and the Phantasms of Early Modern Culture*, ed. Timothy Murray, 171–99. Minneapolis: University of Minnesota Press, 1998.

Quilligan, Maureen. 'The Reader.' In *The Spenser Encyclopedia*, ed. A.C. Hamilton, 770–81. Toronto: University of Toronto Press, 1990.

Quint, David. 'Archimago and Amoret: The Poem and its Doubles.' In *Worldmaking Spenser*, ed. Patrick Cheney and Lauren Silberman, 32–44. Lexington: University of Kentucky Press, 2000.

Ransom, John Crowe. 'Criticism, Inc.' In *The Norton Anthology of Theory and Criticism*, ed. Vincent B. Leitch et al., 1108–17. New York: Norton, 2001.

Rebhorn, Wayne. *The Emperor of Men's Minds: Literature and the Renaissance Discourse of Rhetoric*. Ithaca: Cornell University Press, 1995.

Ricoeur, Paul. *The Symbolism of Evil*. Trans. Emerson Buchanan. Boston: Beacon Press, 1967.

Riggs, David. *The World of Christopher Marlowe*. New York: Henry Holt, 2004.

Roberts, Gareth. 'Necromantic Books: Christopher Marlowe, *Doctor Faustus* and Agrippa of Nettesheim.' In *Christopher Marlowe and English Renaissance Culture*, ed. Darryll Grantley et al., 148–71. London: Scolar Press, 1996.

Robinson, Forrest. *The Shape of Things Known: Sidney's 'Apology' in Its Philosophical Tradition*. Cambridge, MA: Harvard University Press, 1972.

Roche, Thomas. *The Kindly Flame*. Princeton: Princeton University Press, 1964.

Romilly, Jacqueline de. *Magic and Rhetoric in Ancient Greece*. Cambridge, MA: Harvard University Press, 1975.

Rossky, William. 'Imagination in the English Renaissance: Psychology and Po-
   etic.' *Studies in the Renaissance* 5 (1958): 49–73.
Rowland, Ingrid D. *Giordano Bruno: Philosopher Heretic*. New York: Farrar,
   Straus, and Giroux, 2008.
Russell, Jeffrey Burton. *Mephistopheles: The Devil in the Modern World*. Ithaca:
   Cornell University Press, 1986.
Scribner, Robert. 'The Reformation, Popular Magic, and the "Disenchantment
   of the World."' *Journal of Interdisciplinary History* 23, no. 3 (Winter 1993):
   475–94.
Shagan, Ethan. *Popular Politics and the English Reformation*. Cambridge: Cam-
   bridge University Press, 2003.
Sherman, William H. *John Dee: The Politics of Reading and Writing in the Eng-
   lish Renaissance*. Amherst: University of Massachusetts Press, 1995.
Shumaker, Wayne. *The Occult Sciences in the Renaissance: A Study in Intellectual
   Patterns*. Berkeley: University of California Press, 1972.
Silberman, Lauren. *Transforming Desire: Erotic Knowledge in Books III and IV
   of 'The Faerie Queene.'* Berkeley: University of California Press, 1995.
Sinfield, Alan. *Faultlines: Cultural Materialism and the Politics of Dissident
   Reading*. Berkeley: University of California Press, 1992.
Sisson, C.J. 'The Magic of Prospero.' *Shakespeare Survey* 11 (1958): 70–7.
Skura, Meredith Anne. 'Discourse and the Individual: The Case of Colonialism
   in *The Tempest*.' In *Case Studies in Critical Controversy: 'The Tempest,'* ed.
   Gerald Graff and James Phelan, 286–322. Boston: Bedford/St Martin, 2000.
Snow, Edward A. 'Marlowe's *Doctor Faustus* and the Ends of Desire.' In *Christo-
   pher Marlowe's 'Doctor Faustus,'* ed. Harold Bloom, 47–76. New York: Chel-
   sea House, 1988.
Spingarn, Joel. *A History of Literary Criticism in the Renaissance*. 1908. Reprint,
   New York: Columbia University Press, 1963.
Srigley, Michael. *Images of Regeneration: A Study of Shakespeare's 'The Tempest'
   and Its Cultural Background*. Studia Anglistica Upsaliensia 58. Uppsala, Swe-
   den: Academiae Upsaliensis, 1985.
Stephens, Walter. *Demon Lovers: Witchcraft, Sex, and the Crisis of Belief*. Chi-
   cago: University of Chicago Press, 2002.
Stewart, Alan. *The Cradle King: A Life of James VI & I*. London: Chatto and
   Windus, 2003.
– *Sir Philip Sidney: A Double Life*. London: Chatto and Windus, 2000.
Stillman, Robert. *Philip Sidney and the Poetics of Renaissance Cosmopolitanism*.
   Burlington: Ashgate, 2008.
Strier, Richard. '"I am Power": Normal and Magical Politics in *The Tempest*.'
   In *Writing and Political Engagement in Seventeenth-Century England*, ed.

Derek Hirst and Richard Strier. Cambridge: Cambridge University Press, 1999.

Strype, John. *Annals of the Reformation and the Establishment of Religion*. 4 vols. Oxford: Clarendon Press, 1824.

Tambiah, Stanley J. 'Form and Meaning of Magical Acts: A Point of View.' In *Modes of Thought: Essays on Thinking in Western and Non-Western Societies*, ed. Robin Horton and Ruth Finnegan, 3–32. London: Faber, 1973.

– 'A Performative Approach to Ritual.' *Proceedings of the British Academy* 65 (1979): 113–69.

Teall, John. 'Witchcraft and Calvinism in Elizabethan England: Divine Power and Human Agency.' *Journal of the History of Ideas* 23, no. 1 (January–March 1962): 21–36.

Teskey, Gordon. *Allegory and Violence*. Ithaca: Cornell University Press, 1996.

Thomas, Keith. *Religion and the Decline of Magic: Studies in Popular Beliefs in Sixteenth and Seventeenth Century England.* 1971. Reprint, Oxford: Oxford University Press, 1997.

Thomas, Vivien, and William Tydeman, eds. *Christopher Marlowe: The Plays and Their Sources*. New York and London: Routledge, 1994.

Tomlinson, Gary. *Music in Renaissance Magic: Toward a Historiography of Others*. Chicago: University of Chicago Press, 1993.

Traister, Barbara Howard. '*Doctor Faustus*: Master of Self-Delusion.' In *Christopher Marlowe's 'Doctor Faustus,'* ed. Harold Bloom, 77–92. New York: Chelsea House, 1988.

Ulreich, John C., Jr. '"The Poets Only Deliver": Sidney's Conception of Mimesis.' *Studies in the Literary Imagination* 15, no. 1 (Spring 1982): 67–84.

Vickers, Brian. 'Analogy versus Identity: The Rejection of Occult Symbolism, 1580–1680.' In *Occult and Scientific Mentalities in the Renaissance*, ed. Brian Vickers, 95–164. Cambridge: Cambridge University Press, 1984.

Walker, D.P. *Spiritual and Demonic Magic from Ficino to Campanella*. 1958. Reprint, *Magic in History*, University Park: Pennsylvania State University Press, 2000.

Wallace, Dewey, Jr. 'George Gifford, Puritan Propaganda and Popular Religion in Elizabethan England.' *Sixteenth-Century Journal* 9, no. 1 (1978): 27–49.

Walsham, Alexandra. *Providence in Early Modern England*. Oxford: Oxford University Press, 1999.

Walsham, Alexandra, and Peter Marshall, eds. *Angels in the Early Modern World*. Cambridge: Cambridge University Press, 2006.

Waters, D. Douglas. *Duessa as Theological Satire*. Columbia: University of Missouri Press, 1970.

Watt, Ian. *Myths of Modern Individualism: Faust, Don Quixote, Don Juan, Robinson Crusoe*. Cambridge: Cambridge University Press, 2006.

Webster, Charles. *From Paracelsus to Newton: Magic and the Making of Modern Science*. Cambridge: Cambridge University Press, 1982.

Weinberg, Bernard. *A History of Literary Criticism in the Italian Renaissance*. 2 vols. Chicago: University of Chicago Press, 1961.

Welsford, Enid. *The Court Masque: A Study in the Relationship between Poetry and the Revels*. New York: Russell and Russell, 1962.

Willis, Deborah. 'Shakespeare's *Tempest* and the Discourse of Colonialism.' In *Case Studies in Critical Controversy: 'The Tempest,'* ed. Gerald Graff and James Phelan, 256–67. Boston: Bedford/St Martin, 2000.

Wimsatt, William. *The Verbal Icon: Studies in the Meaning of Poetry*. Lexington: University Press of Kentucky, 1954.

Wimsatt, William, and Monroe Beardsley, 'The Affective Fallacy.' In *The Norton Anthology of Theory and Criticism*, ed. Vincent B. Leitch et al., 1387–1402. New York: Norton, 2001.

Wimsatt, William, and Cleanth Brooks. *Literary Criticism: A Short History*. London: Routledge, 1970.

Wind, Edgar. '"Hercules" and "Orpheus": Two Mock-Heroic Designs by Dürer,' *Journal of the Warburg Institute* 2 (1938–9): 206–18.

Wolfe, Jessica. *Humanism, Machinery, and Renaissance Literature*. Cambridge: Cambridge University Press, 2004.

Wootton, David. 'New Histories of Atheism.' In *Atheism from the Reformation to the Enlightenment*, ed. Michael Hunter and David Wootton, 13–54. Oxford: Oxford University Press, 1992.

Yates, Frances. *Giordano Bruno and the Hermetic Tradition*. Chicago: University of Chicago Press, 1964.

– *The Occult Philosophy in the Elizabethan Age*. London: Routledge, 1979.

– *Shakespeare's Last Plays: A New Approach*. London: Routledge, 1975.

Zagorin, Perez. *Ways of Lying: Dissimulation, Persecution, and Conformity in Early Modern Europe*. Cambridge, MA: Harvard University Press, 1990.

Zammito, John. *The Genesis of Kant's 'Critique of Judgment.'* Chicago: University of Chicago Press, 1992.

Žižek, Slavoj. 'Neighbors and Other Monsters: A Plea for Ethical Violence.' In *The Neighbor: Three Inquiries in Political Theology*, by Slavoj Žižek, Eric Santner, and Kenneth Reinhard, 134–90. Chicago: University of Chicago Press, 2006.

Index